JOHN BANVILLE
A Critical Introduction

Also by Rüdiger Imhof

Alive-Alive O! Flann O'Brien's *At Swim-Two-Birds*
Edited by Rüdiger Imhof (Wolfhound Press 1985)

JOHN BANVILLE

A Critical Introduction

Rüdiger Imhof

WOLFHOUND PRESS

First published 1989 by
WOLFHOUND PRESS
68 Mountjoy Square,
Dublin 1.

British Library Cataloguing in Publication Data

Imhof, Rüdiger
    John Banville: a critical introduction.
    I. Title
    823'.914 [F]

    ISBN 0-86327-186-3
    ISBN 0-86327-187-1 p

Cover design: Jan de Fouw
Sketches of John Banville: Rüdiger Imhof
Typesetting: Phototype-Set Ltd.
Printed and bound by The Camelot Press plc, Southampton.

Contents

Acknowledgements

Being a *summa* of sorts, the present study is based on, and makes use of, ideas which I previously expounded in my articles on John Banville's work, in particular "John Banville's Supreme Fiction", *Irish University Review*, 11, 1 (Spring 1981), and "Swan's Way: Goethe, Einstein, Banville — The Eternal Recurrence", *Études Irlandaises* (1987). Some of the arguments I have taken over more or less *verbatim* because I felt they were still valid. The greater part of my earlier findings have gone through a thorough process of revision, and a considerable amount of new material has emerged since and will be offered here for the first time. I should like to thank Professor Maurice Harmon for granting permission to use the material originally published in *IUR*, and Professor Patrick Rafroidi for permission to recycle my discussion of *Mefisto*.

Quotations from various writers cited are credited in the notes or text and are gratefully acknowledged.

My sincerest gratitude goes to Mr Banville for never tiring of answering my queries, no matter whether inane or ingenious, and for allowing me to interview him. He also kindly granted permission to quote from his work. "Niemals sterben, niemals sterben." Mr John McKeown, M.A., sacrificed a lot of his time and energy on reading the typescript; his criticism and his suggestions have been invaluable. I am also indebted to Dr. Jürgen Kamm and Mr Colin Foskett, M.A., who read parts of the study. Mr Robin Robertson, of Secker & Warburg, was most helpful in providing me with copies of reviews of the novels and of other valuable documents. Frau Anke Schmidt, with eagle-eyed perception, spotted a not inconsiderable number of typographical mistakes which I indefatigably smuggled into the script. My deepest thanks, however, must go to my wife, Karin Imhof, for having had the good sense to find consolation in the fact that while I was working on the book I would leave her in peace.

March 1988

Introduction

Things acquire sense and significance only within contexts, writers too, their works no less. For to assess the significance of the writer John Banville, several contexts suggest themselves, the most immediate being that of contemporary Irish literature, and, more specifically, of contemporary Irish fiction.[1]

Irish fiction in the twentieth century has been quite conventional in subject matter and technique, despite Joyce and Beckett and in spite of what has been going on elsewhere in the world. Too much is about Ireland, the sow that eats her farrow, about a priest-ridden God-forsaken race, or about what the vitriolic Myles na gCopaleen called "wee Annie going to her first confession, stuff about country funerals". Too much is in the mould of cosy realism. The exceptions are too few and far between. The majority of Maurice Harmon's "second generation of writers",[2] *i.e.* writers who have emerged posterior to the Fabulous Four O's: O'Casey, O'Connor, O'Flaherty and O'Faolain, are fundamentally ploughing the same clod of clay that the first generation of twentieth-century Irish writers toiled over — writers who, by undividedly concentrating on matters intrinsically Irish, were concerned with helping to find a national identity. Now that this identity is found, one could reasonably expect an opening up of the focus of interest. Such an opening up has still to be accomplished on a larger scale. Banville has shown himself to be among the very few who have sought to attain this goal. With *Doctor Copernicus* and *Kepler*, but also with his efforts at literary derivation in *The Newton Letter* and *Mefisto*, he has turned to incontestably non-Irish subject matter. As a result, some regard him as the black sheep in the family of Irish writers; others, strangely enough, think he is not a typical Irish writer at all, for whatever that may be worth.

A good deal of what was written by the first generation of

twentieth-century Irish fiction writers, whether in the form of short
or fully sustained narratives, is in the old oral storyteller's tradition in
that it is primarily sequential in kind. Almost as a rule, the accounts
start at A and by the end they have arrived at Z in linear fashion. The
novels of O'Flaherty, O'Connor, O'Faolain and others basically rely
on series of short scenes, each of which could claim to be a short story
in its own right. Too seldom is it possible to discern attempts to pull
the constitutive parts into polyphonic and polyvalent relationships.
Relatively rare are the efforts to erect what Henry James called "a
house of fiction", where each section is of vital importance to all the
other sections, not only to those that immediately precede or follow
it.

The situation has scarcely changed today, as becomes apparent
from the works of such writers as John Broderick, Jennifer Johnston[3],
John McGahern, whose *The Leavetaking* in its first version was a compositional disaster particularly as regards Part II, and Edna O'Brien,
whose only original work is *Night*, where she manages to transcend
linear, sequential narration. In this context, Aidan Higgins represents
an exception, although it is dubious whether what seems to be
Higgins' endeavour to put into practice the idea of a 'total' book[4] has
so far been successful. So does Benedict Kiely's brilliant recent novel
Nothing Happens in Carmincross, which by employing Joyce's method(s)
in *Ulysses* convincingly overcomes sequential narration in the
direction of a spatial sort of narrative discourse. From the first,
Banville has not been one to tell his 'stories' in an 'and-then-and-
then' fashion. His work is characterised by a predominant concern
with shape. *Kepler*, for instance, represents an extraordinarily
complex compositional tour de force; *Birchwood* and *Mefisto* are no less
interesting and admirable storyteller's bookwebs. This is one reason
why in the context of contemporary Irish fiction Banville can claim a
front rank among the supreme craftsmen.

*

The contemporary Irish novel is, as far as its mapping by critics is
concerned, still largely a *terra incognita*. The time has been too short for
the grain and the husk to be separated, and analyses of the state of
affairs have been bedevilled by the analysers' being too closely
involved in the events. While the nineteenth century has been quite
reliably scrutinised,[5] hardly anything is as yet available that could be
consulted for information about, for example, what new genres of

the novel have evolved and what older forms are still in use. The appropriate chapters in the literary histories of A. Norman Jeffares and Seamus Deane[6] are disappointing not least because of their concentration on individual authors instead of on genres and modes — an alternative approach that would yield a more reliable picture as it would allow the covering of a wider variety of writers, including those who have so far only produced few, though significant books and who, since their output is scanty, get passed over without further ado. Augustine Martin's *The Genius of Irish Prose*[7], although partly at least focusing on genres, is unreliable and unrewarding for excluding too many and for putting forward erroneous notions, as in the case of Martin's own discussion of the Irish comic-phantastic tradition after Flann O'Brien, which notes that the tradition has ceased to exist,[8] whereas in fact it is still going strong, as *vide* Patrick McGinley, Tony Cafferky, Michael Mullen and others.

If a study of genres were available,[9] it could easily be shown that part of Banville's artistic programme has aimed at transcending Irish narrative genres, much in the sense in which the Russian Formalists, Tynjanov and Shklovsky in particular, conceived of the life and development of genres in literature. There are those who, for their own shady reasons, consider the transcending of Irish conventions, no matter how exhausted these may be, too iconoclastic to be acceptable. For these, Banville is, once again, not a typical Irish writer, as if to be a typical Irish writer was *ipso facto* a recommendation.

*

Richard Kearney is one of the very few scholars and critics to have studied the fiction output of the post-Joycean era with a critical eye.[10] While also noting that "the majority of Irish writers continued in the classical tradition of the novel as quest, unchallenged by the Joycean problematic",[11] he points out that such writers as Higgins, Banville and Stuart "feel that they can no longer take the novel for granted; they feel compelled to interrogate its very possibility".[12] He also includes McGahern among his set of interrogators; but one must definitely draw the before McGahern. Kearney seems inclined to view this change of direction as an indigenous Irish phenomenon. If he does, he is of course wrong. The 'critical' novel represents an international event that has come late to Ireland, at least, that is, in the form in which the 'critical' novel has evolved after Joyce and Beckett. These two writers have been exceptionally instrumental in bringing this type of fiction into being. But the 'critical' part of *Ulysses* does not belong in any Irish tradition.[13] There was no such tradition when Joyce wrote the book; nor was there any such tradition when Beckett, with whom critics have the severest difficulties in proving why his fiction is Irish,[14] started working on his novels. As yet there are too few 'critical' novels in Ireland to speak of a tradition.

The 'critical' novel must be assessed within an international context, for this form of narrative discourse to be given its due. Incidentally, this is where Banville appears to see himself. He has remarked in an interview:

> ... I never really thought about Irish literature as such. I don't really think that specifically 'national' literatures are of terribly great significance. Perhaps for a country's self-esteem.[15]

Furthermore, he has confessed: "... if I were to look about for a stream to be part of I would certainly look to America or Europe ..."[16] He is most keenly aware that as a conscientious artist in the second half of the twentieth century he must not write in the moribund modes of narrative discourse in which the greater part of what is being written in Ireland, but likewise in England, today presents itself. In his review of John Fowles' *Daniel Martin*, for instance, Banville has made this awareness apparent.

> Mr. Fowles knows as well as anyone that we cannot unlearn the lessons of modernism, that the novelist cannot go back to 'realism' and write as if nothing much had happened in the period between, say, James's *The Ambassadors* and Beckett's *The Unnamable*.[17]

Seamus Deane has reproved him for being

> a *litterateur* who has a horror of producing 'literature'. This horror is equalled only by his amusement at the notion that literature might (by accident or innate capacity) reproduce life. He rejects mimetic realism by practising it in the avowed consciousness of its incompetence.[18]

These are rum arguments, of course; they betray something of the ideological premises of Deane's criticism but are less rewarding as a sensible statement about Banville's art.

Banville belongs in that group of contemporary writers who have aspired to develop, and not to flog to death, the art of fiction. It is a group which unites novelists and storytellers who have realised that

> it is ... a symptom (though *not* a cause) of the sickness afflicting fiction these days that it is in criticism *of* fiction that the best work is done.[19]

Fiction may indeed be sick, much of it anyway. These writers, though, write 'critical' fiction to find a cure. It is noteworthy that after his critical exercise in fiction, with *Nightspawn* and to a certain, albeit very different, extent with *Birchwood*, Banville has successfully striven towards developing his own individual narrative voice, his own specific narrative vein.

One effect of such criticism is that fiction becomes literary, relying as it does on quoting from, and alluding to, extant literary texts by other authors. The policy can be observed in the works of a host of 'critical' novelists, or metafictionists, from Cervantes to Vladimir Nabokov and John Fowles. It is likewise conspicuous in Banville's books, from *Long Lankin* to *Mefisto*. Deane seems convinced that "the literariness of John Banville's work [is] its most recurrently weakening feature",[20] and he shows himself by this remark to be obviously oblivious to the indisputable fact that intertextuality is among the oldest strategies employed by writers, to different ends of course.[21] For the contemporary authors, intertextuality fulfils a number of purposes, primary among them to make the point that literature is made from literature.[22] This is part and parcel of the discriminative fathoming of the relationship between art and nature, and such fathoming has been one of the major concerns of Banville's art.

*

If asked whether contemporary Irish fiction displays efforts equivalent to so-called postmodernist experiments in narrative discourse, most critics would probably want to respond in firm denial. Admittedly, the bulk of books published during the last couple of decades is decidedly old-fashioned and conventional, not to say parochial. Moreover, no one as yet seems to have found it worth his, or her, while to investigate this issue. If someone had, it would have been made clear that, surprisingly enough, all the categories of experiment that Annegret Maack was able to establish for the contemporary English novel[23] are also to be found within the context of the contemporary Irish novel. Of the eight categories singled out by Maack,[24] three are represented by the work of Banville. *Nightspawn* and, to a lesser extent and in a somewhat different sense, *Birchwood* belong in the compartment labelled the 'poetological' novel, or metafiction. An adaptation of literary models for the purpose of reinterpreting them has been achieved in *Birchwood, The Newton Letter* and *Mefisto*. The problematic relationship between historical fiction and fictitious histories is thematically virulent in *Doctor Copernicus* and *Kepler*. Still a fourth category of experiment must be mentioned, which Maack subsumes under the 'poetological' novel, but which for various reasons should be made into a compartment in its own right: the transcending of established modes of fiction. *Nightspawn* and *Birchwood* aim at debunking familiar modes, Irish as well as non-Irish.

Banville's true context (*pace* all those critics who believe that the apotheosis of all things Irish is their real business) is the international level of what has, rightly or wrongly, been termed postmodernist fiction, though decidedly not in the sense in which a critic such as Ihab Hassan has defined the phenomenon of postmodernism:

> ... postmodern literature knows silence other than the inhuman imposes. The avant-garde finds ingenious ways to deny language, deny form, deny art ... Let me briefly summarize five metaphors of anti-art: A. Art cancels itself ... B. Art deprecates itself ... C. Art becomes a self-reflexive game ... D. Art orders itself loosely, even at random ... E. Art refuses interpretation.[25]

Most of these metaphors, which are of course not true metaphors, make as little sense as Hassan's catalogue of the features pertaining to postmodernism.[26] This catalogue, which Hassan sets against a comparable list of the characteristics of modernism, is nonsensical. It is so all-embracing as to be preposterous: it enumerates almost every cultural, literary, and social peculiarity of our time. According to Alan Wilde, "... postmodernism seeks in any number of ways to refute — or simply reject — the very bases of modernist beliefs".[27] There is always a tendency to exaggerate the difference between the old and the avowedly novel, and this has helped to conceal the truth that, as Frank Kermode has put it,

> there has only been one Modernist Revolution, and ... it happened a long time ago. So far as I can see there has been little radical change in modernist thinking since. More muddle, certainly, and almost certainly more jokes, but no revolution, and much less talent.[28]

Numerous attempts have been made to refute such convictions, especially by American critics, who are at pains to establish post-modernism as, first and foremost, an indigenous American event and seem prepared to assign it a cosmic significance.[29] But as Nabokov knew, the cosmic is only a slippery 's' away from the comic.

Postmodernism, if there really is such a thing, is at best a cultural, not so much a literary phenomenon.[30] In literature, and specifically in fiction, most of the so-called postmodernist characteristics were implicit in modernism. Much even goes back to romanticism. Self-reflexiveness, that alleged hallmark of postmodernist narrative discourse, dates back further still: to Sterne and Cervantes.[31] Anthony Burgess certainly has a point when he warns that, before we have understood all the implications of modernism, the end of that artistic period has not been reached yet.[32] In that sense, John Banville is a highly conscientious modernist of the post-Joycean, post-Beckettian era, who unlike many Irish fiction writers can hold his own on an international plane of comparison.

The modernist way of conceiving a narrative smacks of the experimental, and the term 'experimental' applied to a literary work almost invariably means that that piece of writing is irksome, unrewarding to read, inferior in quality, in short, that it belongs to the avant-garbage. Experimental literary texts demand a creative response and active participation on the part of the reader. He simply cannot lean back and, in a consumer's pose, 'enjoy' the book as if it were a big beribboned box of chocolate-coated Culture. Banville is certainly not an easy writer. He has the reputation of being a writers' writer, which categorisation is, more often than not, nothing but a silly excuse for people who are too lazy to make the effort. Each new book of his, while in many ways intricately connected with its predecessor, is always good for a surprise. Banville has so far managed to remain a moving target for his critics.

*

Lastly, the significance of the writer Banville, and his work, should be assessed within the context of theories of, or notions about, art. Naturally, a detailed discussion of what art is, or what various theoreticians and artists have thought that art is, falls outside the scope of this study. All that it is feasible to do here is to try and discern Banville's own ideas about art and the craft of fiction from his critical writings. The task is difficult enough, as it has to rely mainly on Banville's reviews and must be confined to converting covert statements into overt ones. The whole will most likely be to Mr Banville's gleeful amusement. Even so — the attempt will be made in the following chapter. It should be borne in mind, though, that the purpose of the undertaking is quite modest: all it seeks to achieve is to lay some sort of basis in theory for the remaining parts of this study to be able to explore the ways in which the theory has been put into practice by the individual books as well as to show wherein the excellent of Banville's craft resides.

CHAPTER 1
A *Principia* of Sorts:
Reflections on Art and the Novel

'*Principia*' means basis, foundation, fundamental principles. Whether the ideas that will be discussed here are in fact principles fundamental to Banville's way of thinking ultimately remains for Mr Banville himself to decide. Yet they are contained in his theoretical statements and thus can claim some measure of authenticity as being straight from the horse's mouth, to put it somewhat facetiously. As for their *ex cathedra* quality, they are offered here to be taken with a grain of salt. Views tend to change, and what may have been a conviction in the '70s may now be no longer valid.

The central question for every serious artist, as Banville saw it in 1977, is whether to "choose realism or formalistic experimentation, social sanity or morbidity", or whether to follow the method of Kafka or Thomas Mann.[1] "Ought *angst*", he asked, "to be taken as an absolute, or ought it to be overcome?"[2] Formalism leads inevitably to the inward obsession with *angst*, while at the same time it helps to renew art and expand its frontiers. Traditional realism tends towards technical stasis, yet enables a writer, "the finest of the few", to engage the social problems of his time.[3] Banville himself seems to be in favour of formalism and against traditional realism. For he believes that the main concern of the novelists in this century has been "to cut the novel free from the clutter of its Victorian inheritance — ethics, manners, didacticism".[4] The process of liberation and purification was begun at the turn of the century, and one writer in particular was singularly instrumental in developing a revolutionary manner of writing that relied on economy and order and that turned the craft of fiction into an art form. The writer was Henry James, for whom Banville seems to have a great admiration and to whom he may be indebted for his own preoccupation with shape.

Henry James, a man of some discernment and critical acumen,

dismissed *War and Peace* as a "large, loose, baggy monster". That novel and others of its kind have, he conceded, life, but "there is life and life, and as waste is only life sacrificed and thereby prevented from 'counting'. I delight in a deep-breathing economy and organic form ..." Reading these books (*i.e.* Margaret Drabble's *The Ice Age*, Thomas Keneally's *A Victim of the Aurora*, Olivia Manning's *The Danger Tree*, and Marion Engel's *The Bear*), or three of them at least, I realised, with some force, that James was a voice intoning in the wilderness, for on the evidence of these ... novels, the revolution which he effected, by turning into an art form the baggy monstrosity of the 19th century novel, might never have occurred.[5]

The need for formal experimentation to the end of arriving at narrative techniques which are appropriate for expressing thematic issues relevant to the twentieth century, instead of adopting anachronistic devices, this is a concern that permeates most of Banville's theoretical statements and characterises his practical efforts. After James and Joyce and Beckett, no writer can continue to write in the old way. "Most of us do. Most of Irish writing is within a nineteenth-century tradition where the world is regarded as given."[6] Today the world is no longer given, and a writer must account for this loss of certainty and stability by exploring the medium of narrative discourse for adequate formal means that make it possible for him to go on writing.

Experimenting with the novel form is indispensable, but it must have its limits. "The whole linguistic experimental thing" of recent years has, according to Banville, died, not least because its effect was obfuscatory, whereas the efforts behind it should have aimed at introducing a greater amount of clarity. "We're going back to a state in which clarity will be the prime criterion ..."[7] It failed also because it represented a case where the experiment dictated the necessity; instead the necessity should dictate the experiment. Banville finds that desideratum realised in Joyce. With him, "the experimenting was a necessity, there was simply no other way for him to write, and it shows."[8] It does not show in the experimenting that has gone into the *nouveau roman*, for instance.

One of the odd things about the 'new novel' is that the theory is always more exciting, more interesting, and even more entertaining, than the actual novels.[9]

The great failure of the *nouveau roman* is that, in the face of its avowedly novel exploratory endeavours, "it is unable to deal adequately, in a way that measures up to daily experience, with ordinary things".[10]

The purpose of a novel, for Banville, is to communicate the sense of a world being carefully scrutinised and described. "Novels are about *life*, they *teach* us things."[11] Could that aim not be accomplished best by a committed kind of literature, through what could be termed a political kind of fiction? Banville does not think so, or rather he would first want to know what the term 'political' is meant to convey. Politically motivated artists he finds weighed down like Sisyphus by his stone.[12] Art or action, which to choose?

> ... I shall, I suppose, appear simple-minded if I say straight away that I have never been able to understand why it must always be one or the other that one must plump for, since, frivolous creature that I am, I cannot rid myself of the quaint conviction that art *is* action.[13]

Art may be action for Banville, though not action in the sense in which, say, Marxist writers and critics like to conceive of the purpose of literature. The novel, literature, has no dealings with the soap-box. One cannot put politics, or at least politicking, into a novel without contaminating it. "There is no such thing as polemical art: one destroys the other."[14] Art simply will not grind axes.[15]

Not least as a result of this, the novel is, of all art forms, in a particular way "the purest, since it is the one which most nearly manages to contain itself adequately within its own limits".[16] The prime reason why it can do so arises from the role that style and shape must play in fiction, in art generally. Style should possess a balletic quality, "full of sharp points and sudden leaps and startling comic turns", and copious "obsessive wordy playfulness".[17] Style should be the outcome of a tenacious obsession with words, with the power and beauty of language, but it is an obsession that must not become its own end: it should work towards redeeming us from the disaster that is our age. For Banville, the power and beauty of language is the only remedy — something that Beckett has taught him:

> ... it is Beckett's supreme achievement to have shown us that the horror and cruelty of the world ... can be redeemed through the beauty and power of language — language and nothing more, not progress, optimism or delusion, but words alone.[18]

Perhaps this is neither here nor there; Hamlet would say: "Words, words, words", or Nabokov: "*Worte, worte, worte.* Warts, warts, warts".[19] And then again, such a conviction is possibly derived from the belief that in fiction "the thing said must always be subordinate to the way of saying".[20] If this demand is met, a novel will be imbued with the most important quality in writing: density,[21] and it will be "some enormous intricate thing dancing, in sadness, brief happiness, pain".[22]

Shape is of overriding import for Banville. He is interested in, and fascinated by, the shape of an idea, just as Beckett is said to be, for instance as regards the idea of the two thieves, in *Waiting for Godot*, one of whom was saved and the other lost.[23] "In art", he has written in his article "Physics and Fiction: Order from Chaos"[24], "the only absolute criterion is shape, form, ratio, harmony, call it what you will. Call it order." Notably Banville does not so much have in mind a sequential, linear kind of order, but a spatial one, a kind of order relying on multiple planes of relationships. This becomes obvious in his discussion of how Joyce reintroduced "the mediaeval method of moving stasis, the ideal symbol of which is the circle", into fiction writing dominated by the "Renaissance notion of linear progression, personified in the invention of perspective in painting (and basic to the novel still for instance in the techniques of 'plot', 'psychological depth', 'character', etc.)".[25] It also becomes obvious in Banville's work.

Art, for Banville, is first and foremost about form.[26] Art has nothing to do with personal, or intimate, self-expression.

> As Kafka put it, the artist is the man who has nothing to say. What Kafka, with his usual reticence, left out is that only by saying nothing does he succeed in saying anything worthwhile. I am speaking, of course, of saying out of one's personal life, as it were, of using art as a vehicle for personal opinions and emotions.[27]

Art is a cold fish, not interested at all in the artist's personal affairs.[28] Banville's creed as an artist is perhaps best encapsulated in some lines from Rilke's *Duino Elegies*, which Banville himself has quoted on two occasions when referring to the essential purpose of art.[29]

> ... Sind wir *hier*, um zu sagen: Haus, Brücke, Baum, Tor, Krug, Obstbaum, Fenster — höchstens: Säule, Turm ... aber zu *sagen*, verstehs, oh zu sagen *so*, wie selber die Dinge niemals innig meinten zu sein ...
>
> [... Are we, perhaps, *here* just for saying: House, Bridge, Fountain, Gate, Jug, Fruit tree, Window, — possibly: Pillar, Tower? ... but for *saying*, remember, oh, for such saying as never the things themselves hoped so intensely to be ...][30]

It is the saying that makes all the difference, the way words are used in literature to express the quintessential nature of things, what

Banville in "A Talk" refers to as the Kantian *Ding-an-sich*, so exceptionally important for his protagonists from Ben White, in *Nightspawn*, onwards, and most notably for Doctor Copernicus. Like the Rilke of the *Elegies*, Banville wants to praise the world to the Angel, and he is aware of the tension "between the desire to take things into ourselves by *saying* them . . . and the impossibility finally of making the world our own", and out of that tension "poetry springs, and that other poetry which some of us disguise by not justifying the right-hand margin of our books".[31] That other poetry is the poetry of prose. Banville's aim has, from the first, been to make the words sing in his novels, to write prose as if it were poetry. Only in that manner can such saying be achieved as never the things themselves hoped so intensely to be.

A literary artist is someone who can make a stone glow by describing it in a specific manner, so that we as readers can see it glow.[32] Art is not 'about' reality. "Art . . . is about ways of looking, of comprehending, or *making reality comprehensible*"[33]. But to try and say the things as they themselves never hoped to be, to try and make reality comprehensible, this entails for the artist — as Banville shows in *Nightspawn, Birchwood*, and *Mefisto*, but likewise with the shift in perspective in *Doctor Copernicus, Kepler*, and *The Newton Letter* — that he is engaging himself in a never-ending process of failure. Like White, Godkin, Koppernigk, Kepler, and Swan, the artist in the end must come to terms with his predicament in redemptive despair.

*

Banville once remarked in a letter that there is "the fear of cosiness, if I may put it so: of the artist and his critic climbing hand in hand into an ivory tower for two".[34] That kind of fear must be dispelled. In what follows this critic wishes to be thought of as playing Virgil to the reader's Dante in guiding him through John Banville's 'houses of fiction'.

CHAPTER 2
Long Lankin

A prefatory note to *Long Lankin* explains that the title comes from an old English folk song, "based on the old belief that a leper can heal himself by spilling innocent blood into a silver cup".[1] The blurb takes up the thematic basis of the song, or ballad rather, and comments that

> [by] relating this theme, itself stemming from the Grail legend, to the modern obsessions with guilt, atonement and salvation, the author attempts to illustrate the timelessness of human preoccupations.

It is even bold enough to suggest that the illustration affords "the reader new and deeper insights into their [*i.e.* the characters] essentially tragic, and often funny, conditions in modern Ireland". There is something deplorably wrong about both the note and the blurb.

In most variants of the traditional ballad "Long Lankin", or "Lamkin", such as those collected in F.J. Child's *The English and Scottish Popular Ballads*[2] or the one in *The Oxford Book of Ballads*[3], the titular hero is "a mason good", who, having built Lord Wearie's[4] castle, is refused payment. By way of revenging himself for the injustice, he seeks access to the castle, which he gains with the help of a "fause nourice", while Lord Wearie is away. Lankin first kills Wearie's "bairn" and then the lady of the castle, who comes down from her chamber when she hears her child crying in terror. Whether all this has anything to do with a leper who heals himself by spilling innocent blood is more than doubtful. The ballad is about injustice, revenge, destructiveness and self-destructiveness, and so are the nine stories and the novella, or longer tale, that go to make up Banville's first book.

The unfortunate thing is that *Long Lankin* suffers from having too heavy a burden thrust upon it in the blurb: guilt, atonement, salvation, the timelessness of human preoccupations. In actual fact it is a collection of atmospheric character studies about what in "Island" is termed "the fragility of ... existence" (p. 83), or, more specifically, the fragility of personal freedom, human love and happiness.[5] These thematic concerns are treated in a rather ponderous fashion, relying too frequently on arbitrary symbolism, which seems to indicate that the author was aiming to be sophisticated although in fact he was not. That Banville is not too happy with part of the material in the original version of Long Lankin can be discerned from his decision not to republish "Persona" and "The Possessed" in the revised edition of 1984.[6] He may, in retrospect, also have had second thoughts as to whether the thematical substance implicit in the leper business is significant enough to base a complete book upon it. The case is contestable, but even more contestable is how the stories and the novella in Long Lankin should afford deeper insights into the essentially tragic, and often funny, conditions in modern Ireland.

*

The nine stories have each a cast of two characters who are closely involved with one another. They are friends, they are in love, they are married, they hate each other. Their relationships are destroyed, or disturbed in some radical way by the interference of a third character, the Long Lankin figure. In the longer tale, "The Possessed", the perspective is changed, so that now the account is rendered from the point of view of the interloper figure, "and what is examined is the effect on *him* of his disturbance of the lives and relationships of others".[7] All the stories, as well as "The Possessed", are constructed in such a way as to make the main characters at one particular moment come to terms with the precarious nature of freedom, love, and happiness.

Long Lankin seems greatly indebted to Joyce's Dubliners, not so much because the author, like Joyce, has written the moral history of his country, with Dublin as the centre of paralysis, but because the stories form groups which strikingly correspond to those in Joyce's collection: childhood, adolescence or early manhood, and maturity. The twin themes: the destruction of human happiness and the dissolution of a close relationship between two persons hold them together. In "Wild Wood" the friendship between two dissimilar boys is destroyed. "Lovers" depicts the destruction of the love between a young man and a young woman by the wicked, egotistical

scheming of the man's father. "A Death" highlights that the relationship between a married couple who are expecting a baby has long
gone sour. "The Visit" deals with the loss of innocence and happiness
experienced by a little girl. "Sanctuary" treats of how the relationship between two women breaks down and how one of them loses the
confidence of the other. "Nightwind" shows a married couple on the
last lap of their deadly serious manoeuvres towards mutual
destruction. "Summer Voices" has two children come to terms with
the bitter and violent truth about life and the concomitant destruction of their insouciant life as children. "Island" presents another love
relationship gone awry; and "Persona" focuses on the shattering of a
character's belief in a friend in a moment of extreme despair.
Additionally, at least some of the stories are linked to each other by
reading like an elaboration of possibilities inherent in a preceding
one; they are follow-ups, in a sense. "A Death" could be assumed to
depict what has, or may have, become of the 'lovers' who did not go
away after all, but remained in Ireland on account of the father; he
has died and so has their love. "Persona" could be a follow-up to
"Island", showing what sort of a development Ben could have undergone to end up like Norman Collins. "Persona" possesses thematic
parallels with "Sanctuary", since in both stories one character calls
on another character for help, but is compelled to realise that the
other does not truly feel for her, or him.

In addition, the stories are related through a likeness in compositional design. Seven of them have a three-part texture underlying
the narrative, while "A Death" and "Nightwind" are divided into
four thematic units. With the exception of "Sanctuary" and
"Summer Voices", they begin with what may be termed an
'atmospheric' description, setting the scene; for instance "Wild
Wood": "A fine rain began to fall, it drifted soundlessly through the
tangled branches and settled on the carpet of dead leaves on the
ground" (p. 9). Or take "Lovers": "Birds were going mad in the
square, spring and the recent rain had them convinced that they were
enchanters" (p. 17). Frequently, as with the near-Gothic opening in
"Persona":

> A storm was gathering, he could feel it as he drove homeward
> through the evening city. There was a bitter taste of sulphur in
> the air, and in the west the sky was blood-stained ... (p. 88)

the atmospheric description has a direct bearing on the main issue of
the story. In the case of "Persona", the incipient thunderstorm fore-
bodes the inner turmoil of the protagonist. The madness of the birds
in "Lovers" prefigures the cunning madness of the old man by means

of which he thwarts the lovers' plans. Either in this indirect manner or by dint of more direct reference, Banville, in almost all the stories, plants the main motif, or theme, at the very outset. The "dull crack of an axe wounding wood", in the first paragraph of "Wild Wood", subtly foreshadows the murder-motif. The antagonism between Muriel and Peter's old man is anticipated in the second paragraph of "Lovers" when an old man, stepping out of the house in which Peter lives, slams the door in Muriel's face (p. 17). Or "the glimpses of the closed, secret world he would never enter" (p. 58), early in "Nightwind", hint at Morris's personal predicament as a result of having married into a world to which he can never belong.

Yet another common denominator of all the stories is that they display a circular narrative movement. The "mad birds" that open "Lovers" also conclude it. The allusion to Alice's pregnancy at the beginning of "A Death" is taken up at the end. Julie's avowed wish to get married frames "Sanctuary"; the reference to the "wild wind" occurs at the start and close of "Nightwind", and the same applies to the description of the boy looking out of the window in "Summer Voices".

These composition features clearly enhance the artistry in the stories and evince Banville's keen sense of form. Although not yet developed to full fruition, they are an unmistakable indication of the author's artistic potential.

But the stories have their weaknesses. One of these results from an excessive use of metaphors, images and symbols. At times, the metaphors and symbols appear to run wild, or at least to fall short of tying up into recognisable semantic patterns. For example, references to birds and the sea permeate "Sanctuary". The female protagonist is terrified by the sounds of the sea and the seagulls. This would seem to lend metaphorical, or symbolic, import to them, but what import is difficult to determine. For the reference, if a reference is intended, is left all too ambivalent. Towards the end of "Nightwind" there is a moment during which Morris experiences some kind of epiphany, in the Joycean sense. It is brought home to him with stark truth how much he has had to sacrifice by marrying into a world in which he could never find roots and which would require from him a betrayal of his convictions. The epiphanic moment is rendered by means of a series of images, some of which are quite successful:

> Long ago when he first saw this room he had thought it beautiful, and now it was one of the few things left which had not faded. The shaded lamp took from the warm walls of lilac a

soft, full light, it touched everything, the chairs, the worn carpet, with gentle fingers. On the table beside him a half-eaten sandwich lay beside his bottle. There was an olive transfixed on a wooden pin. Muted voices came in from the hall, and outside in the fields a shout flared like a flame in the dark and then was blown away ... He felt something touch him, something of the quality of silence that informs the saddest music. It was as if all the things he had ever lost had now come back to press his heart with a vast sadness. (p. 67)

The olive transfixed on a pin is aptly suited to carry metaphorical repercussions with regard to Morris himself, who in the world of his wife resembles that olive. The end of the passage is finely wrought. The comparison of the something touching him with the quality of silence that informs the saddest music skilfully prepares the way for the climactic acknowledgement on Morris's part of what he has lost. But the first and middle sections betray an artistic insecurity. The image of the few things left that had not faded simply does not work, if only because the reader is left puzzling over why this should be, when the entire world Morris has married into is hateful to him. The image may have an effect as an atmospheric set-piece, in particular the "gentle fingers" of the light succeed in evoking a feeling of comfort, ease, safety and a sense of belonging; yet it is no more than a set-piece, or an unsophisticated attempt at conjuring up an intricate and delicate emotional situation. The unnecessary repetition of 'beside' in: "On the table beside him a half-eaten sandwich lay beside his bottle" is very clumsy indeed.

Two further deficiencies of the collection of stories are apparent in "Nightwind". One has to do with the claim in the blurb concerning the alleged insights into the conditions in modern Ireland. While most of the pieces, because of their universality of theme, could take place in any part of the western world where there is a sea, for the sea is prominent in quite a few of them, in "Nightwind" there is an overt attempt, albeit a feeble one, to introduce something like the Ireland-theme. Morris tells his wife: "Look at it. The new Ireland. Sitting around at the end of a party wondering why we're not happy" (p. 61). But this remark and the fact that a tinker plays some secondary role in the events are all there is to suggest the theme. The second shortcoming involves some of the titles in Long Lankin. If one subscribes to the idea that a title should either name the central concern of a narrative or give the reader a crucial clue as to how he is meant to understand what is offered, then the title "Nightwind", for one, is of no apparent help at all. The same could be said of "Wild

Wood", "Sanctuary", "Summer Voices", "Island", and "Persona", or of "De Rerum Natura".[8]

If it is correct that every story has a Long Lankin figure,[9] in "Sanctuary", "Island", and "Persona" it remains somewhat vague who is meant to be cast in this role. In the other pieces the identification of the interloper is fairly easy. As for "Sanctuary", here the constellation of characters suggests that the red-haired youth who comes to say good-bye to Julie is intended to represent Lankin. For it is he who causes Julie's faith in Helen to crumble to pieces by revealing that last year another girl with similar personal problems stayed with Helen. "Island" and "Persona" pose the greatest difficulties. In "Island" there is no convincing Lankin figure. It would not really make sense to identify the Negro as Lankin, tempting though this may be. For he remains teasingly elusive. Almost the same applies to the mysterious "dark implacable pursuer" in "Persona". He is one of those things full of sound and fury signifying nothing. If he is meant as some class of dark angel of destruction, the reader is surely reluctant to accept this implication since it is never adequately expressed.

*

The prime problem with the stories is that they were written when Banville was quite young. Some of the pieces date from the time when he was seventeen years of age.[10] And it shows. This criticism no doubt sounds presumptuous when stated by someone who, like this author, has not published one imaginative piece of creative writing. However, the case surely gains plausibility when one takes into account the fact that Banville himself has professed his reservations about *Long Lankin*, in particular about "The Possessed".

*

"The Possessed" is certainly fraught with severe artistic deficiencies. In all, though, the novella is not so dreadful as the author himself makes it out to be.[11]

The quotation from André Gide's *L'Immoraliste* about "objectless liberty" being a "burden" pithily sets the central theme of Part II of *Long Lankin*. The novella, told from the perspective of the Lankin figure, Ben White, is concerned with how Ben frees himself from the influence of his sister, Flora, has been exercising over him so far as well as with the question of what to do with this newly-found freedom. Another apt description of the thematic issue in "The Possessed" is given in *Nightspawn*. There, Ben White, who is surely meant to be identical with the Ben White of the novella, tells the story of Cain. When Cain, following the advice of the old man in the mountains, has opened his brother's head with an axe and goes back to his adviser to ask: "Now what shall I do?", the following brief dialogue exchange ensues:

"'Now you're free', the old man answered softly.

"And what shall I do with freedom?"

The old man smiled.

"I told you how you might be free", he said, "But I can tell nothing to a free man, and you must find your own ways.'"[12]

At the end of "The Possessed", when Ben has successfully, as he and his sister are given to believe, undergone his exorcistic experience, he tells Livia Gold:

I applied the name freedom to the thing I was searching for. But it wasn't freedom. Whatever it really was I didn't find it and by some weird logic what I did find was indeed freedom itself. And now I don't know what to do with this consolation prize. (p. 184)

Ben White's exorcism is effected in the course of a mad hatter's party, involving a prodigious army of leprechauns and a ritual reminiscent of the cruel party games in Albee's *Who's Afraid of Virginia Woolf?* and organised for "the displaced persons set" (p. 124). It is a macabre Dostoyevskian ritual of "guilt and atonement" (p. 176), supposedly planned and supervised by Livia Gold for the purpose of opening a lot of "old wounds that needed reopening" (p. 176). Ben is cast in the role of Lankin; Livia, in whose house the party is given, acts as the false nurse who lets Lankin in, setting up a "regal entry" (p. 107) for him; Flora plays the part of the lady of the ballad. In a feat of contrived coincidence, when one guest at the party, called Jacob, is reciting a couple of stanzas from "Long Lankin" and is singing:

My lady came down she was thinking no harm

Long Lankin was ready to catch her in his arm (p. 133)

Ben and Flora are manoeuvred so as to meet for the first time:

She saw him then, and her laughter ceased, but the smile remained frozen on her face. He stepped forward, vaguely conscious of them watching him ... (p. 134)

At the climax of the excruciating and hallucinatory incidents, Ben tries to kill Flora, more figuratively than literally, even though a breakneck drive in an old Ford car on the beach is involved.

Irish and English critics, not obsessionally or unduly troubled by theoretical distinctions, have tended to regard a novella as some form of narrative midway, as it were, between a short story and a novel, as something longer than a short story and shorter than a novel. *The Encyclopedia Americana*, for example, defines it as encompassing 20,000 to 40,000 words. German critics, on the other hand, notorious for their urge and seemingly inborn predilection for neat categorising and all-pervading theorising, have of old felt dissatisfied with specifying a genre on the basis of such profane criteria as mere length. So instead of relying on unsatisfactory taxonomy, they have been at pains to apply poetological considerations of composition in order to come to terms with the question of how a novella can be differentiated from related, shorter forms, such as the short story, the tale, the anecdote etc. and of course also from longer modes.

Thus, for instance, Friedrich Theodor Vischer, in his *Aesthetik*, sees the relationship between the novella and the novel as similar to that of a beam of light and a diffuse 'corpus' of light. Whereas the novel offers a comprehensive picture of a large social area, one that would be illuminated by a 'corpus' of light, a novella concentrates on one particular aspect, which is rendered with intense and momentary force.[13] Johann Wolfgang Goethe, who with *Unterhaltungen deutscher Auswanderer* (1795) tried to continue the successful tradition of novella-writing which had been inaugurated by Boccaccio, considered a novella to be nothing other than the recounting of a particularly striking and surprising event. Ludwig Tieck, sometimes termed the father of the genre, believed the characteristic feature of the novella to consist in the 'turning-point' within the narrative. What he meant by this compositional device is a stage or a point in the course of the account where the incident narrated is placed in the realm of the miraculous, the strange and unfamiliar; where, in other words, the events initially rendered quite objectively, realistically or literally, assume a symbolic, subjective or wondrous meaning. Developing Tieck's ideas, Paul Heyse advanced his "Falkentheorie", after Boccaccio's novella involving a falcon as a permeating motif and an indicator of the turning-point. For Heyse, a novella is concerned with one group of characters, with one conflict, a fateful event or a fateful question, or with a strictly limited character portrait.

The sad result of all the theorising efforts is that they have not yielded one acceptable theory of the genre. None of the theories is fully convincing, because each tends to be applicable only to those works which served to deduce it. The same drawback mars comparable poetological attempts with regard to the short story or the one-act play. Benno von Wiese, in his excellent brief study,[14] which manages to say more than others of three times its length, has clearly expressed the view that defining and pinpointing is altogether alien to the stylistic as well as structural scope of the novella.

Impossible though a normative theory is, a common denominator for a majority of cases can be found in the dramatic design of the narrative movement and the supra-realistic, symbolic nature of the events, much in Tieck's sense. "The Possessed", too, betrays these artistic characteristics. The narrative is modelled on a dramatic pattern almost Freytagian in its pyramidal form, and it seeks to imbue its incidents with symbolic value. The latter intention, however, does not always come off convincingly.

Ben White's ritual of guilt and atonement is roughly divided into three parts, which are distinguished by Ben and Flora first being at the party, then on the mad night-journey to a stretch of beach in Killiney Bay, and lastly, back at the party, or rather back in Livia's house to take part in the aftermath of the midsummer night of casualties. Part I contains the exposition and the rising action. Livia Gold, the false nurse, lays the ground situation for the organised midsummer night's madness, significantly with a ritualistic opening intended to appease the "household gods" (p. 102). In following her subsequent moves, the reader is introduced to the main characters and their plans one after another, first Ben, who has come back from Greece to rid himself of the "devils" that have been haunting him; then Flora, his opponent in the exorcistic liberation, who feels herself persecuted by the spirit of her dead mother; and thirdly, Flora's fiancé, who is a rival for Ben and, in social respects, to the displaced persons set: his convictions and style of life are contrasted with the decadence of Livia's circle. The news of Patrick's death introduces the inciting force. For he is the first in a series of casualties, and from the announcement of his untimely death, the events build up to their devastating climax. In a brief conversation, Ben and Wolf challenge Colm on his beliefs, and Ben plays a foul trick on him: he schemes an encounter between Colm and a homosexual guest.

The middle part provides the climax and starts the falling action. Flora and Ben set off on their nightmarish drive through Dublin during the midsummer night when "the spirits are out" (p. 145), for example a totally inebriated American, who reiterates his view that Ireland is a swell, little country and who has a horde of leprechauns in the boot of his immaculate white Mercedes, and a mysterious stranger called Sylvester, who has a habit of carrying "a phone receiver complete with its ragged flex" (p. 153) in the pocket of his shabby mackintosh and whose ambiguity may owe something to the man in the mackintosh in *Ulysses*. The climax of the main conflict in "The Possessed" is reached when Ben tries to kill Flora, or the two of them, by forcing her to drive the car into the sea.

With their return to Livia's house, the falling action sets in. Ben learns from Wolf that the night has resulted in a number of casualties, for which, strangely enough, everyone has held Ben responsible. The moment of final suspense is effected by Colm taking his revenge on Ben and punching him on the jaw. The remaining part of the story, involving mainly Ben and Livia, could be said to present the catastrophe, if catastrophe were not too strong a term for what actually happens. Flora, liberated by her experience with Ben on the beach from the traumatic influence of her mother, departs with her fiancé. Livia is cured of her guilt complex at having caused the death of her boy-child by having sex with Ben; and Ben himself is quite confident of having attained his freedom from Flora, so that he can start again by embarking on the career of a writer. With this decision in mind, Ben says farewell to Livia and Ireland, "to start out on his long journey home" (p. 189), that curious echo from Joyce's "The Dead".

The novella is given further structural coherence by a small number of thematic reverberations, used in such a way as to bring about circular patterns. At the beginning of "The Possessed", Livia predicts that she will be "the only one here when it's all over" (p. 105), and so she turns out to be at the end; she is the first to greet Ben and the last to be liberated by him. Equally, the room in which Ben has sex with Livia is the very room in which he stays alone with Flora before they set out on their trip at night. The compositional practice of planting the main motif, or of evoking the crucial thematic concern, very early on, sometimes — as in quite a few of the stories — in the first paragraph, is also noticeable in "The Possessed". Livia's ritualistic shower in the garden to appease the household gods sets the tone of the account and points to the strange ritual which is about to get under way.

It is a ritual that is informed by two mythical folk-customs. The events take place on Midsummer's Eve, which is to say on June 23rd, when fire-wheels, signifying the sun, used to be rolled down hills to denote the descent of the sun as from that day onwards.[15] Or enormous bonfires would be lit. The general purpose of the fire was to promote the growth of the crops and the welfare of man and beast by averting the dangers and calamities which threaten them.[16] Two theories have been constructed around the midsummer ceremonies: the solar theory and the purification theory. According to the first, fires are kindled as a charm to ensure an abundant supply of sunshine for man and beast, corn and fruit.[17] According to the latter, fire is used as a destructive agent to consume evil things and burn, or repel, witches, who were believed to hover invisibly in the air.[18] No matter which theory was held responsible, the purification and fertility rites were reason enough for the people to indulge in outrageous merry-making. The outrageousness of the events and the belief in the purificatory effect of midsummer night's rites seem to lie behind "The Possessed". But a second traditional custom appears to have gone into the novella. It is the ceremony known as "carrying out Death", originally performed on the fourth Sunday in Lent to ensure a prosperous year,[19] and involving the throwing of an effigy of Death, often a puppet embodying winter, into the water. The incident on the beach seems to have a parallel in this rite, just as the general idea of the ritual scapegoat, designed to remove all ills that have infested a people, is responsible for some aspects of the character of Ben White.

With the exception of Colm, the characters who have gathered for the midsummer night's party are of a particular sort:

> They are just trying to prove they are real. Look around you. What it is you see is a bunch of unhappy people making a little world of happiness and fond friends. It's all a lie but in a way they are succeeding because this is the only place they belong. Right here and now. Ireland or England or — Greece is all the same. They are an international breed. The displaced persons set. (p. 124)

Its most important exponent is Ben White. He is introduced as "an intricately made, unhuman creature" (p. 107), "balanced on the edge of a private darkness" (p. 107). Quite soon after meeting Livia, he makes his intentions clear. He is the Ben of "Island", who has been brought back from Greece by certain dark forces he sought to escape from.

> I thought I could get away but they followed me. They brought me back. Always they bring you back to where you started. Like a murder. A murderer is what they want to make of you. Kill and you will be free they whisper. Free. I want to be free Mrs. Gold and so I'm here to see if they can keep a promise. (p. 108)

Later on, in almost identical words, he says the same to Flora (p. 142). When he meets her, the text states in meaning-laden words: ". . . he

... went through the frame into the past" (p. 134). And indeed all sorts of private obsessions connected with the past are brought to bear on Ben. Quite a few are convincing, as far as they go, but there are some which are truly disappointing. One of his obsessions has to do with the sea and drowning. This is possibly a parallel to the Shakespearean idea of "sea change and death" in *The Tempest*. If it is intended in such a way, it does not work acceptably. Nor does the notion from Eliot's "The Love Song of J. Alfred Prufrock" of hearing mermaids singing and lingering in the chambers of the sea "Till human voices awake us, and we drown".[20] It is this notion that seems to have inspired the passage where "voices ... from the black reaches of the sea" come to Ben via Sylvester Pettit's disconnected telephone receiver. The passage may have been designed to help substantiate Ben's fear of drowning one day (p. 157), a fear that has been plaguing him ever since, as a child, he saw a drowned man on the beach (p. 157). But even this aspect seems too unmotivated to be believable. The only point that does come off is the allusion to an event from "Summer Voices" to establish Ben's haunting past. He mentions to Flora that when they discovered the body of the drowned man, she laughed at the sight, whereas he himself "saw some rumour of the future" in it (p. 157). In the story, the boy and the girl undergo precisely these experiences.

What has pre-eminently been holding him in thrall and has induced him to return to Ireland is Flora.

> I want you to leave me alone ... I want to be free of you. Wherever I go you follow me. A thousand miles was nothing. (p. 158)

There are, it would seem, unambiguous hints of an incestuous relationship between Ben and Flora. For instance, her provocative showing of her thighs in an erotic manner, which is accompanied by the remark: "You still want me" (p. 160). Near the end, he confesses to Livia Gold:

> Did you ever see two trees growing so close together that their trunks joined and twisted through each other. I loved her in all sorts of ways and certainly there was more than a little hate in it. (p. 184)

Strong bonds of profound love are responsible for Ben's state of affairs. A hint is given in the account of Apollo's love for Hyacinthus. It tells of Apollo's unrestrained affection for Hyacinthus and of how Apollo, infatuated by Hyacinthus' beauty, tried to teach him everything he knew. But the West Wind had also fallen for Hyacinthus, and when one day Apollo was instructing him to throw the discus, the West Wind was filled with excruciating jealousy and fury, and he made Hyacinthus' first throw turn back upon him. The discus smashed Hyacinthus' forehead and killed him. Of course one is tempted to apply the story to the constellation Ben *versus* Colm for Flora's love. But the analogy does not really work. If Ben is Apollo, it does not make much sense to equate Colm with the West Wind. And if Colm is associated with Apollo, Ben cannot be the West Wind, for he does not really kill Flora. He may assume he has done so, but the assumption like the entire exorcism is somewhat hard to swallow.

The events intended to denote Ben's breaking loose from Flora, with the sinister Sylvester emitting "a wailing ... punctuated by yelps that seemed of ecstacy" (p. 162) appear to have got out of hand. They simply fail to imbue the otherwise realistic incidents with symbolic overtones which are plausible. The wild hazardous drive on the beach, preceded by Flora and Ben eating chips, drinking rum with an American and so forth is seriously flawed. Nor will any but the most gullible of readers accept Ben's decision to go away as being the true outcome of his midsummer night's experience. It is all too glib. The contriving machinery of the author's manoeuvring the events to click into place can be heard creaking too loudly, and the coincidences make the mind boggle, as for instance when, after the exorcism, the sun is said to be rising to greet a new day, one that will find a new liberated Ben White. Too much of the middle section is unsatisfactory. Too much is simply asserted by the author, but not shown. There is, notably, a considerable amount of string-pulling at work to make the character of Ben not only into a Long Lankin figure, who is forced into the role of the victim, but likewise into some sort of Byronic "Childe Harold", characterised by demonic individualism and unmitigated *Weltschmerz* (p. 118); but the whole effort is a bit too clever to ring true. Too many casualties are strewn along Ben's path.

An outstanding one is Livia. She has traumatic obsessions of her own. Repeatedly she is haunted by car sounds, a squeal of tyres, and a voice frantically calling (p. 109). Before too long, the cause of these noises becomes evident. They occur in her head and remind her of how she killed her boy-child by running him over with her car. At one point, she sums up her problem of guilt:

> But lately I've made a discovery, she said slowly. The world do you see is full of death and in order for me to live at all I have to die just a little. I'm empty now. I am not happy nor unhappy. I feel nothing. But you know nature abhors a vacuum so maybe

> something will come to fill the barren spaces. Who knows.
> Maybe a miracle. (p. 185)

So far her character delineation is credible, even if it does not add up
to much. But when shortly after making her confession to Ben, she
succumbs to his efforts at making love to her, sporting "a slow,
wicked smile" (p. 187) on her face, her behaviour is too puzzlingly
unaccounted for. It is quite conceivable that Banville intended her
sexual infidelity to signify one instance of where she is forced to "die
a little", an act of moral depravation. Still, one has difficulty in
accepting her decision in favour of extra-marital sex as a true
atonement for her feelings of guilt.

Slightly more credible, though again not altogether successfully
realised, is the character of Flora. Not surprisingly, she is also disturbed by a ghost from her past in an Ibsen-like way. Her mother,
who died giving birth to her, bedevils her to such an extent that she
suspects her poltergeist of having barged into the room into which
she and Ben have withdrawn from the party hubbub (p. 144). Only
when Banville has stretched his exercise in deliberate mystification
to its very limits is Ben made to give away the information necessary
for the reader to understand Flora. While it may be cleverly effective
to withhold the true familial relationship of Ben and Flora until the
climactic moment on the beach, the delay in providing details
concerning her obsession is feckless. Neither on a figurative nor on a
metaphorical level is it convincing when Flora argues after her
experience on the beach:

> You see Ben I think I needed last night more than you did. I
> learned a lot. I learned it's possible to live without games. There
> is a real world, I've grown up at last. I think I'm happy now —
> yes I'm free too . . . You see really you did kill me. At least you
> killed one part of me. But — well death is a kind of freedom
> really isn't it. I mean some kind of death. (p. 173)

Well, yes, another liberated soul in the displaced persons set, but the
reason why the liberation has been effected is too shady. To be sure,
there is some mention of Flora and Ben having grown up in a world
of their own, a dreamworld (p. 183), which she may have been
compelled to leave behind after the encounter with Ben. But since
she is engaged to be married to Colm, who is socially-oriented,
down-to-earth and the opposite of everything Ben represents, she
would surely have been introduced to the real world much earlier
through Colm; at least she would logically have been confronted
much earlier with the realization that "there is a real world". And to
embellish Flora with "the powers of magic" and an ability to "call up

the dead" (p. 183) would seem feasible in a fairy tale only. The embellishment rings false in a narrative the blurb of which maintains that it affords the reader new and deeper insights into conditions in modern Ireland.

If such insights can be said to be provided at all in "The Possessed", they are connected with the character of Colm. In Livia Gold's ménage of highly-strung, decadent and idiosyncratically wilful people, Colm is an outsider. He is introduced as being unable to forget his "social conscience" (p. 111); he is "all for the working-man and the starving masses and he can't forget it for a moment" (p. 112), when the others at the party try their best to forget it and be concerned solely with their private interests. The difference between Colm and the rest of the cast is probably best expressed by Colm himself in his debate with Wolf:

> I was born in a little house in a row of other little houses all the same. There was a dry lavatory out the back and a big tin bath we all washed in Saturday nights. My father was a drunkard and my mother died of a heart attack. There was a connection — you know. I was left to get along on my own and I'm proud of what I've done. Sure it's corny. It's not fashionable to be an accountant is it. But if some of these here tonight had to live for a week like my mother did all her life it might wake them up a bit. I'll tell you one thing. There would be less of this fashionable claptrap you've been giving out. (p. 124)

There is surely inherent here an occasion for social criticism, but no one can seriously be expected to take the characters Colm is inveighing against as true representatives of modern Ireland. Besides, Colm is not at all fleshed out by the author to the stature of a possible spokesman either for, or against, any sort of conditions, funny or tragic, connected to modern Ireland. Whereas most of the supporting cast remain too shady, Colm remains too wooden to be of interest. He is built up as one among many other prey that the vulturous Ben tears to shreds. The point is, of course, that the blurb is fatuous. Banville probably never intended to convey any such insights.

*

Perhaps more apparently in "The Possessed" than in the stories, Banville can be observed striving for his personal artistic idiom. There are passages of verbal brilliance and there are others where the metaphorical and rhetorical pyrotechnics clearly misfire. One chain of symbols and metaphors involves light/fire and water. It is nicely established in the very first paragraph, where the concepts of light/ fire and water are evoked and remarkably modulated and blended. When Livia is standing under the silver arrows of water which emit from the sprinklers, light and water are said to flash against each other (p. 101). Her hair becomes heavy "with the cold flames of water", while "crystals of ice [are] burning the sky" (p. 101). Whether consciously or unconsciously chosen, fire and water are particularly appropriate symbols and metaphors in connection with midsummer night rituals, for the reason that mythical expulsion of evil has customarily been associated with these elements. Through-out "The Possessed" there are recurrent references to them in various forms, ranging from such seemingly accidental coincidences as the choice of the name 'Livia', which recalls the Joycean embodiment of water and flux "Anna Livia Plurabelle", to such dauntingly unusual descriptions as "Ben looked, light flashed on the shards, blood and ice" (p. 133). What differentiates the style of "The Possessed" from that of *Doctor Copernicus*, say, is that in the former certain chains of symbols are built up and continued for a considerable time but not sustained throughout.

There are also quite a number of single metaphors of considerable excellence, for instance this one: "Glasses clattered, punctuating the phrases of the drinkers and laying jagged edges against their words" (p. 115), and further, quite a few masterly observations which manage to encompass paradoxes, in Cleanth Brooks' sense of the term — the comic, pathetic and the sad: "John Gold was polishing his spectacles and at the same time grinning all around him to prove that he could see perfectly well without them . . ." (p. 121). Yet, sadly, the stylistic achievements are outweighed by too many shortcomings. An annoying number of questions which the text prompts the reader into asking are left open. What thematic purpose do the leprechauns have? Are they just a throwaway joke? What is one to make of the character of Sylvester Pettit? Is the story about Hyacinthus really worth the telling in the context of Livia Gold's ritual and Ben's ordeal? Is it really necessary for him to have sexual intercourse with her in order to top the bill of his efforts to provide "blood and death tonight" (p. 128) at the party? There is also the question of whether the policy of gathering many of the characters from the stories in *Long Lankin* at Livia's party really helps to link the novella with the stories and make the narratives combine into an artistic whole: Morris and Liza of "Nightwind", Jacob and Norman of "Persona",

Ben and Flora of "Summer Voices", Julie and Helena of "Sanctuary".

Another deficiency lies in the recurrent reference to Flora's hair. Almost every guest at the party observes that she has cut it (pp. 112, 113, 140, 183), but the significance of the reference is left exasperatingly obscure. Colm always takes "a reckless gulp of whiskey" (pp. 115, 123). Too many characters, including Ben and Colm, are observed "sucking their teeth" (pp. 124, 155, 182) or looking down at their hands. When Ben, trying to find his way around in the dark room, trips over some object and accompanies his exertions with words like "Can't you put on the bloody light. Ech. O I'm going to — going to — ach chuh. Ah. The dust. Chaach. Christ" (p. 139), the effect is cheap.

In *Doctor Copernicus*, the astronomer is frequently assailed by visions of nightmarish horror, many of them involving "monstrous hawklike creatures ... flying ... on visible struts and wires ..."[21] There Banville has managed to incorporate them meaningfully into the organic whole of the narrative. Almost as if in anticipation of such visions, Ben is troubled by a similar figment of his imagination during a brief period of sleep:

> The room was in darkness, and when he looked down he saw animals surround the bed, squat black creatures that grovelled and snarled, and snapped their pointed, glittering teeth ... (p. 143)

But this hallucinatory mirage does not tie in with any other aspect of the story, apart from Ben's hearing Eliot's mermaids singing down Sylvester Pettit's disconnected telephone receiver.

*

Banville is probably right in regarding "The Possessed" as a disaster. The novella is probably meant to be an imitation of Joyce's "The Dead" and was composed under the influence of "the mighty Russians"[22], principally among them Dostoyevsky, who in his novel *The Possessed*, or *The Devils*, has a similarly calamitous fête. But it did not quite all work out.

CHAPTER 3
Nightspawn

The theme of *Nightspawn*, according to the first-person narrator, Benjamin S. White, is contained in the solution to the riddle he sets the reader at the beginning of Part III:

> Perceive. One word, three syllables. The first is a wager. The second a fish. The third is one third less than everything, and the whole is my theme. What is it?[1]

A wager is a 'bet', the name of the fish is 'ray', and one third less than everything is 'al'. The theme, therefore, would be 'betrayal'. Seamus Deane thought that *Nightspawn* was "fundamentally concerned with pursuit and immunity"[2], and he does not seem to have liked the manner in which Banville has treated this allegedly fundamental concern:

> Instead of finding a way in which the commentary on time and freedom will arise naturally from the story and its circumstances, Mr. Banville makes the story into an exotic mode of talking about these problems.[3]

And:

> His is a Portrait of the Artist as a Cryptic or as a Corrupt Young Man, but Mr. Banville forgets Ben's youth and forgives it as Joyce never does Stephen's.[4]

Nor did most of the reviewers like what they encountered. The review in *Oxford Mail* remarked: "White is strong medicine, and it is difficult to decide whether his doings are to be interpreted on a real or symbolic level".[5] The reviewer in *The Daily Telegraph* betrayed himself to have been no less at sea as to what to make of the account: "But what precisely the ambiguous narrator and supporting cast of nasties are up to remained for me an enigma shrouded in ennui".[6] *The Financial Times* objected to the book as "a load of ripe, verbose Irish hokum, exuberantly insincere, almost heroically overwritten".[7]

Auberon Waugh, in his vitriolic vein, panned it without pardon: "The only purpose, so far as one can judge, of this utterly pointless book is to impress the gullible reviewers with its own cleverness ... a blinding bore to read".[8] Brendan Hennessy, however, was sensible enough to realise that *Nightspawn* is "a novel about how to write a novel. The magic is in Banville's mastery of construction and language, confirming the starting promises of his first book, *Long Lankin*."[9]

The reason why so many reviewers dismissed the novel was presumably that they really felt betrayed. *Nightspawn* is, apart from anything else, about betrayal, though betrayal of a specific sort. Banville himself has made the point succinctly in an interview:

> *Nightspawn* is a kind of betrayal, of the reader's good faith in the writer's good faith, and also it is a betrayal of, if you like, the novelist's guild and its secret signs and stratagems.[10]

Nightspawn is an inside-out novel; "it wears its skeleton and its nerves on the outside".[11] The book represents a meta-novel and is, besides Flann O'Brien's *At Swim-Two-Birds* (1939) and Ralph Cusack's *Cadenza* (1958), one of the very few novels of this class to have been written in Ireland after World War II. It was published when the self-reflexive mode of narrative discourse was running rampant, especially in the United States, but also in England and elsewhere. Notably enough, Banville, presumably writing under the influence of Samuel Beckett[12] and Vladimir Nabokov, offered his contribution to the 'critical novel', to the narrative stock-taking of what fiction can, or cannot achieve, long before a writer such as John Fowles, that admirable metafictionist, did with *Mantissa* (1982). Just like *Mantissa* and most other meta-narratives, *Nightspawn* is fundamentally about art, throwing into stark relief the question if, and how, it is feasible in literature to transfix beauty, capture reality in its essence, and laying bare the conventions, some of them at least, by dint of which conventional fiction creates an illusion of *mimesis*. *Nightspawn* plays havoc with those conventions, is essentially play, seemingly modelled upon some kind of intricate narrative chess-game, involving characters named White, Weiss, and Black; there is even a Knight, and there are any number of pawns, which is to say fictional personages who are shown to be at the mercy of what Nabokov, chess connoisseur *extraordinaire*, would call "an anthropomorphic deity impersonated by [himself]".[13] At one point, Ben White discovers an unfinished chess-game in a room at Julian Kyd's villa (p. 87). The game is unfinished because it metaphorically represents the fiction game in which he figures as head pawn, which at that stage is only half way through. Chapter 13 of Part II reads: "White pawn to black king one. Look at this." (p. 188)

For an unsuspecting, undiscerning readership, steeped mainly in nineteenth-century realism, to offer a game is to commit an act of betrayal. But to write a novel in the post-war era as if nothing had happened in fiction since the turn of the century is even a grosser act of betrayal. Partly in order to show up the exhausted nature of the established narrative conventions, the narcissistic narrative emerged particularly in the '50s and '60s of this century, even though the idea goes back to Sterne and even further back to Cervantes and *Don Quijote*.[14] Metafiction should be seen as a serious endeavour to develop the art of fiction, and not as an aberrant attempt at solipsism as a result of which narrative discourse is inexorably manoeuvred into a blind alley.

Ben White remarks on one occasion:

> ... I must say here, in fairness to myself, even though I do not deserve it, that things were not so obvious as I have made them appear in these pages. The process of artistic selection sometimes eliminates the nuances which misleads. I have tried to retain a few of them, but they have a fishy smell. Anyway, I think that it should be ... look, what am I excusing? What do I care? I am the boss around here, of course I am, and I shall do as I like, so put that in your column and criticize it. (p. 175)

One may, as those reviewers did, put it in one's column and criticise it; but there can be no gainsaying that the implications of the statement constitute the very heart of *Nightspawn*. Elsewhere the narrator divulges that what he is after in his "sinister pages" is the issue of how "time [can] be vanquished" (p. 107) through art; and still elsewhere he points out that he is "talking about the past, about remembrance ... about Mnemosyne, that lying whore" (p. 113); at the end of his account he notes: "I am talking about art" (p. 224). *Nightspawn* is about all this, and about a *coup d'état* in Greece.

*

In a letter to his American publisher, W.W. Norton & Company, Banville has explained at some length why he felt it necessary to undertake this extraordinary narrative enterprise.

> Anyone writing today, who cares at all about his craft, is conscious of how this half century has shifted the battleground of art. Fifty years ago, writing was a struggle with the raucous

voice of language; today it is a struggle with the insidious whisper of silence. Total silence seems the only really honest way to speak about Buchenwald and Hiroshima; silence has now come to seem, not failure, but honesty . . . All right, silence is fine; but what do you do if you have a voice and it won't stop still? First of all, in my case at least, one has to use that voice to speak about that voice; one has to build up a base which is nearest to the honesty of silence, and begin from there. NIGHTSPAWN, for me, is that base. I have written a book which, for all its fruity flavor, is as near to silence as I can get, at the moment.[15]

Whether silence is in fact the only really honest way to speak about the atrocities of Buchenwald and Hiroshima is surely arguable. What is less arguable is that the struggle with the insidious whisper of silence, that the notion of using the voice to speak about that voice, is strongly reminiscent of how Beckett has characterised the creative predicament of the contemporary artist.

The expression that there is nothing to express, nothing with which to express, nothing from which to express, no power to express, no desire to express, together with the obligation to express.[16]

Banville's concern with failure recalls another of Beckett's statements:

. . . to be an artist is to fail, as no other dare fail, that failure is his world and the shrink from it desertion . . . I know that all that is required now, in order to bring even this horrible matter to an acceptable conclusion, is to make of this submission, this admission, this fidelity to failure, a new occasion . . . and of the act which, unable to act, obliged to act, he makes, an expressive act, even if only of itself, of its impossibility, of its obligation.[17]

"In Nightspawn", Banville has submitted, "I set out to fail. What was important was the quality of the failure".[18] In that letter to W.W. Norton & Company, he goes on to explain:

On more immediate levels, I wrote a book so that it would be puzzling; yes, you do have to read it again, and if, after the second, third or twentieth reading, you feel cheated, that, too, is intended. Art is cheating. I could have tied up all the knots in it with one of those Agatha Christie scenes where all the suspects gather in one room, and that insufferable little prick, Hercule, will point to one . . . the other one again.

And:

. . . let me just echo Ben, and say that the book far from being about Greece, or violence, or love, is about the whisper of forgotten music, the transference of art, the smiles of Botticelli's maiden.

One further self-comment may help to place the artistic efforts responsible for the writing of *Nightspawn* into a meaning-giving context.

> When I came to write my first novel . . ., the attitude which I adopted was one of extreme distrust of the novel form itself. I set out to subject the traditional, nineteenth-century concept to as much pressure as I could bring to bear on it, while remaining within the rules. I made a wildly implausible plot. I chose stock characters. I brought in a political theme — the Colonels' coup in Greece — precisely in order to make nothing of it . . . There are many reasons for proceeding in this way, but one of the principal ones was that I was interested to test, to *bend* close to breaking, the very curious relationship which exists between a reader and his author. I wished to challenge the reader to go on suspending his disbelief in my fiction in the face of an emphatic admission on my part that what I was presenting *was* fiction and nothing more — and everything more.[19]

The point is clearly made: *Nightspawn* was conceived of as a meta-fictional attack on the nineteenth-century conventions of fiction — those conventions that, for better or for worse, still hold sway over a good deal of what is being written today, especially in Ireland. Concomitantly, the novel is also an attack on, a deliberate betrayal of, the reader expectations provoked by these conventions. The question, though, is whether the experiment was worth doing. The author himself seems, now in retrospect, to have his doubts.[20]

*

One way of assessing *Nightspawn* is to consider it as a thriller, or novel of suspense. The self-conscious narrator at one stage admonishes himself: ". . . wait now, wait, I am getting carried away with all this thriller stuff" (p. 177). It is also possible to find affinities with the novel of pursuit, as epitomised by William Godwin's *Caleb Williams* (1794). For instance, the openings of the two novels are quite similar.[21] But then, the novel of pursuit is of course the precursor of the thriller, or novel of suspense. Or *Nightspawn* could be grouped among that species of novel which P.N. Furbank, in his discussion of Godwin's book, has called "the dramatized history of a state of mind".[22] This represents a form of confessional literature, comparatively rare in either Irish or English literature, which can claim Dostoyevsky as its most prolific practitioner. Incidentally, the first sentences in *Nightspawn* are a paraphrase of the beginning of *Notes from Underground*. There the narrator insists: "I am a sick man . . . I am an angry man. I am an unattractive man. I think there is something wrong with my liver . . . No, I refuse treatment out of spite."[23] Ben White notes: "I am a sick man, I am a spiteful man. I think my life is diseased . . . [etc.]" (p. 7).

Nightspawn features a Prufrockian protagonist. In trying to set down his unusual and complicated involvement, as a pawn in someone else's sinister game, in an attempt at a *coup d'état* by the army in Greece and in certain efforts by an English businessman to counter that attempt, he is "[spitting] out all the butt-ends of [his] days and ways".[24] As with Prufrock, we are faced with a character of considerable intelligence and humility who is seeking to decide the significance of his own life. White is fatigued by his worldliness: "Do I dare/Disturb the universe?"; he means to affirm his existence amidst all its obvious decline. Like Prufrock, White is paralysed "like a patient etherized upon a table"[25]; he is characterised by passivity and activated by external forces. He is a new Lazarus, come back from the dead, overwhelmed by his own spiritual death.

But Ben White's account, although employing the customary paraphernalia of the genre — conspiracy, murder, persecution, love, drinking bouts, mysteries galore, punch-ups, last-minute revelations, narrow escapes, and a sensation-scene full of blood and gore and gunsmoke — is not an ordinary thriller; it is, as was suggested above, a thriller which deliberately wears the conventions of the genre on its sleeve.

The obvious metafictional intention is carried out on two levels: on the level of the story, and on the level of the authorial intrusions. These levels coincide with the two different levels of time. There is what appears to be a present time plane, constituted by Ben's conjuring up the events in Greece — "I open the box and there it is . . ." (p. 7); "I am about to conjure up another world" (p. 107); and there is a past time plane, concretised by the events White recounts. To some extent, what is narrated about the revolution and Ben's involvement in it is not so important as the way in which the recounting is being effected. Ben's thriller is full of contradictions, incongruities, deliberate mystifications, revelations that are not revelations, explanations that are not explanations. The perpetrators of the coup and their opponents advanced towards their various goals by intricately circuitous routes. Ben follows their practice in the manner of his account.

About most things regarding the political conspiracy Ben is kept in the dark. Much importance is attached to "a little thing" (p. 25, *passim*) the two parties are in search of. For a long time Ben, and likewise the reader, has no idea as to the nature of that little thing. Eventually he learns that it is some document Julian Kyd, the English businessman, desires in order to spike the Colonels' guns. Repeatedly messages are brought to White which he is unable to decipher, as when a child offers him a scrap of paper on which he finds "strange hieroglyphs ... printed, a message without meaning" (p. 32). At times he may be able to decode the communications, but then he leaves the reader in ignorance as to their contents. Or there is the woman Helena, with whom White falls in love. Is she Kyd's daughter or wife? At first, she is introduced by Kyd as his wife, and she herself claims to be his wife, while evidence accumulates that she is his daughter, playing a macabre joke on White. Even when near the end of the novel Kyd confesses that Helena is his daughter, too much remains unexplained, in the face of a profusion of explanations, for both Ben and the reader to be fully convinced. After all, Kyd admits to being an obsessional practical joker. When Ben believes some kind of revelation has been, or is being, offered to him concerning the mysterious battle for power between the Colonels and Kyd, either he is incapable of verifying what the revelation was about (p. 132), or the revelation is cut short before it reaches its most decisive stage.

Then there is a sizeable number of contradictions and incongruities in which Ben as well as the reader find themselves entangled, for instance the one about, again, a message, this time from Erik Weiss, with whom Ben has some dealings:

> It was from Erik. His handwriting, which I had never seen before, surprised me with its neatness and docility, its deference, almost, to the reader's eye. The tall letters demurely bowed their heads, the others were fat and fulsome. It was written in violet ink. That German was full of little surprises (of which, by the way, this was one, for it was not he who had written the note). (pp. 137f.)

The reader is led to believe that the note has been written by Erik, even though he may have doubts as to how Ben is able to tell, having never before seen Erik's handwriting. Because of the comments on the ink and the letter, though, he will convince himself that his doubts are unfounded, only to find, surprisingly, that he *was* right after all.

A perfect summary, as Ben suggests (p. 219), of the events centred around the coup as well as of the narrative process which recounts them is offered in the penultimate section of the book. Ben has been asked to visit Colonel Sesosteris on his death-bed to receive some explanation from the Colonel about the revolution and his involvement in it. But quite symptomatically of Ben's narrative, before the Colonel can divulge anything he dies. Once again, White is forced into the role of a stupid ignorant pawn in a farcical game "where nobody trusts anybody" (p. 83). The reader's position is little better.

Ben says of himself: "I was born in the darkest hour of the darkest night in a black year . . ." (p. 41). The title of the novel may refer to his being a spawn of the night. But obviously and no matter whether meant as a throwaway joke, there is a pun contained in 'nightspawn': it may also be 'night's pawn', or 'knight's pawn'. The last possibility proffers some telling comment on Ben's situation, for he is indeed at one stage a pawn of one Charles Knight, an associate of Kyd's to whom he gives the valuable document, that "little thing". Both 'night spawn' and 'night's pawn' invite the reader to speculate on connotative connections with the events. Such speculations, however, are, it appears, only called for by Banville to lead the reader on an interpretive wild-goose chase. But then White, and through him Banville, warns that the account is about betrayal.

Banville's narrative strategy is such that the reader is manoeuvred into a position which exactly equals Ben's in the context of the incipient political upheaval in Greece — the upheaval which finds its counterpart in the upheaval wrought upon the narrative conventions.

*

In Part I of Nightspawn, Banville creates a potentially rich ground-situation for a suspense fiction, encompassing secret meetings to hand over valuable documents, murder, the ransacking of rooms, moves and countermoves, love and sex. Moreover, the ground-situation leaves open any number of probable ways in which the intrigues and conspiracies could be developed. Part II transfers the action from the island of Part I to Athens, and it serves largely to further the love-relationship between Ben and Helena, while also providing opportunity to get Ben involved with Julian Kyd and his plans. This section culminates in an hilarious climax that bears unmistakable resemblance to a mad hatter's party: Ben sees, or thinks he sees, Julian

Kyd beating Colonel Sosesteris and Erik Weiss' amanuensis, Andreas, with a cane while Erik comes galloping through the room and crashes through the window. Part III purports to present the finale: the resolution of the various conflicts. Admittedly, the document, much sought after in the previous parts, is explained and handed over by Ben; the love affair is brought to an end; each of the main characters reveals what role he played in the coup; Erik is killed because he was a traitor; the revolution has started; Ben avenges himself on Kyd by inadvertently killing his son whereas he meant to kill Julian and Helena. It is a finale all right, but one that resolves as much as it leaves unresolved.

The openendedness of the suspense action fulfils two functions. It is one more of those devices employed by Banville to send his reader on bootless interpretive speculations. The unresolved aspects provoke him to consider the events afresh, from the start, in the hope of discovering something previously overlooked that may explain the hitherto unexplained. The second function of the openendedness has to be assessed in connection with the novel's argument about the role of art. On three occasions, Ben White asserts that there is something wrong with the chronology of his account (pp. 139, 206, 223). Referring to this alleged deficiency for the last time, he even suggests: "To judge the veracity of the book, take a look at the time sequence" (p. 223). The point is, though, that this clue involves an intentional misleading of the reader. Apart from some clearly identifiable flaskbacks there is nothing especially deficient about the chronology. Or if there is, Banville does not provide the means for the reader to ascertain where the time sequence goes off the rails.

The novel is a practical joke in more than one way, but a practical joke as Julian Kyd understands and explains the phenomenon: as something "where no conditions are manufactured, but the complete thing is conjured out of the air" (p. 195). To demonstrate that a novel is something "conjured out of the air", as it were, this is the principal purpose pursued by Banville. White is correct in considering his book to be a metaphor (p. 223), but not so much of despair, as he first ventures to submit before quickly retracting the suggestion; rather it is a metaphor of the futility of endeavouring to capture reality through fiction, even art in general. Significantly, Ben's last Beckettian remarks concern this futility. He urges himself on to try yet another time to transfix it all.

Come, one more effort to transfix it all, to express it all. Try. I cannot. The world is ... Art is ... No, no use, I cannot. You must, there must be a conclusion. A word, even. Try. Try now,

here. Could I? Try. Chapter one. My story begins at a —
(p. 224)

The effort is useless. Reality may be organised, shaped into art, but once it has been subjected to this transformation, it is no longer reality; it is art, an entity distinctly different from so-called reality, a reality of its own while at the same time part of that phenomenological reality.

The futility of capturing reality through fiction is, among other narrative strategies, expressed by means of a circular narrative movement. Circularity of texture is evoked in the very first chapter; it is sustained throughout the novel and fully brought into the open at the very end. Additional support is lent by a number of thematic echoes and recurrent references, most prominent among them the mystery regarding the Godot-like character James H. Twinbein. He is mentioned first in section 3 of Part I, when Erik Weiss meets Ben White and mistakenly thinks he is Twinbein. True to the novel's ludic spirit, James H. Twinbein is one of Julian Kyd's practical jokes, the name being an anagram of Ben's full name: Benjamin S. White.

Ben's efforts at narrative discourse are unconventional indeed. Advancing from the conviction that "art is, after all, only mimicry" (p. 217), he places his main interest in demonstrating how this mimicry is accomplished.

*

The metafictional elements can roughly be divided into two classes. Whereas the laying bare of the general narrative conventions is effected through explicit commentary, the turning inside-out of the conventions pertaining to the thriller is brought about by dint of parodic treatment.

The concept dominating the metafictional activities in *Nightspawn* is that of the novelist as magician, or Aristophanic sorcerer. As early as in the second chapter, the notion is evoked, when Ben, speaking for the first time of the island, maintains: "I open the box and there it is, an image cut from jewels, quivering between the azure lid and bed of sapphire silk" (p. 7). The novelist opens his box of tricks and conjures up a self-sufficient world. Ben contends he is the ring-master in his fictional ménage, but this is only half the truth, and Ben knows it. His freedom of choice is curtailed by the conventions which have to be observed in order for a specific kind of fiction to come into its own. At one point, he abruptly interrupts a dialogue passage and reasons:

> How tedious this is. Could I not take it all as understood, the local colour and quaint customs, and then get on to the real meat of things? But I suppose the conventions must be observed. (p. 36)

And yet this issue also involves a matter of choice. That Ben is only prepared to follow the conventions up to a point is quite evident from the nature of the account. Otherwise his fabrication would not be metafictional. In one case he may be eager not to infringe upon the dictates of the genre, as when he gets carried away by a subject and forgets the normative narrative procedure for a moment, but then admonishes himself to present everything in its proper place, so that the reader's belief remains unshattered (p. 29). In another, however, he deliberately wreaks havoc with plausibility and throws into relief the artifice nature of his book by halting the narrative movement in order to repeat a sentence, or a scene he takes delight in:

> ... I reached forward and touched her hand.
>
> 'I'll teach you to laugh again.'
>
> I said that, I did. I really did. Let us have it once more, for the joy of it.
>
> 'I shall teach you to laugh again, Helena.' (p. 120)

One may be reminded here of how Tristram Shandy arrests the action of his uncle Toby's knocking the ashes from his tobacco-pipe for a considerable time in order to attend to matters that are happening in another part of the Shandy household at the same time.

Not surprisingly, almost all the issues and self-conscious commentary in *Nightspawn* were previously explored by Sterne and Beckett and to similar thematic ends. Take the overt evaluation of a given description: "Clumsy description, try again, no time ..." (p. 88); or a remark such as this one: "Later I shall fill in the details ... all these things when I get to the smut" (p. 40); or announcements of the type that tell the reader what part of the novel is about to follow (cf. p. 156).

Such instances basically serve two functions. One is to point out to the reader and make him never forget that he is contemplating an artefact. The second function is to challenge the reader's critical awareness. Sterne, by incorporating possible responses to his story into his book, which responses he attributes to the fictitious Madam or Sir, satirises these ways of reading his novel by disclosing their fatuity, and he indicates more adequate receptive efforts. Similarly, discussions of style and descriptive technique in *Nightspawn* provoke the reader to examine whether the narrator's judgement is correct. An examination of this sort inevitably necessitates a deeper involvement and a more attentive participation in the receptive process. The reader is unrelentingly drawn into the book, so to speak.

By far the most telling example of the kind of game the self-conscious narrator in *Nightspawn* plays with, and on, the reader concerns the thematic, stylistic and compositional elements of great excellence with which White claims to have invested his account. "There are", he maintains, "pearls here strewn among this sty of words. Time enough to rend and tear, time enough" (p. 36). Shortly afterwards, he even augments his claim by arguing: "Did I say pearls? Diamonds, for god's sake, rubies" (p. 39). Probably only the most inattentive of readers would not jump at the suggestion and be sent off in search for those diamonds and rubies, and there are indeed enough to be found. There are those diamonds that reflect the artistic skill of the writer Banville: descriptive passages of great beauty and evocative power, or the intricate ramification of plot. Contrary to the customary practice, where such constitutive elements of a fiction are pulled together into polyphonic relations by the dynamics of the aesthetic purpose connected with the story they bring into being, in *Nightspawn* they are employed for their own sake. The aesthetic end they strive towards is not so much the story itself, but how a story is *made*.

Then there are those rubies which, once the secret springs of fiction are revealed, serve to bring home to the reader what effect these have on him in conditioning his creative participation in the communicative act between himself and the text. One example will suffice. It involves the connotative, or symbolic quality of a literary work. Banville plays here with the habit of reading between the lines. On his visit to Delos with Erik, Ben is made to bear witness to the slaughtering of a little lamb (p. 41). There is a considerable amount of talk about "ritual and magic", of "anastenarides", "a pagan St Sebastian" and of ancient rites, too. Little wonder if a reader is tempted to interpret the events in the light of the Christian belief in the ritual sacrifice of a lamb, or of related notions he may have derived from *The Golden Bough*, for instance the idea of the ritual slaying of the old king. The temptation is only the more understandable since White, after describing how the throat of the lamb was slit, comments: "Sweaty pencils poised, panting hunters of symbols? There is wealth in store" (p. 45). And indeed there is wealth in store, not only with regard to this event. The point, though, about the sacrifice of the lamb, as well as about the other occasions of seemingly symbolic import, is that the decoding of their connotative meaning yields little of real significance for the story at hand. Instead of furthering the reader's understanding of the book's thematic design, the interpretive pursuit of possible symbolic implications manoeuvres the reader into a situation in which he finds himself barking up the wrong tree.

*

The parodic intention informing *Nightspawn* is signalled at the very beginning by the paraphrase of *Notes from Underground*. The narrative is largely designed in such a manner that it exploits, while at the same time undercutting, the stock-features of the thriller. Quite early on, the indebtedness of the book to the cloak-and-dagger class of novel is hinted at in a conversation between White and Weiss.

> 'When are we to meet this man?' he asked.
> 'Tonight, on Delos, at the festival.'
> 'The festival?'
> 'Yes. We won't be noticed in the crowds.'
> 'Ah. Very cloak and sword.'
> 'Dagger.'
> 'Dagger.' (p. 17)

Furthermore, a conspicuously rich number of incidents seem to be modelled on commonplace features of gangster movies. Some of these incidents are even prefaced by references to the usual practice of films, or are compared with them. There is one such incident where Erik first wrestles with someone who holds him at gunpoint before killing him. It is the way in which Erik outwits his opponent that is closely reminiscent of comparable happenings in an endless series of films. Erik tells Fang, the man holding him in check: "Fang, you are a fool, and you see too many films" (p. 84), and then the narrative continues thus:

> But Erik, like all of us, had also been a student of the cinema. A handful of dust, whoosh in the eyes, Bob said the gun, and then Erik was on his feet and kicking Fang in the stomach. *Poh*, and the sailor's breath and breakfast flew out of his mouth. Erik wrenched the gun away and fired one little bullet straight down into the top of Fang's head. (pp. 84f.)

Or there is that hilarious scene when Ben comes home, finds Charlie Knight there and gets involved in a fight and becomes aware of a "little vicious man" inside himself, whom he calls "Al for the connotations that are in it" (p. 183) and whose voice he adopts to get the truth out of Knight.

There are, in particular, five motifs and plot devices which, as essential ingredients of thrillers and thriller movies, play a most influential part in *Nightspawn*, albeit again in an undercut form. The revolution is excruciatingly ridiculed in its seriousness at one stage by being presented as relying on no more than a preposterously undersized arsenal of ammunition and weapons hidden in a hole in the ground (p. 81). Most thriller movies contain, towards the end, a wild chase starring the hero-agent and his opponent. *Nightspawn* offers such a hot pursuit in the form of a slapstick game of cat-and-mouse Julian Kyd plays with Ben. Meeting him in his drawing-room first, Julian goes to fetch him a drink, but does not return. The next thing that Ben sees is that Julian has gone into the yard to poke at the underbody of his car. He rushes downstairs, since he wants to question Kyd on some vital issue; but he trips over a suitcase and, in Laurel-and-Hardy fashion, skids along the hall on his chin and arrives at the car only to find Kyd gone. Now he is standing in the window upstairs where Ben stood prior to his disastrous gallop (p. 192). This routine is carried on for quite some time. It is a sequence that may be indebted to the show-down scene in Nabokov's *Lolita* between Quilty, the rapist, and Humbert Humbert, the therapist. There would seem to be a similar indebtedness in the case of the passage in which Ben remarks: "I would leave her, or she would leave me, or we would leave us, or they would leave them, or it would leave you ... bah, we knew nothing of the kind" (pp. 127f.). Describing his wrestling with Quilty, Humbert notes: "We rolled all over the floor, in each other's arms, like two huge helpless children ... I rolled over him. He rolled over me. They rolled over him. We rolled over us."[26] In both cases the absurdity of the discourse is meant to mirror the fatuous and exhausted nature of such scenes.

Most thrillers have, towards the end, confession scenes, in which the baddies explain the reasons that made them what they are. Such scenes are also contained in *Nightspawn*, for instance the one involving Kyd, which is deliberately made to lapse into melodramatic sentimentality when Kyd talks of his late wife, Nana (cf. also Andreas' confession, p. 208).

As a rule, thrillers force the events to a climax near the end. In this practice they follow the nineteenth-century melodramas, which culminate in colossal sensation scenes. In *Nightspawn*, Prufrockian Ben White tries to force the moment to its crisis by attempting to kill Kyd. But his efforts effect the conventional outcome of the thriller climax only in Ben's deluded imagination: "On the pavement, Julian, Helena and Knight lay snapping and kicking, clawing at each other in agony, wallowing in blood" (p. 212). Soon he is forced to dispel this chimera: "Something was wrong with this farce. A wing collapsed. No creatures writhed on the ground" (p. 212). For in reality, he has merely managed to puncture the front tyre of Julian's car with a bullet from his gun.

A thriller cannot do without a love-plot, naturally; one need only think of James Bond's amorous escapades. The love-plot in *Nightspawn*, like all the other elements from suspense fiction and films, has too many absurd turns to be taken, and meant, straight-facedly. Take the scene in which Ben and Helena practise their first sexual intercourse. Before it became permissible to present sex scenes on the screen in unabashed frankness, the camera would swing away from the lovers and, to the accompaniment of appropriate music, focus on blue skies, budding branches and murmuring brooks. Correspondingly, in *Nightspawn* the focus is shifted away, while Ben and Helena are rolling and writhing on the clay, to lizards and the limitless sky.

> All round about us the air was singing, and through the leaves and the bitter fruits, something slowly moved. The lizards saw it and were still, transfixed by a hypnotic throbbing of the air and light, the yellow sun, the music and weird chanting high in the limitless sky. (p. 64).

In the main, the parody of the love-plot is brought to bear through outrageous exaggeration and through exposing the emptiness of the lovers' conversation. For instance, Ben tries to launch a sexual assault on Helena; yet being "too enthusiastic" (p. 65) he lands himself in a ditch. While Julian is away, Ben and Helena make "violent and lunging love, causing the bed, the window panes, the very walls to rattle" (p. 129). There is scarcely a conversational exchange in the course of which Ben is not forced to comment in dismay: "O Jesus, I can reproduce no more of this twaddle" (p. 93). In order to point out the hackneyed character of the love relationship, he likens Helena to "Anna K. [*i.e.* Karenina] preparing to dive under that train" (p. 93).

*

The question one feels ineluctably compelled to ask when confronted with a metafiction such as *Nightspawn* is this, and if one were Gulley

Jimson one would probably phrase it in these terms: it is "like farting Annie Laurie through a keyhole. It may be clever but is it worth the trouble?"[27]

Banville's artistic endeavours in *Nightspawn* seem fundamentally indebted to two notions. One is the age-old idea that only through art can time be conquered, or as White himself has it: "Only here, in these sinister pages, can time be vanquished" (p. 107); the other is a concept of fiction writing that is inseparably linked with the artistic efforts of Beckett. If Banville can be criticised for anything in his first novel, it is for the ground-situation out of which he has made his narrator compose his unusual suspense fiction.[28] This situation bears too much the imprint of Beckett, without Banville being able to offer any recognisable progression from such novels as *Murphy*, *Watt*, and the trilogy. Beckett's narrators strive towards telling the truth, but without resorting to the old lies of story-telling. They want an art form that is true to itself, and whatever truth may be, for them it has to do with expressing only those subjects for which their artistic medium is suited; and those subjects are about art itself and about how sensual perception is transformed into art. Beckett's narrators try to conquer time inasmuch as they persist in keeping on talking in order not to lapse into silence. For silence means death. So they keep on telling themselves stories. Theirs are stories that make no real claim to being representative. For instance the beginning and the end of Part II of *Molloy* patently contradict one another, thus slyly hinting that Jacques Moran, the narrator, may already be lying with his very first sentences and that therefore his entire report may be one of those old storyteller's lies.

Like many a Beckett narrator, Ben White urges himself on, while at the same time admitting to his impotence: "He blundered about the room. I cannot go on. I watched him. On, on, you cunt." (p. 209). In the very last section of the novel, he is compelled to acknowledge that his efforts to transfix a period of his life having been born out of a desire to escape the "suffocating void" (p. 223) of silence, which will engulf him as soon as he has set down his last word. Therefore, he makes his words go on and on "until we are all up to our balls in paper" (p. 224) — a situation evoked also at the end of Nabokov's *Bend Sinister*. Telling stories is being alive, but they should be stories that have no other pretensions than to be artifice. As soon as they attempt to transfix, or represent, reality, "to express it all" (p. 224), they are bound to fail. This is the final lesson Ben White is constrained to learn. He would be no more successful in saying through fiction what the world is if he tried another time: "Try. Try

now, here. Could I? Try. Chapter one. My story begins at a —"
(p. 224). Art consists in a repetitive, progressive progress of failure.

*

Yacinth, Julian Kyd's son, holds an extraordinary attraction for Ben White. There is also the somewhat incredible fact that hardly has he made the acquaintance of Erik Weiss than he realises that he loves him (p. 35). Should all this be interpreted as evidence of Ben's homoerotic bent? Scarcely so, for Yacinth serves as a personification of Beauty. The boy is on two occasions associated with "a single red rose" (pp. 87, 117), and he prefigures Gabriel Godkin's "rosy grail", in *Birchwood*, as Ben White's anticipates the predicament of Godkin. Ben, at one point, recalls with extraordinary vividness how Yacinth had stood on the landing in the grey dawn hour and bared his teeth at him (p. 132), and he thinks some revelation was offered him there. Later, he sees the boy bent over a paper,

> writing swiftly, smiling, with that smile, so perfect, so absorbed, a thing which seemed to exist, like himself, like music, without reference to anything else in the world. (p. 200)

Julian Kyd is aware that Ben really desired Yacinth, not Helena, taking her — a "poor imitation of a flower" (p. 117) — as a substitute for what was beyond his reach (p. 201). Then Ben accidentally kills the boy, bemoaning his loss: "Yacinth, my Hyacinth" (p. 212). Thumbing through Erik's file against humanity, he comes across a saying of his that Erik has committed to paper: *"What the heart desires, the world is incapable of giving"* (p. 214).

As he is an artist, a writer, his heart desires truth and beauty, but the world is incapable of giving him the means to preserve truth and transfix beauty once and for all. Yacinth bares his teeth at him; beauty defies the artist. And in the end the artist kills beauty through his necessarily inadequate efforts.[29]

*

Nightspawn represents Banville's first attempt to deal with the manner in which the artistic imagination comes to terms with the world. *Birchwood* approaches the problem from a similar and yet so different angle. Whereas the godfathers of *Nightspawn* were Nabokov and, above all, Beckett, the godfather of *Birchwood* is Marcel Proust.

CHAPTER 4
Birchwood

Birchwood is Banville's "brilliant novel of Ireland in chaos". Or so Grafton Books have seen fit to advertise their paperback edition of the book.[1] But the account is really not of Ireland in chaos, the idea being thoroughly misguided, as is the widely-held belief that *Birchwood* is a big-house novel.[2] Thus, for instance, in David Hanly's novel *In Guilt and Glory* there is the following line: "... their demise [i.e. of the Irish ascendancy] was now being delineated with fluent compassion by John Banville and Jennifer Johnston".[3] Quite a few readers may have been persuaded to embrace this erroneous belief by the unfortunate blurb to the original hardback edition, which reads: "Birchwood is the Big House, a fortress behind whose weeping walls the Godkins enact the last rituals of a crumbling Irish dynasty".[4] True, the Godkins are a crumbling Irish dynasty, and they enact what could be termed "the last rituals". True also that myriad conventions of the Irish narrative genre of the 'big-house novel', as established by such writers as Maria Edgeworth, Somerville & Ross, Elizabeth Bowen and others, are employed and exploited by Banville. But it is the manner in which these conventions are used that makes all the difference. *Birchwood* all but represents a straight rendition of the big-house *sujet*. If it intended to, Part II, "Air and Angels", would be curiously and damagingly out of place. What is delineated there has next to no connection with the big-house genre. The truth of the matter is that the big-house novel is, together with other narrative genres, exploited by Banville, and of course by his narratorial substitute, Gabriel Godkin, for a very specific purpose; and this purpose emerges above all from the first and last chapters in the novel.

*

These two chapters constitute a referential and thematic frame. According to Seamus Deane, "Mr. Banville has provided, in *Birchwood*, a complicated metaphor of the world as book and the author as God".[5] Yet, *Birchwood* is not so much a complicated metaphor of the world as a metaphor of a way of coming to grips with the world; and the author, not of course Mr Banville himself, but the implied author of the entire account, Gabriel Godkin, who is shown as being engaged in this epistemological quest, emerges not at all akin to God, or of God's kin. To be exact, Gabriel's is first and foremost not an epistemological quest, but one directed at making sense of the past by remembering it and, more importantly, by writing it down in the form of a sustained narrative. All this is established in, and by, the frame.

It is a very Proustian undertaking. In his review "Adieu Tristesse", Banville comments on Patrick Modiano's novel *Villa Triste*:

> *Villa Triste* is a sly, deceptive book. It is, in its miniature way, a Proustian search for lost time, and also a celebration of that time, not as it *was*, however, but as it seems to be, and as it seems now in retrospect.[6]

He might have been referring to his own novel. Like Marcel, in *A la recherche du temps perdu*, Gabriel Godkin is in "search of time misplaced" (p. 5). In Proust, the realization of *temps perdu* becomes the incentive to a search for the essential nature of the past as well as of time; and memory — in Gabriel's case *mémoire volontaire*, not as in Marcel's *mémoire involontaire* — becomes the medium of finding it. Gabriel tells his stylised story in order to get to the bottom of his life in terms of sense and purpose; he tells it from memory, and that strategy brings to bear the difficulty of drawing upon one's memory, the unreliability of one's memory (memory, like women, being "usually unfaithful", as a Spanish proverb has it), and the teething troubles in communicating one's experience through language. Gabriel notes:

> I spent the nights poring over my memories, fingering them, like an impotent casanova his old love letters, sniffing the scent of violets. Some of these memories are in a language which I do not understand, the ones that could be headed, *the beginning of the old life*. (p. 3)

Another very famous book of memory, namely Dante's *La Vita Nuova*, heads the section "after the first pages, which are almost blank": *"Incipt vita nova"* — here begins the new life.[7] For Gabriel, the fundamental impetus to remember derives from a modified Descartes quotation: "I am, therefore I think" (p. 3), and since for

him "all thinking is in a sense remembering" (p. 3), he is simply bound
to think and in thinking to remember. With remembering, though,
there comes the problem of whether what one recalls is in fact
authentic. Gabriel denies this possibility: "We imagine that we
remember things as they were, while in fact all we carry into the
future are fragments which reconstruct a wholly illusory past" (p. 4).
T. S. Eliot expressed a comparable conviction in these terms:

> What might have been is an abstraction
> Remaining a perpetual possibility
> Only in a world of speculation.[8]

The epistemological difficulty notwithstanding and in spite of his
professed inability "to discern a defensible reason for [his] labours"
(p. 4), Gabriel nonetheless takes them on, in fact shows himself in the
very process of doing so, gathering those Proustian "madeleines"
(p. 5), comparing them to his memories of them, adding them to the
mosaic, for the sole purpose of arriving at "these extraordinary
moments when the pig finds the truffle embedded in the muck" (p. 3),
of discerning the "thing-in-itself" (p. 5).

Gabriel is thus the first of Banville's characters to occupy himself
with a search for sense, for the whatness of things. Copernicus after
him will also be greatly pre-occupied with the thing-in-itself; and so
will Kepler, Newton, the fictitious Newton biographer, and
Gabriel's namesake in *Mefisto*. And like all of them, Gabriel Godkin
associates this search for the thing-in-itself with the discovery of a
sublime form of beauty and harmony. After having inadvertently
stumbled upon his mother and father making love in Cotter's
dilapidated cottage, he believes he has discovered not love, "or what
they call the facts of life", but "the notion of — I shall call it
harmony" (p. 25). Notably, this notion comprises an ability, or rather
a desire to be able, an almost Faustian incessant striving, to "see, with
vision clear,/How secret elements cohere,/And what the universe
engirds".[9] Trying to explain this idea of harmony, Gabriel suggests:

> How would I explain, I do not understand it, but it was as if in
> the deep wood's gloom I had recognised, in me all along,
> waiting, an empty place where I could put the most disparate
> things and they could hang together, not very elegantly,
> perhaps, or comfortably, but yet together, singing like seraphs.
> (p. 25)

It should be borne in mind that the Gabriel Godkin's striving
anticipates Gabriel Swan's Faust-like efforts in *Mefisto*. Like
Copernicus, Kepler, the historian in *The Newton Letter*, and Gabriel
Swan, the narrator in *Birchwood* is convinced that, even though the

world is chaotic, there are moments, rare moments, when some order, some aspect of the quiddity of life shines through:

> Listen, listen, if I know my world, which is doubtful, but if I do, I know it is chaotic, mean and vicious, with laws cast in the wrong mould, a fair conception gone awry, in short an awful place, and yet, and yet a place capable of glory in those rare moments when a little light breaks forth, and something is not explained, not forgiven, but merely illuminated. (pp. 25f.)

Lastly, like all subsequent Banville protagonists to date, Gabriel is driven on in his endeavour by the question: "What does it mean?" (p. 72). Kepler, near the end of his life, will come to recognise the appropriateness of what his friend, the Jew Winklemann, told him: "Everything is told us, but nothing explained. Yes. We must take it all on trust. That's the secret."[10] Godkin, about midway upon his imaginative journey through the foreign land of his past, realises:

> There is never a precise answer, but instead, in the sky, as it were, a kind of jovian nod, a celestial tipping of the wink, *that's all right, it means what it means*. (p. 72)

However, he continues by asking himself: "Yes, but is that enough? Am I satisfied?" It is not enough, and he is not satisfied, hence his search for time misplaced.

The search is very Proustian not only on account of the aspects mentioned above. There are further echoes of, and correspondences to, *A la recherche*, for example in the form of textual quotations or near-quotations, such as the "madeleines", which Marcel eats with his linden tea, and the smell of which inaugurates the *mémoire involontaire*, or the very notion of time misplaced. Gabriel, furthermore, refers to the chairs in the library as "crouched in menacing immobility" (p. 4); Marcel speaks of "the immobility of the things that surround us".[11] Gabriel and his Proustian counterpart have comparable parents: the mothers exercise a far greater emotional hold over the boys than the fathers, who more or less remain unidentified eminences. Or *Birchwood*, like *A la recherche*, is modelled on patterns of circularity.[12] Lastly, in both cases, the efforts of the narrator-protagonist bring about the narrative account in a most literal sense.

*

Gabriel's reflections and recollections are intended to make up for what he failed to attain during the time he lived through the events.

He feels that life is, and has been, terribly swift. Commenting on Granda Godkin's death, he notes:

> But I felt as I have felt at every death, that something intangible had slipped through my fingers before I discovered its nature. All deaths are scandalously mistimed. People do not live long enough. They come and go, briefly, shadows dwindling toward an empty blue moon. (p. 53)

Two things are especially noteworthy about these reflections and recollections: first, the repeatedly articulated fictionality of the memories, which in turn throws into relief the fictional character of the entire account, showing Gabriel in the process of weaving a web of words; and, second, the fact that the search for sense is slyly and deftly transferred from the narrator to the reader. The recurrent questions and permeating mysteries on which the story hinges provoke him into searching for sense and a *raison d'être* himself.

Yet for the reader and the narrator alike, the issue concerning the sense of Gabriel's life remains unresolved. Gabriel at the end, as diligently and painstakingly as a sleuth in a detective novel, clears up the mysteries, solves all the riddles with which he so expertly has spiced his narrative. The most essential question, though, namely: "What does it mean?", is left as open as at the outset. Or perhaps this is not quite true. What *Birchwood* seems to suggest is that the answer, the result of the effort is not as important as the effort itself. When Gabriel at the beginning of his search fails to discern a defensible reason for his labours but supposes "that there must be one ... buried somewhere" (p. 4), then at the end he comes to realise that this reason resides in the particular and very specific manner in which he has taken on and conducted those labours. It is the effort that counts, not the outcome, which can at best be an approximation of the quintessential nature of truth.

He may arrive at passable, even most accurate views on memory, the unreliability of mnemosyne, or on time, for instance when he recalls how he became aware of the destructive as well as transient nature of time while eating blackberries:

> Down in the green gloom under the bushes, where spiders swarmed, the berries were gorgeous, achingly vivid against the dusty leaves, but once plucked, and in the basket, their burnished lustre faded and a moist whitish film settled on the skin. If they were eaten ..., it was only in that shocked moment of separation from the stems that they held their true, their unearthly flavour. Then the fat beads burst on our tongues with a chill bitterness which left our eyelids damp and our mouths

flooded, a bitterness which can still pierce my heart, for it was the very taste of time. (p. 60)

He may, furthermore, live through one of those rare moments when the pig finds the truffle embedded in the muck, and experience "fixity within continuity":

> ... it came to me with the clarity and beauty of a mathematical statement that all movement is composed of an infinity of minute stillnesses, not one of which is exactly the same as any other and yet not so different either. It was enormously pleasing, this discovery of fixity within continuity. (p. 122)

And he may apply this insight to his whole existence, which consequently must appear to him as if he were stumbling through it for the greater part in utter darkness, except for those rare moments when something seems to have been illuminated:

> And I saw something else [he goes on to note] namely that this was how I lived, glancing every now and then out of darkness and catching sly time in the act, but such glimpses were rare and brief and of hardly any consequence, for time, time would go on anyway, without *my* vigilance. (p. 122)

Time will not be conquered.

The Elizabethans, for example, believed that art could defeat the bloody and devouring tyrant Time. Although far from being an Elizabethan, Gabriel would share that belief, if only he were able to arrive at, as well as master, an artform appropriate enough for capturing his time, all time. The narrative discourse in which he features and for which he is responsible, as it were, represents a supreme effort at testing such various artforms. But as it turns out, they are ultimately all of little avail. At the end, Gabriel is constrained to acknowledge: "There is no form, no order, only echoes and coincidences, sleight of hand, dark laughter. I accept it." (p. 171) He acquiesces in the fact that whereof he cannot speak, thereof he must be silent. His journey thus is from the Cartesian certainty of "I am, therefore I think" to the Wittgensteinian despair of "whereof I cannot speak, thereof I must be silent" (p. 171). But that despair emerges at the end only.

*

Prior to the end and within the thematic frame thus established there is precisely form, order, echoes, coincidences, prodigious sleight of hand and copious dark laughter.

In shape *Birchwood* equals a clockwork device: wheels-within-wheels, Chinese-box fashion.[13] The wheels are, by and large, constituted by the narrative genres Gabriel exploits in the course of his *recherche*. There is, firstly and most obviously, the big-house genre, which features prominently in Part I and, to a lesser degree, at the end of Part III. Part II develops the account into a quest romance, or a romantic mystery story with distinctive traits pertaining to the picaresque novel and the Gothic novel. It is a quest *romance* on account of the romantic search for the twin sister, whom Gabriel, who looks upon himself as "a knight errant" (p. 112), regards as his *alter ego*; ultimately, of course, the search is for Gabriel's own identity. Romantic, furthermore is the use of the *Doppelgänger*-motif. "There was", the narrator points out, "something always ahead of me ..." (p. 119) and that something turns out to be his twin brother, Michael. Finally romantic about the mystery story is that it *is* a mystery story and that it should be embellished with Gothic elements, glamour, glaver, gloom and all. The adroit manner in which, throughout the novel, anticipations, clues, mysterious hints are dropped, then later taken up and elaborated, or the way in which the strategy of fore-shadowing is employed and the motif of the twin-sister quest is slyly and subtly established, all this is especially reminiscent of the rationalised Gothic and its offshoots — the tale of ratiocination and the detective novel. Part III, in particular, is very ratiocinatory, assiduously tying up all the loose ends and solving all the carefully planted riddles. "There is no girl. There never was ... I believed in a sister in order not to believe in *him*, my cold mad brother." (p. 168) Thus Gabriel commences his final unravelling of the plot, and by the end of his revelation, the reader, unlike Kepler, can say: 'Everything is told us, and all is explained.' This is a supreme triumph of art, but it is a triumph that has no bearing on reality, as Gabriel himself comes to understand. The withered wizard Prospero has never existed, but Gabriel wanted to keep him, "with his cloak and his black hat", and so he "became [his] own Prospero, and [ours]" (p. 168) — a magician, a wizard with words.

The similarity of part of *Birchwood* to a tale of ratiocination, or to a detective novel, is made specifically conspicuous through the fact that the narrator writes his account in retrospect and, before he begins, knows everything he purposely keeps the reader in the dark about, much in the manner in which the narrator in a whodunnit embarks on his narrative venture after the murder is committed and the culprit caught. Gabriel is of course fully aware that he never had a twin sister, but a twin brother.

Birchwood as a whole resembles an autobiographical *Entwicklungs-roman*, charting Gabriel's intellectual development from certainty to despair, or, to be exact, a specific kind of despair — the despair of the artist at never being able to find the "rosy grail" of truth and perfection. Gabriel, it is important to note, is an artistic figure. For after all, it is he who pens "the story of the fall and rise of Birchwood", all of it, and in a decidedly artistic vein into the bargain. Thus, in the final analysis, *Birchwood* can also be considered a *Künstler-roman*, dealing predominantly with the possibility of expressing and capturing the essence of one's life in a creative, artistic way.

The individual parts of the book as well as the various genres adopted therein are held together by an intricate system of leitmotifs, allusions, anticipations. The very first chapter presents most of the significant thematic issues; it lays the foundation for all future events, explains the fundamental narrative situation, voices the intention informing the account, plants a rich number of meaningful clues. To mention only some of them in addition to those already discussed, Gabriel informs the reader that he has "gone down twice to the same river", slyly echoing and inverting Heraclitus' tenet about change: "You cannot step twice into the same river, for other waters are continually flowing in."[14] He goes on to remark: "When I opened the shutters in the summerhouse by the lake a trembling disc of sunlight settled on the charred circle on the floor where Granny Godkin exploded" (p. 3), thus foreshadowing Granny's unusual death in Part I, Ch. 14, and obliquely anticipating his father's death in Part III, when he discovers him, presumably throttled by Cotter (cf. p. 167):

> The windows in the summerhouse were faintly lit, and the door was wide open. I crept up the steps . . . On the bed Papa lay in his black suit and waistcoat with a blue face and staring eyes and a thick protruding tongue. (p. 165)

Or the passage: "My fists were wet with tears. I was not weeping for those who were gone . . . I wept for what was there and yet not there. For Birchwood." (p. 4) — this passage prefigures Gabriel's return to Birchwood in Part III, when for the first time in his life he weeps, having all the time been asked by various people whether he does not weep at all (cf. for instance p. 42); now his tears flow copiously while he is bearing witness to how Cotter and the Molly Maguires slaughter the Lawlesses. The mention of a photograph of "a young girl dressed in white", which "Mama said was a picture of her as a child" (p. 5), but which Gabriel himself assumes was of "a lost child, misplaced in time" (p. 5), is the first in a series of references and allusions to a lost sister by means of which the leitmotif of the twin sister quest is established. The remarks about Rosie, whose "furry damp secret" (p. 5) he fingered and "found not so much a hole as a wound" (p. 5), heralds his affair with Rosie, while at the same time forming a link between Rosie and his alleged twin sister. Aunt Martha, when teaching him, reads out to Gabriel the story of *"The Something Twins"* (p. 42), which is about the twins Gabriel and Rose, "who lived in a big house by the sea. One day, when she was very young, little Rose disappeared, and Gabriel went away in search of her ..." (p. 42). The story provides the basis for Gabriel's *idée fixe* that he has a twin sister who mysteriously disappeared and whom he has to find. On the same day, he discovers "on a little low table by the bookshelves ... a small framed photograph of a young girl in white standing among leaves in a garden ... In one hand she held a flower. A rose." (p. 43). Later on, when he is laid up with pneumonia, "on the table by [his] bed a single red rose, mysterious and perfect" (p. 78) stands in a glass, and his

> fevered brain [goes] back through many years ... gathering fragments of evidence, feeling [his] way around certain dis- crepancies ..., collating all those scraps that [point] unmis- takeably ... to one awesome and abiding fact, namely, that somewhere [he has] a sister, [his] twin, a lost child. (p. 79)

He goes on to explain:

> This discovery filled me with excitement ... Half of me, some- where, stolen by the circus, or spirited away by an evil aunt, or kidnapped by a jealous cousin — and why? A part of me stolen, yes, that was a thrilling notion. I was incomplete, and would remain so until I found her. (p. 79)

This, then, is a prime example of how Banville, or Gabriel, works by dint of "those echoes bound to cause confusion" (p. 9), as he terms it: the echo of the girl in white, the rose Rosie, his juvenile love, the circus which he joins in Part II to search for his sister, the possibility that an evil aunt may have spirited her away, which in turn prefigures his later assumption that the twin sister was Aunt Martha's invention, or the figure of the "jealous cousin" who, one may at first suppose, is Michael, until it is revealed that Michael is Gabriel's twin, but no less jealous for all that. The echoes are taken up in the end, in the denouement: "... so, instead of fratricide, he [*i.e.* Michael] played with Martha her sly game, and between them they sent me off in search of a sister" (p. 170).

Additionally, in his first chapter Gabriel refers to "that mighty maid who many years later [he] met along the road" (p. 5). The mighty maid is Mag with whom in Part II he has, in a symbolically portentous environment, a singularly unfruitful sexual experience. He mentions Silas and his band and, not to be forgotten, he anticipates that situation when, after Cotter and the circus people have left Birchwood, he finds himself confronted by a mysterious "creature in white", standing under the lilacs with one hand on the back of a seat, leaning into the sunlight smiling (p. 6). At the end, this creature is identified as Michael, whom Gabriel shies away from killing with the Sabatier (pp. 163ff.).

Wheels-within-wheels, circular patterns; Gabriel's questionable quest is of course also circular, bringing him back empty-handed to where he started. These constitute the admirable form of the story which Gabriel copies, of the fall and rise of Birchwood and of the part Sabatier and he himself played in the last battle.

*

Circular patterns are, however, not the only salient compositional device in *Birchwood*; they are assisted by binary patterns, sets of pairs, twins, dualities, mirror symmetries. The Lawlesses used to be the masters of Birchwood before the Godkins took over. Towards the end of the book, the Lawlesses have surreptitiously regained possession of the estate, and finally Gabriel Godkin inherits all. There are two archangels, Michael and Gabriel, and a Holy family, Joseph and Martha, a servant called Nockter and a peasant called Cotter; there is a Beatrice-Sabatier near-anagram; the circus has a Justin and a Juliette and an Ada-Ida twin; there is a Mario and a Magnus, Silas and Sybil, Angel and Sophie. Part I and Part II end in fires. At the close of Part II Magnus is killed when an exploding bullet hits the back of his head; the same thing happens to the last of the Molly Maguires. Mario loses his child in a similar way, or so one is tempted to conjecture, to how the girl in the story gets lost. Gabriel begins with the description of a girl in a white dress, at the close he sees his twin brother in a white gown. There are mirrors everywhere, literal as well as metaphorical ones.

The metaphorical mirrors consist in an impressive number of allusions to, quotations or near-quotations from, literary works. There are also phrases which seem to be lifted from, or seem to recall, the works of other writers but without there being a way of identifying their sources, such as "Did I spy, in the darkness of one of their poky windows, the glint of a merry eye regarding me?" (p. 6), or: "I feel I have already lived for a century and more" (p. 3). The book opens with an inverted reference to Descartes' "Cogito ergo sum" as well as to Dante's *La Vita Nuova*; midway upon his journey across a famine-ridden Ireland Gabriel alludes to the opening canto of Dante's *Inferno* (p. 132); at the very end of his labours he quotes Wittgenstein's dictum: "Wovon man nicht sprechen kann, darüber muß man schweigen."[15] There is the inverted Heraclitus citation, and a Shakespearian Prospero who quotes from *The Tempest*: "our revels now are ended" (p. 110). Sybil recalls Yeats' Cathleen ni Houlihan, bodying forth "the sorrow of the country" (p. 139). At one point, Gabriel feels like Eliot's "Tiresias in the city of plague" (p. 70). Gabriel's family name may be a covert reference to Stephen Dedalus' description of the artist as God. In the first chapter, there is a mention of a white cloud sailing into a blue bowl of sky; a similar thing happens in the first chapter of *Ulysses*. The photograph Gabriel notes at the start is of a girl who smiles dreamily, "as though she were listening to some mysterious music", like Gretta Conroy, who married a Gabriel. At the narrator's birth, there is an apocalyptic moment which resembles the central scene in "Circe", and it is followed by a policeman's skull being split by an ashplant. Gabriel, like Stephen Dedalus, goes on his quest "in silence cunningly" (p. 104). Michael is Gabriel's "cold mad brother" (p. 168), the words Anna Livia uses to describe her father at the end of *Finnegans Wake*. Silas relates of a feast which his friend Trimalchio laid on for him in words supplied by Petronius Arbiter; he even curses in Latin. Gabriel is referred to as "Caligula", or little boots. The book opens with a poem by Catullus and contains many echoes of the Oedipus myth.

But *Birchwood* is in fact much richer in metaphorical mirrors than the examples listed here can suggest; it is indeed a happy hunting ground for all those who take delight in source-hunting. What all the examples go to prove is that Banville, or Gabriel, betrays himself in the act of making literature out of literature. It is one way of making the reader aware that he is only inventing (p. 13). Another is the specific manner in which he adopts and, in doing so, flaunts the conventions of extant literary forms.

*

The big-house section delineates "the fall and rise" (p. 3) of a big-house. The very circumstance that the customary course of events seems to have been turned topsy-turvy, that, in other words, the story should not be about the rise and fall of Birchwood points, if only in an oblique fashion, to an inversion of the genre.

It is the story of a "baroque madhouse" (p. 7), of a perpetual lacerating battle, fired by hatred and jealousy and greed, for the possession of the estate. As such, it contains most of the thematic issues as well as compositional means which have come to be associated with the big-house novel or story, such as drunkenness, penury, incest, the boldness of the peasants (p. 44), and madness. Brian Donnelly has noted in this respect:

> Gabriel Godkin gives a classic description of the Ascendancy House in its decline as found in the Irish novel from Maria Edgeworth onwards: "Of course our genteel slide towards penury was never mentioned, not in my presence, but the silent evidence of it was everywhere around me, in the cracked paint and the missing tiles, the dry rot that ate its way unchecked across the floor and up the stairs, in the games of musical chairs which Mama played, switching them from the front room to the back in a circle of increasing degeneracy until the day when, groaning and croaking, they regained their original places and the wheel ceased to turn ... [etc., p. 44][16]

Birchwood, in fact, bears close comparison to such exponents of the genre as Maria Edgeworth's *Castle Rackrent* (1800) and, interestingly because of its Gothic elements, Joseph Sheridan LeFanu's *Uncle Silas* (1864). Listed in brief, the parallels are these: like Thady Quirk, Gabriel tells his tale from memory, and he begins by divulging his name: "The name is Godkin, Gabriel" (p. 3). Edgeworth's narrator starts off by noting: "My real name is Thady Quirk".[17] Sir Murtagh comes into the possession of Castle Rackrent by marrying "one of the co-heiresses" (CR, p. 7); Joseph Godkin marries Beatrice Lawless and thus installs himself as master of Birchwood (p. 8). Like the Rackrents, the Godkins have "a great deal of sparring and jarring between them" (CR, p. 10). There is land speculation in both novels, and Beatrice is almost as mad as Sir Condy's wife (CR, p. 30). Gabriel's father, Joseph, is as fond of the bottle as Sir Condy is of whiskey-punch (CR, p. 31). Birchwood falls to rack and ruin as Castle Rackrent does — because of penury and debts; and whereas in Edgeworth, Quirk's son, Jason, secretly pays Sir Condy's debts and buys up the land, thus becoming master of the estate, the Lawlesses finally manage to regain Birchwood by similar means.

The parallels to *Uncle Silas* consist for instance in the way in which mysteries are generated which are deliberately left unresolved for considerable stretches. This is in both cases achieved through enigmatic foreshadowing, ominous allusions and the use of tension-creating questions:

> Was it really the arrival of the governess? Was that apparition which had impressed me so unpleasantly to take the command of me — to sit alone with me, and haunt me perpetually with her sinister looks and shrilly gabbles?[18]

The father of the girl who comes into Uncle Silas' care goes on an "unknown knight-errantry"; Gabriel regards himself as a knight errant. Silas becomes Maud's *custos*, Silas, Gabriel's; LeFanu's Silas is "a child of the Sphinx" (US, p. 117), Banville's Silas, too, has something of the Sphinx in him. The portrait of Uncle Silas "with his enigmatic smile" (US, p. 60) finds its counterpart in the enigmatic photograph of the girl. The antagonism between Martha and Gabriel is comparable to the antagonism between Madame de la Rougierre and Mâud. Both Maud's father and Gabriel's die under mysterious circumstances. There is a Prospero and there is blackberry-picking in *Uncle Silas* (pp. 192, 198) as well as in *Birchwood*, and Gabriel as well as Maud repeatedly refer to a darkness that is of their own making and that surrounds them (cf. US, p. 289). Maud, like Gabriel, recounts her story of a big house, Bartram-Haugh, in retrospect: "I have penned it. I sit for a moment breathless ..." (US, p. 435), and she, too, unravels the plot in the very last chapter. *Uncle Silas*, in a different way but like *Birchwood*, represents a specimen of rationalised Gothic.

The plentitudinous parallels between *Birchwood* and the (gothic) big-house tradition have mainly been responsible for misleading gullible and undiscerning readers into regarding Banville's novel as a straightforward and straitlaced attempt to write in this vein, much in the sense in which Jennifer Johnston never tires of doing or in which Aidan Higgins has come up with in the brilliant achievement of *Langrishe, Go Down*. The crux, though, is that the story, or a considerable part of the story in *Birchwood*, is precisely of a "baroque madhouse", is of "the intricate *farce* [my italics] being enacted under its roof" (p. 65), featuring no less noteworthy, Dickensian oddities.

There is, to begin with, Granny Godkin, the dominant figure at Birchwood, who drives her daughter-in-law to madness and lives on "only despite us" (p. 28), until the house grows tired of her and she dies of "spontaneous combustion" (p. 75), a most extraordinary way to depart, but one which occurs also in Dickens' *Bleak House*. Doc McCabe says he has "read of one or two similar cases, you know, in America" (p. 75), and he is right. One such case features in Charles Brockden Brown's novel *Wieland*. Or there is Granda Godkin, who regards his wife across "the chasm of silence that separated them with the grudging air of one who suspects he is being cheated" (p. 28). He has taken to drinking on the sly and slouching around the house, producing "an odd choked cooing little noise, like a rusty hinge" (p. 29). The curious manner of his death is comparable to that of Granny Godkin, the consequence of a farcical accident brought about when Joseph pursues a poacher who, in his flight, runs into Granda and knocks him to the ground. Granda goes soft in the head and deems himself visited by God and subsequently by an enormous woodlouse (p. 51). One morning he is found in the birchwood

> curled like a stillborn infant in the grass. His mouth was open, caked with black blood, and it was not until they were moving him that they discovered, in the tree beside which he lay, his false teeth sunk to the gums like vicious twin pink parasites in the bark. (p. 54)

There is Gabriel's mother, who wanders through the rooms of Birchwood in mad Ophelia fashion; or take Joseph, who has never had any real interest in the estate, but lives on drink and his "jaunts to the city" (p. 64); when he finds out that his wife is barren, he accepts the fact with "mixed relief" (p. 168) and fathers "a *real* Godkin" (p. 169) on his sister, Martha; only this real Godkin turns out to be twins, an unforeseeable result which sets the whole tragedy of the battle for Birchwood in motion. The arrangement that Martha and he had agreed on, namely "that I would be the son of the house but Michael must be the heir" (p. 169), was thoroughly thwarted by Joseph's "unwillingness to let pass the opportunity of laying the framework for a perfect delayed action joke" (p. 169) — the changed will.

In addition to peopling Birchwood with oddities, or stock figures: the dark, angry father; the long-suffering mother; the ghastly grandparents; the artistic son; the wild son; the strange aunt,[19] Banville works towards upsetting, parodying or flaunting the big-house genre and likewise the Gothic tradition by the mock-heroic vein in which he adapts the conventions. A comic note pervades Part I in particular. Think of the description of how Beatrice and Joseph kiss for the first time: "they grappled awkwardly in a stunned silence, her teeth clattering against his" (p. 10). Or think of how the Lawlesses attend the wedding party (p. 11), of Angel sitting on a little antique chair inside the door, "her arse overflowing the seat" (pp. 12f.) There is also the moment when Gabriel, engrossed in "the startling and menacing intricacy of a daddy-longlegs going mad against the glass in the corner of the window", suddenly sees his "own long-legged daddy approaching through the wood" (p. 20). Or there is Granda and the woodlouse:

God had come to visit him in the night.

'That's nice', said Mama. 'Did he have anything to say?'

He gave her a crafty sidelong look, became suddenly morose, and changed the subject by petulantly demanding his false teeth.

...

'Where's Joseph?', he cried, clacking his choppers. 'I want to talk to Joseph.'

But when my father was found the old man had forgotten what he wanted to say ... An enormous woodlouse, he told us, was lumbering around the room with elephantine tread, blind antennae feeling the fetid air, searching for him. The louse, it seems, was god come a second time. (p. 51)

To give one last example, there is papa stranded on the lavatory after two floorboards have crumbled to dust underfoot.

'Nockter! Jesus Christ almighty. *Nok* — there you are. Get me a hammer, nails, a couple of planks, hurry up, we have a job to do. I could have been killed. Like that! Jesus can you imagine the laugh they'd have. *Broke his arse on his own lav, ha!*' (p. 64)

The "intricate farce being enacted under [the] roof" of Birchwood is thus by various means deliberately turned into a farce, or rather a parody, of the genre. While a comic, mock-heroic note is prevalent in the big-house section mostly, in Parts II and III this is replaced by a terrifying, gothic mood.

*

This is, however, not to say that humour is completely lacking in these sections of the novel, or that the turning inside out of literary genres and conventions has been abandoned. The romantic quest is revealed as a vain ploy, and what may seem as a serious description of a specific part of Ireland's sorry history teems with anachronisms.

Gabriel is sent on his quest for his twin sister as a consequence of the intricate plan his aunt, Martha, who is really his mother, and his twin brother have devised in order to regain the inheritance of Birchwood. The intricacy of the plan finds its formal expression in the intricate way in which the twin-sister motif is built up: from a cryptic mentioning of a photograph portraying a young girl, via a seemingly casual reference to the book *The Something Twins*, a random coincidence in name between his girlfriend and the sister, permeating allusions to roses, and finally the delirious dream of his twin sister after which Gabriel is convinced he has in fact a twin sister. The search for her is the main subject of Part II, and it takes on the character of a quasi-picaresque series of adventures.

Of the features which have been established as characteristic of a picaresque story,[20] the following are the most relevant here. The picaresque novel is said to be partly an *Entwicklungsroman*, treating of the initiation of the *picaro* from a simpleton to a *schelm*, or worldly-wise person. Gabriel sets off in a state in which he blindly believes in his twin sister, as becomes evident, say, when he explains to Silas that he is "searching for someone ... My sister" (p. 104). It is a state of enchantment, similar to the enchantment of the people who attend the performance of the circus, a fantasy necessary for lending a feeling of sense to his life. As he notes:

> I also [like the people who visit the circus] wanted to dream. I knew too that my quest, mocked and laughed at, was fantasy, but I clung to it, fiercely, unwilling to betray myself, for if I could not be a knight errant I would not be anything. (p. 112)

This marks the stage when he begins to doubt the reality of a sister, or when his initiation begins. This is an initiation to the extent that Gabriel acknowledges the futility of his quest and the fantasy character of his sister:

> The story of my sister, the stolen child, had been laughed at. The laughter woke me from a dream. No, not a dream precisely, but a waking, necessary fantasy ... I admitted at last that the search for this doubtful sister could no longer sustain me. (p. 132)

And when Rosie, as it appears, is carried to the graveyard, Rosie who by way of association is linked with the sister-quest, his dream has died (p. 147). The initiation is complete when he admits: "There is no girl. There never was ... I believed in a sister in order not to believe in *him*, my cold mad brother" (p. 168). Actually, the initiation encompasses far more than the shattering of a dream. It also entails the facing up to his abilities and shortcomings as an artist.

But to come back to the characteristics of a picaresque novel, the adventures the *picaro* is made to undergo on his journey do not usually form a thematically or compositionally harmonious unit, but are loosely strung together like pearls on a string; they are not causally concatenated, do not lead to an inevitable climax and thus could be continued indefinitely. Gabriel's adventures are serial in nature; the quest could easily be prolonged by adding more links to the chain. The only difference is that Banville has wrought the chain into the shape of a circle as a formal manifestation of the utter futility of Gabriel's quest.

Thirdly, the *picaro* relates what happened to him, while journeying from one place to the next, meeting people of all social strata from the perspective of an underdog. To be a member of a circus gang is surely to be an underdog. Fourthly, it has been argued that the genre of the picaresque novel flourishes best in times of social upheaval. The time when *Birchwood* was written was certainly not a time of social upheaval. But the novel is nonetheless true to the picaresque tradition by rendering a panoramic picture of an Ireland shaken to the roots by famine.

The reference to a famine may lead to the assumption that *Birchwood* was concerned with a particular period in the history of Ireland, namely, the famine of the years 1845-48. It is a misguided assumption. For the social as well as political background remains teasingly vague, opaque. The salient socio-political features are established as recurrent phenomena. A famine was also depopulating Ireland during the days of Gabriel's namesake, great-great-grand-father Godkin (p. 7). There are, moreover, repeated references to a famine throughout Part I, and since Gabriel, on his quest, is also troubled by a potato shortage, the famine and, together with the famine, the social picture of Ireland is generalised, or universalised. It is an Ireland permanently plagued by shortage and want. The covert allusion to Yeats' Cathleen ni Houlihan is especially informative here. Gabriel feels that unhappy Sybil is an apt symbol of sorrow-ridden Ireland. He has

> the insane notion that it was perhaps on her, on Sybil, our bright bitch, that the sorrow of the country, of those baffled people in the rotting fields, of the stricken eyes staring out of hovels, was visited against her will and even without her knowledge so that tears might be shed, and the inexpressible expressed. (p. 139)

The picture given is of a Dante-esque inferno, and it is quite appropriate that Gabriel should allude to the first canto of *Inferno*.

Although most of the socio-historical phenomena have been universalised, there are some chapters in Part II which seem to fulfil the function of raising more specific issues. These concern the contrasting pub scenes. The first one (pp. 120f.) satirises one aspect of Irish life, the conviviality of Irish pub life in its "wild mordant gaiety" (p. 121), which appears to Gabriel "to carry the savour of the country itself, this odd little land" (p. 121):

> Much raucous laughter tumbled out of gap-toothed mouths, and the voices and the strange macaroni talk clashed in the smoky air like the sounds of battle. A fat woman with a red face was copiously weeping, rocking back and forth on a stool between two sheepish, speechless men. The cadaverous piper, hunched

over his reeds, swung into a gay dance tune, but his long face registered only a deeper melancholy. There is in the happiest of that music a profound thread of grief, never broken, equivalent to but not springing from the sustained drone note, an implacable mournfulness, and so, although the jig made the glasses sing, the fat woman wept and wept, rocking her sadness to sleep, and the two old men, with their hands on their knees and their jaws munching, sat and stared, with nothing to say. (p. 121)

The curious blend of boisterousness, melancholy, sadness and grief is marvellously captured in this passage. "Tears and laughter, they are so much Gaelic to me", as Beckett's Molloy notes.[21] The second time the circus people come to the pub, the picture is entirely different. The place is deserted; there is no longer merriment and melancholy all in one; the silence of the dead reigns now. Gabriel feels that "something was dying here" (p. 149). The sounds of levity of the previous scene have been turned into a "Tötentanz [sic]" (p. 149). An entire era is dying, the era of the landed gentry; the "new-found boldness of the peasants" (p. 44f.; cf. also pp. 16, 68) has taken over.

Yet such more specific allusions notwithstanding and in spite of clear references to rebels, "the new State" (p. 55), the Molly Maguires, and more oblique ones to the Whiteboys Movement, the Young Ireland Movement, and the Land League, the point is valid that the socio-cultural background remains obscure, schematic. It would even be true to assert than the chronology has deliberately been distorted. As Francis C. Molloy has pertinently pointed out: "... the period details which in a serious historical work of fiction assist the reader in placing events only confuse in this novel"[22]; and Sean McMahon has given a summary of the historical jumble: "Cigarettes, bicycles and telephones are in quite common use, the Molly Maguires figure in the plot and the British soldiers have rifles and refer to the Irish as 'Fucking Micks'".[23] McMahon may be wrong about the cigarettes, for there does not seem to be a mention of them in the book; otherwise, though, he is correct. All this would appear to place the events as happening after 1880 at the earliest. At one point Gabriel identifies a gossamer frock his mother is wearing as "straight out of the gay nineties" (p. 81). Yet the famine described is so excruciating that it must be the Great Hunger of the forties, trapdoor coffins and all.[24]

The universe of *Birchwood* is a timeless one that does not coincide with any one historical period. The anachronistic aspects, primary among them the quotations from, and references to, twentieth-

century literature and philosophy, bring home the point unmistakably. Whether the book should be read as "an allegory of a
troubled land"[25] is rather questionable. For Banville seems not to be
concerned with an allegory of this kind; instead he would appear to
have been aiming at an allegory of art and the artistic imagination.
This possibility is suggested by the role of the circus in Part II.

*

When Banville sent *Birchwood* to his American publisher he received
the most extraordinary four foolscap pages of suggested changes
which an editor had probably ever written:

> She'd written it as she was reading the book and you could see
> the dawning sense of horror as she said: 'What's all this circus
> business? Perhaps we could leave out Part 2.' She simply did not
> know what was going on.[26]

So much for the discernment of editors.

The circus is billed as a magic circus, in fact as "PROSPERO'S
MAGIC CIRCUS" (p. 99). Prospero, one later learns, does not exist;
he is the supreme magician and represents the imagination, from
which stems the creativity of the circus members and which, as
Molloy has noted, is also the means whereby the artist pursues
Beauty.[27] The circus is the world *in nuce*, consisting, as Gabriel's
world and story does, of sets of pairs, twins: Mario and Magnus, Ada
and Ida, Justin and Juliette, Sybil and Angel, Silas and Prospero. Silas'
band comprises magicians and jugglers; they conjure up a world that
does not exist, a make-believe world, just as Gabriel himself does.
Hence it is most appropriate for him to fall in with them. Throughout
the book, he has been a Prospero for himself and for the reader. His
aim has been not only to find Rose, his twin sister, but the "rosy
grail" (p. 168) as well. In both he fails. The rosy grail stands for
beauty and truth, the rose being the symbol of beauty and the grail of
truth.[28] Gabriel is the artist in search of order and harmony. The quest
for the twin sister is a metaphor for the artistic quest for perfection.[29]
His efforts are through art, hence the exploitation of a sizeable
number of literary genres and conventions. What is more, Gabriel is
all the time aware of making the efforts and he throws this awareness
into relief. He shows himself in the process of writing — writing as a
way of establishing sense and order, life being all inclusion and
confusion and art being all discrimination and selection, as Henry
James has it in the Preface to *The Spoils of Poynton*.

Metafictional comments interspersed throughout the account lay bare the creative process. "Be assured that I am inventing", Gabriel twice signals to the reader (pp. 13, 170). At one point, he comments on a passage depreciatorily: "Words" (p. 19). Or he interjects: "No, that is not true" (p. 33), thus leaving something in that a conventional narrator would have taken out. Furthermore, he reflects on what he has written down: "Does that seem a ridiculous suggestion? But I do not suggest, I only wonder" (p. 139); and he expressly communicates with the reader: "Listen, listen to me . . ." (p. 147; cf. also p. 82), thus throwing into relief that fiction, art, comes about in a communicative act between a real, or implied, author and a reader. By dint of certain stylistic devices — for example in the form of a propensity for alliterative word combinations such as "a hollow horn of silence sounded throughout the house" (p. 17) or "withered wizzard" (p. 168) — Gabriel evinces that his account is a deliberate textual construct involving a certain amount of play. He also includes commentary on the conventions exploited, as when he has Sybil remark about the romantic search for the sister: "That's very . . . romantic" (p. 137). Lastly, the metafictional aspect of *Birchwood* becomes conspicuous through the use of intertextuality.

*

There is an Ada in the book, and like Nabokov's novel *Ada*, itself also a book about the madeleines and madlanes of memory *Birchwood* is, in the final analysis, about the literary, or artistic, imagination and about how the artistic imagination tries to come to grips with the world, life, truth. Gabriel has, just like that paradigmatic magician Prospero, conjured up a world. He has done so by means literary. He has tried out a wide variety of different literary genres, conventions and stereotypes to see whether these could assist him in his quest for perfection, to see whether they would help discover "a form which would contain and order all [his] losses" (p. 171). But the conventions and strategies did not stand up to the task. All they were suited for was to be parodied, in order that their exhausted nature may be discerned. At the end Gabriel resigns himself to the fact that there "is no form, no order, only echoes, coincidences, sleight of hand, dark laughter. I accept it." (p. 171) This admission can be read in at least two different, equally valid ways. He has failed because the old forms were of no use to him, and new, more adequate ones he has as yet not been able to discover. He has also failed because each and every artistic effort — and his narrative represents one such effort — to arrive at perfection can at best be an approximation. The rosy grail forever eludes the artist's grasp. Fresh attempts have to be made, and each fresh attempt will mark yet another stage in the progressive process of failure — an insight Gabriel shares with Canon Koppernigk; the painter Lucian Freud has expressed it in these terms:

> A moment of complete happiness never occurs in the creation of a work of art. The promise of it is felt in the act of creation but disappears towards the completion of the work. For it is then that the painter realises that it is only a picture he is painting. Until then he had almost dared to hope that the picture might spring to life. Were it not for this, the perfect picture might be painted, on the completion of which the painter could retire. It is this great insufficiency that drives him on. Thus the process of creation becomes necessary to the painter perhaps more than is the picture. The process in fact is habit-forming.[30]

*

Saying may be inventing. But such an assumption, as Beckett's Molloy knew, would be:

> Wrong, very rightly wrong. You invent nothing, you think you are inventing, you think you are escaping, and all you do is stammer out your lesson, the remarks of a pensum one day got by heart and long forgotten, life without tears, as it is wept.[31]

CHAPTER 5
Doctor Copernicus

The opening sentences of *Doctor Copernicus* invoke two of the novel's major thematic concerns. There is, first, what may be termed the 'language theme', meaning the inability to express through language the quintessential nature of things. Beckett has the narratorial voice in *Molloy* adumbrate the problem by the remark: "there could be no things but nameless things, no names but thingless names".[1] There is, second, the theme of the search for "the thing itself, the vivid thing",[2] an anticipatory reference to Copernicus' indefatigable endeavour to discern the truth about the universe. In addition to those two themes, the novel is of course about Nicolas Koppernigk[3], faithfully following the historical sources in order to draw a picture of the great astronomer as a sourpuss and a recluse.

This latter thematic interest has misled some readers and critics to regard the book principally in terms of an historical novel. But *Doctor Copernicus* is not so much an historical novel, if by that term one means to denote a form of narrative discourse, the major intent of which is what Wolfgang Iser calls "die Verwirklichung historischer Wirklichkeit" ('the realization of historical reality'), or "die Vermittlung von historischer Wirklichkeit" ('the communication of historical reality').[4] Instead, it should be more appropriate to approach the account as a 'novel of ideas'. To relativise the claim somewhat, one may add — as Banville himself has suggested[5] — that "the quotation marks are important". For, after all, there is a good deal of historical 'reconstruction' in the novel; but this clearly takes second place behind the elaboration of other, more significant pre-occupations, among them the language theme and the theme of the search for the thing itself, the latter being perhaps a predominant concern of Banville's entire oeuvre to date: it was of the utmost

74

importance for *Birchwood*, and will be so for *Kepler, The Newton Letter*, and *Mefisto*.

*

Copernicus is first shown grappling with the same linguistic, but ultimately epistemological, problem as Stephen Dedalus, in *A Portrait of the Artist*: he, too, becomes aware that words are but arbitrary signs for things and ideas.

> Tree. That was its name. And also: linden. They were nice words. He had known them a long time before he knew what they meant. They did not mean themselves, they were nothing in themselves, they meant the dancing thing outside. In wind, in silence, at night, in the changing air, it changed and yet was changelessly the tree, the linden tree. That was strange. (p. 3)

The matter is as strange to young Koppernigk as it is strange to young Stephen that the words 'suck', 'cold', 'hot', 'kiss' should denote certain things and ideas, or that God should in one language be called 'God' and in another 'Dieu'.[6]

The question involved is whether language as an epistemological and communicative medium is capable of accommodating reality in its essense. Phrased differently, the issue would seem to be this: language is recognised as the means by which the world is comprehended. But it is an ambidextrous means, as it brings about a falsification, at best a subjective assessment of what there is. The categories of one's thinking and one's cognitive faculties are dictated by language as a categorical instrument and also by one's individual linguistic competence. In being able to comprehend reality only by dint of one's system of linguistic signs, one is bound to subjectivise reality. The act of cognition consists of a casting over what one perceives as constituents of the world in its objective as well as ideational manifestations, epistemological categories which are linguistic in kind. These categories prestructure reality as an individualised, subjective reality. As Wittgenstein knew: the limits of one's language are the limits of one's world, and whereof one cannot speak thereof one must be silent. Before he dies, Copernicus imagines his brother, Andreas, telling him: "We say only those things that we have the words to express: it is enough" (p. 240), thus echoing Wittgenstein's dictum, as it were. According to Benjamin Whorf,

> we dissect nature along lines laid down by our native language
> ... The categories and types that we isolate from the world of

phenomena we do not find there . . .; on the contrary, the world is presented in a kaleidoscopic flux of impressions which has to be organized by our minds — and this means largely by the linguistic systems in our mind.[7]

The acquisition of language is a mixed blessing. The blessing is mixed since the things around us are robbed of their ontological purity and we of our epistemological innocence and certainty. An object that is part of the world, this young Koppernigk learns, "cares nothing for its name, [has] no need of a name, and [is] itself only" (p. 3).

It is when words interpose themselves that the essential quality of things gets lost. The idea is as old as, if not older than, Locke, who wrote in Book III, Chapter IX, of *An Essay Concerning Human Understanding:*

> At least they interpose themselves so much between our understanding and the truth which it would contemplate and apprehend, that, like the medium through which visible objects pass, the obscurity and disorder do not seldom cast a mist before our eyes, and impose upon our understanding.[8]

According to Fritz Mauthner, ordinary language, which we cannot go beyond, is of no use to us in our quest for truth. "Only in language do these two words 'mind' and 'body' exist, in reality they cannot be separated"[9]; as a result, "the so-called self-observation has no organs"[10]. Since for Mauthner there is "no thinking without speaking"[11], and since, when we speak, there is no distinguishing between the report and that which it is supposed to be a report of, we are continually uttering meaningless statements. Only by transcending the limits of language (which Mauthner considers impossible) will we get to know things as they really are. And this can only be achieved by a critique of language, which Mauthner describes as "the heavenly stillness and gaiety of resignation and renunciation"[12], a phrase reminiscent of Schopenhauer, but even more prophetic of Beckett. The problem for Mauthner is that this desideratum can only be articulated through language. The critique's success coincides with its own destruction; as Mauthner phrases it, "the critique of language is not the solution to 'the riddle of the Sphinx'", but "it is at least the redeeming act which forces the Sphinx into silence".[13]

The opening of *Doctor Copernicus* introduces the idea of such a critique of language. Moreover, Mauthner's notion of the gaiety of resignation and renunciation possesses a striking pertinency for Banville's 'Life' of Koppernigk, as will be seen, but equally so for his narrative account of Kepler, the Newton biographer, and Gabriel Swan in *Mefisto*.

Without a name, that 'thing' which the child Koppernigk observes dancing outside the window of his room is still "the thing itself, the vivid thing". Through the act of its being given a name: "the linden tree", it is deprived of its whatness. Copernicus' way, as charted by Banville, is the way from the certainty as a child about "the thing itself", via a loss of that certainty as a result of the acquisition of language and the acquisition of the epistemological categories attached thereto, to a striving to regain the knowledge of the "vivid thing". "What he was after", the text notes, "was the deeper, the deepest thing: the kernel, the essence, the true" (p. 79). Copernicus' entire theory basically represents an attempt to discern and explain the thing itself that is the universe, or the world. To Girolamo he remarks questioningly: "I mean you do not think that I am capable of formulating a theory which shall reveal the eternal truths about the universe . . ." (p. 81). His work leads him to the certainty, albeit only a putative one, to have rediscovered that thing itself in his theory of the universe:

> What mattered was not the propositions [expressed by the theory], but the combining of them: *the act of creation*. He turned the solution this way and that, admiring it, as if he were turning in his fingers a flawless ravishing jewel. It was the thing itself, the vivid thing. (p. 85)

We shall have to return to the fact that the combining of the propositions, the act of creation, should matter more than the propositions themselves. For the moment, though, it is more relevant to point out that later on, near the end of his life, Copernicus is brought to the realization that his theory does not really express the truth about the world, but is only found useful for 'saving the phenomena'. At best, his theory — this is the shattering result of his final stock-taking — can account for his very own and highly subjective idea about "the essence, the true". He admits: "It [*i.e.* the book] is a failure. I failed in that which I set out to do: to discern truth, the significance of things" (p. 234). Still more unequivocally, his brother, Andreas, sums up the fruits of all that star-gazing in Copernicus' last hallucinatory vision:

> You thought to discern the thing itself, the eternal truths, the pure forms that lie behind the chaos of the world. You looked into the sky: what did you see?
>
> I saw . . . the planets dancing, and heard them singing in their courses.
>
> O no, no brother. These things you imagined. Let me tell you how it was. You set the sights of the triquetrum upon a light

shining in the sky, believing that you thus beheld a fragment of reality, inviolate, unmistakable, enduring, but that was not the case. What you saw was *a light shining in the sky;* whatever it was more than that it was only by virtue of your faith, your belief in the possibility of apprehending reality. (pp. 238f.)

At the end of his life, there thus stands the acknowledgement of having failed in the endeavour to discern and speak the truth. For Copernicus also realises that he was at least partly bound to fall short of attaining his ambitious goal because he was dependent upon communicating his findings through language. He consequently finds himself a victim to the inexorable fact that language falsifies the truth. "Do you understand?", he asks Osisander. "A hundred thousand words I used, charts, star tables, formulae, and yet I said nothing ..." (p. 235). Earlier on, when he had been summoned to Torum, where his uncle the Bishop was lying ill, he had already been assailed by similar doubts: "He had believed it possible to say the truth; now he saw that all that could be said was the saying. His book was not about the world, but about itself" (p. 116). But at that stage in his life, his enthusiasm for setting up a new kind of astronomy, one that would explain, rather than save, the phenomena, had tided him over his epistemological as well as communicative qualms.

Before his death, though, he is made to suffer the more severely for it. For there he is constrained to admit to himself that another reason why he was determined to fail was that the world is essentially chaotic and absurd, and because the world is chaotic and absurd its essence, the thing itself, cannot be discerned. The universe is, for the dying astronomer, no longer imbued with that "marvellous grave gaiety" (p. 22), as he had believed as a child; the universe is no longer a creation whose "eternal truths" (p. 81) can be known, but it is of that chaotic kind that he had experienced on his walks through Torum and that had fascinated him about the life at the wharf:

Here was not a world of mere words but of glorious clamour and chaos ... The boy was entranced, prey to terror and an awful glee, discerning in all this haste and hugeness the prospect of some dazzling, irresistible annihilation. (p. 7)

At the end of the way there is, thus, the unexpressed insight on the part of Copernicus — and that incidentally anticipates the end of Gabriel Swan's way — that the words of Canon Wodka, the words of that teacher in his school in Wloclawek, who introduced him to astronomy, were true all along:

I believe that the world is *here* ... that it exists, and that it is inexplicable ... For you see, when we are dealing with these

matters, truth becomes an ambiguous concept ... all theories
are but *names, but the world is a thing.* (p. 23)
In a sense, *Doctor Copernicus*, like *Birchwood*, moves from epistemological certainty to despair, or more precisely, as will be seen, to
redemptive despair. The search for the thing itself cannot be
successful, the chaotic nature of the world and the deficient means
we have to express that thing having put paid to one's endeavours.

*

Copernicus' search for the thing itself is fundamentally a search for
order, harmony, a unifying system by dint of which he can come to
grips with, as well as account for, the phenomena. Given the chaotic
nature of the world, it is a search for a supreme fiction.

As early as during his schooldays, Koppernigk becomes fascinated
by "the grave cold music of mathematics, ... the stately march of the
Latin line" (p. 19); and there, "in logic's hard bright lucid, faintly
frightening certainties" (p. 19), he dimly perceives "the contours of
some glistening ravishing thing assembling itself out of blocks of
glassy air" (p. 19), and it is then that he experiences "within him a
coppery chord of perfect bliss" (p. 19). When Canon Sturm sets the
class the conundrum featuring two blindfold men, one blind man,
three black and two white hats, he is filled with excitation not
because he can easily solve it, but because the solution is such a
splendidly harmonious one.[14] Canon Wodka, on their walks by the
river, sketches for him the long confused history of cosmology. But
Koppernigk hardly listens. Unperturbed by the scruples besetting his
friend, he hears the firmament sing to him, and he becomes convinced
that "nothing that he [knows] on earth [can] match the pristine purity
he [imagines] in the heavens" (p. 22) just like Kepler after him. And
like Kepler, he is "seeking a means of understanding" (p. 23) the
"intoxicating, marvellous grave gaiety" (p. 22) which he sees when
looking up into the limitless blue, "beyond the uncertainty and the
terror" (p. 22). Kepler will discover a means in geometry, and the
Gabriel Swan of *Mefisto* first in mathematics and later in symmetrical
and mirror-symmetrical patterns. No particular unifying system is
attributed to Copernicus by Banville other than that whereby the
astronomer seeks to introduce a new science, one no longer consisting of sweaty dreams as well as the old reactionary dogmas and
therefore aiming at describing the world only as we observe it.
Instead, being verily persuaded "that the physical world is amenable

to physical investigation" (p. 36), Copernicus' efforts are firmly directed at setting up a theory which *"explains* the phenomena" (p. 36), rather than *saves* them.

Copernicus' basic premise is this:

> Ptolemy, you see, misled us, or we misled ourselves, it hardly matters which, into believing that the *Almagest* is an explanation, a representation — *vorstellung* [sic], you know the German term? — for what is real, but the truth is, the truth is, that Ptolemaic astronomy is nothing so far as existence is concerned; it is only convenient for computing the nonexistent. (p. 81)

In holding this opinion, Copernicus is "out of step with the age" (p. 27). The dispute with Professor Brudzewski throws vividly into relief the aspiring astronomer's revolutionary stance. Brudzewski represents the old concept. He objects to Copernicus' expounding his dissentient view by pointing out: "Ptolemy, young man — you made no mention of Ptolemy, who has after all, as is well known, resolved for us the mysteries of the universe" (p. 33); and Copernicus counters by insisting:

> Yes but but but *magister*, if I may say so, it is not true, has it not been suggested, that there are certain, how shall I say, certain dispositions of the phenomena that nothing in Ptolemy will explain? (p. 33)

All this time, Copernicus is convinced, the old astronomy has "not been able to discern or deduce the principal thing, namely the shape of the universe and the changing symmetry of its parts" (p. 34). But according to the opinion of the professor, such an endeavour, namely to discern the principal thing, is irredeemably doomed to failure since between man, the observing astronomer, and the universe, the discernible constituent parts of the universe, there is no connection: "We are here and the universe, so to speak, is there and between the two there is no sensible connection, surely?" (p. 34).

This opinion, which exactly recalls Canon Wodka's words of warning at the address of Koppernigk, is interpretable in at least two ways. It is, first, an expression of the view prevalent at the time, according to which man himself was only capable of discerning and explaining the nature of, as well as the truth about, the phenomena that go to make up the sublunary sphere, but not those constituting the supralunary sphere. These were thought to be solely the object of divine understanding, and their secrets could only be divulged to man through divine revelation, and not won by rational efforts.[15] The opinion is, secondly, very modern, helping, as do the various anachronistic quotations from Kierkegaard, Einstein, Eddington, Planck and Wallace Stevens, to establish a context of contemporary significance for Copernicus' epistemological predicament. It contains the basic idea of Camus' existentialist philosophy, more precisely the central thesis of *Sysiphos*. This holds that man is incapable of discerning the sense of his life and the truth about the universe because the universe reacts with inscrutable silence to his enquiring approaches, thus erecting an insurmountable barrier between itself and man. Or as the narrator in Carlyle's *Sartor Resartus* remarks of Teufelsdröckh, after the professor has uttered the 'everlasting No':

> Thus has the bewildered wanderer to stand, as so many have done, shouting question after question into the Sibyl-cave of Destiny, and receive no Answer but an echo.[16]

Both interpretations are aptly borne out by the narrative, for example by its ending. There Copernicus would appear to acknowledge the appropriateness of Brudzewski's conviction. That unbridgeable gap between man and the universe is one of the reasons why his theory is a failure. Whereas in his youthful zest he had been singularly determined to discern the truth about the world, now as a dying man he admits to Rheticus: "Ah, truth, that word I no longer understand" (p. 209). Using arguments strikingly reminiscent of Brudzewski's, or for that matter Canon Wodka's, he explains, again to Rheticus:

> You imagine that my book is a kind of mirror in which the real world is reflected; but you are mistaken, you must realise that. In order to build such a mirror, I should need to be able to perceive the world whole, in its entirety and in its essence. But our lives are lived in such a tiny, confined space, and in such disorder, that this perception is not possible. There is no contact, none worth mentioning, between the universe and the place in which we live. (p. 206)

The tragic irony of the lifelong efforts of Copernicus consists in the fact that in the end he should find it incumbent upon himself to curb the zeal of Rheticus, who in his determination to get the *De revolutionibus* into print clearly recalls Copernicus in his attempts to explain the phenomena employing the very same words that Brudzewski employed to curb Copernicus' own youthful zeal (cf. pp. 205, 208, 186, 37 & 184).

When he was twenty-two, that zeal had been nourished by his glimpsing in the writings of antiquity "the blue and gold of Greece, the blood-boltered majesty of Rome" (p. 27) and he had been allowed

briefly "to believe that there had been times when the world had
known an almost divine unity of spirit and matter" (p. 27). But he
had, from the first, feared deep down, deep beyond admitting, that
"if such a harmony had ever indeed existed, ... it was not to be
regained" (p. 27). And yet regain it he must, as a consequence of a
"dreadful need to discern in the chaos of the world a redemptive
universal unity" (p. 55). Although believing "that the world is
absurd" (a very Camusean belief), he had to strive for "the deepest
thing: the kernel, the essence, the true" (p. 79), experiencing all the
while and battling against "the familiar feeling of dislocation" as a
result of the lack of "a connection between the actual and the
imagined" (pp. 120f.). Perhaps it is true that Copernicus "*did not believe
in truth*", as Rheticus insists on two occasions (pp. 163, 176), but then
again, the assessment may simply be the outcome of Rheticus' biased
views. What is less doubtful, though, is that he based his work on the
firm conviction according to which

> the physical world is amenable to physical investigation, and if
> astronomers will do no more than sit in their cells counting upon
> their fingers, then they are shirking their responsibility. (p. 36)

It is this conviction that, given the dogmatic division between
sublunary and supralunary spheres, makes Copernicus's scientific
stand a truly revolutionary one. Still another theory which aims only
at *salvare apparentia* was completely unacceptable to him; it had to be
one which explains the phenomena. And so he became one of "the
makers of supreme fictions" (p. 136).

*

Copernicus became a maker of a supreme fiction because, for one, his
theory was not true. He did not, contrary to common belief, set the
sun in the centre of the universe. That centre, according to the
arguments submitted in *De revolutionibus*, is the centre of the earth's
orbit, which is situated at a point in space some three times the sun's
diameter distant from the sun, as Rheticus correctly asserts (p. 217).
The planets, therefore, do not revolve around the sun, but around a
hole, a void, a nothingness. Copernicus became, secondly, a maker of
a supreme fiction because, as Banville sees it, he was ultimately not so
much concerned with establishing a new science, was essentially less
interested in the propositions of his theory than in the combining of
them, in "*the act of creation*" (p. 85). His is an interest which is above all
motivated by "a dreadful need to discern in the chaos of the world a

redemptive universal unity" (p. 55). It is of course the overriding interest underlying the creative efforts of an artist.

The manner in which the scientific imagination, as represented by Copernicus, works is likened to the way in which the creative imagination grapples with the problems that confront it. Copernicus comes by the solution to the cosmic mystery — as Kepler will after him — not by painstaking drudgery, but by chance and inspiration and intuition: when least expected.

> And then at last it came to him, sauntered up behind him, as it were, humming happily, and tapped him on the shoulder, wanting to know the cause of all the uproar ... it came ... like a magnificent great slow golden bird alighting in his head with a thrumming of vast wings. It was so simple, so ravishingly simple, that at first he did not recognise it for what it was. (p. 84)

Copernicus' supreme fiction, or what Einstein called 'free creations of the human mind'[17], is the consequence of, significantly, "a creative leap" (p. 85). He treats the solution as if he were an artist, a sculptor, say, marvelling at the beauty of his finished work and deriving an immense aesthetic pleasure from it.

> He turned the solution this way and that, admiring it, as if he were turning in his fingers a flawless ravishing jewel. It was the thing itself, the vivid thing. (p. 85)

Copernicus' labours, like the incessant efforts of a creative artist, are described as "a progress of progressive failure" (p. 93). The artist cannot but fail, since every attempt at discerning and expressing the truth as the only true and worthwhile objective of his vocation must needs represent an approximation only. Still — he has to go on and will go on: "What matter! He dipped his pen in ink. He bled." (p. 93) His book is "not science — it is a dream" (p. 207) — Kepler will entitle one of his books "Somnium": a dream bodying forth the perennial dream of the artist to be able to force the chaos that is the world into some harmonious whole which will lend sense to it by opening up the way to perception (cf. p. 207).

The making of supreme fictions, the efforts necessary for arriving at outstanding, world-shaking scientific discoveries or for making a superb creative achievement, can only come to full fruition at the expense of a total withdrawal from ordinary life. This is the dire dilemma that Copernicus finds himself in, and that Kepler, the historian in *The Newton Letter*, and, to a somewhat lesser degree, Gabriel Swan, in *Mefisto*, will find themselves in.

*

Copernicus is the first of Banville's "high cold heroes who renounced the world and human happiness to pursue the big game of the intellect".[18]

From early on, when still a boy, Nicolas suffers a "contemptuous detachment" (p. 10) from the life that all the other boys are leading. He cannot manage to join in their games, where even the part of victim would have been preferable. Later he will deliberately cultivate "an enviable immunity" (p. 63), while at the same time hankering after "that mysterious self that had eluded him always" (p. 65). Nonetheless, he determinedly shies away from "the thick green stench of humankind" (p. 11), fearing the world: "His flesh crawled at the thought of it" (p. 11). He takes refuge in thinking as a way of scrambling higher and higher away from the loathsome part of life, where he feels dragged by his brother, Andreas, into "rarer and rarer heights of chill bright air" (p. 12). But that thinking cannot obliterate the feeling that he is living only half his life at Wloclawek; rising in the mornings in the mewling dormitory, he becomes grievously and yet pleasurably aware "that somewhere a part of him [is] turning languidly into a deeper lovelier sleep than his hard pallet would ever afford", believing all the while "that someday his sundered selves must meet in some far finer place" (p. 17).

Meanwhile, however, his mind is centred on the purity and brilliance of the sky. Having carried his numbed and lightened spirit up the winding stairs to Canon Wodka's observatory and looking through the single window which opens out like a trapdoor on the firmament, he is ravished by the experience of all tending upward here as if on the point of flight: the sky a dome of palest glass, the sun sparkling on the snow. All the happiness in his as yet brief life, the "foolish happiness" (p. 25), arises from the "infinite possibilities of the future" awaiting him; and his young soul swoons, "and slowly, O, slowly, he seemed to fall upward, into the blue" (p. 25). It is thus that he arrives at the firm decision that, even though the real world will not be gainsaid, being the true realm of action, "he must gainsay it, or despair" (p. 28). On his way across the Alps into Italy, he is not at all pained by the sufferings, the dead and the maimed, all those terrible scenes, the blood and mud, the bundles of squirming flesh. The emptiness within him horrifies him (cf. p. 44). Nor does he desire to get involved in the political affairs of the world. "Action is necessary", Novara and his fellow-conspirators besiege Copernicus, trying to win his active support in overthrowing the present bad Pope and appointing a Pope of their making. Nicolas becomes briefly engrossed in the wonderfully ridiculous image of himself and Bishop

Lucas, his uncle, deep in dark discussion of a plot to bring down the Pope, but then he curtly dismisses the whole idea, backing out with the mealy-mouthed remark: "Sir, you do not know my uncle" (p. 60).

The desire to cultivate "a contemptuous detachment" from the world is an important thematic issue of at least two of the other books that make up Banville's tetralogy. In *Kepler*, after his son Heinrich has died in infancy, the protagonist is described standing by the bedroom window, hearing vaguely his wife's anguished cries behind him "and listening in awe to his mind, of its own volition, thinking: My work will be interrupted".[19] In *The Newton Letter*, the historian, like Newton, is loath to become genuinely involved with other people. "I had", he states at one point, "not contracted to be known as she [*i.e.* Ottilie] was trying to know me."[20] Gabriel Swan, in *Mefisto*, is somewhat of an exception. For, although he perceives and experiences the world vicariously, as it were, by dint of figures, he nonetheless seeks to become involved with the people around him and their affairs.

In *Doctor Copernicus*, this thematic aspect seems to be tied to the motif of metaphorical shining birds and hawklike monsters. "Monstrous hawklike creatures ... flying on invisible struts and wires" are first mentioned in connection with young Nicolas masturbating, pulling "at that blindly rearing lever between his legs ... pulling himself back into the world" (p. 24). Next in a letter to Tiedemann Giese, written two and a half years before his death, Copernicus states: "... the filthy world that will not let me be, that comes after me always, a black monster, dragging its damaged wings in its wake" (p. 155). Then, later, the monstrous creatures turn into "a huge steely shining bird":

> it was soaring on motionless outstretched great wings, terrible, O, terrible beyond words, and yet magnificent, carrying in its fearsome beak a fragment of blinding fire, and he cried out, to utter the word, but in vain ... (p. 229)

In his last conversation with Osiander, he finds himself once again assailed

> by the great steel bird, trailing flames in its wake and bearing in its beak the fiery sphere, no longer alone, but flying before a flock of others of its kind, all aflame, all gleaming and terrible and magnificent, rising out of darkness, shrieking. (p. 236)

Lastly, the "terrible birds [sail] in silence into the dark" (p. 241) during Copernicus' hallucinatory vision of Andreas visiting him as an angel of redemption. As the lines written to Giese suggest, the hawklike creatures metaphorically signify the world: they are monstrous because the world is monstrous to Copernicus; their hostile attacks body forth the hostile attacks of all that Copernicus desires to stay aloof from. They turn into magnificent shining birds when it is borne home to Copernicus, late, in fact too late in his life and at first only subconsciously, that the world will not be gainsaid: the world, like the shining bird, is magnificent; it is the vivid thing that he all along mistook for something else. The fragment of blinding fire the bird carries in its fearsome beak signifies the realization of the truth. Compassion for, and love of, the world, the people in the world, emotional commitment — they are what Copernicus has been lacking throughout his life, and 'thou' is the word that, when assailed by the huge steely shining bird, he tries to cry out, "but in vain":

Word!

O word!

Thou word that I lack! (p. 229)

The dilemma of Copernicus as a humane human being, or the problems resulting from his "enviable immunity", are paradigmatically worked out in the novel through the relationship with Girolamo and, more even, with Andreas. When he first meets him, Girolamo is on his way home after a "misspent" night of drink and debauchery. Or so he tells Copernicus. Later it becomes obvious that this was not the case: he lied because he knew that Copernicus wanted him "to be a rake, a rich wastrel, something utterly different from [himself]" (p. 82). Copernicus accompanies Girolamo to the tumble-down palazzo, where in one of the rooms he discovers, under the sagging canopy of a vast four-poster, a naked young man asleep in a tangle of sheets. He is struck by the patrician indifference and ease of Girolamo, and although his "lean grey troubled soul" suddenly aches with envy of "this young man's confidence and carelessness, his disdain for the trivial trappings of the world" (p. 69), he shrinks back into his black cloak. But in spite of this initial, inborn defence mechanism, Girolamo makes Copernicus cast his contemptuous detachment to the winds. He feels intimately drawn to the young man, and for the first time in his life he experiences a human happiness that is distinctly different from the vicarious happiness he is able to derive from what Andreas disparagingly calls 'stargazing'. Significantly enough, it is an "inexpressible something" which swells within him. But immediately this novel experience is sorely over-shadowed by the fear that the fine frenzy he finds himself caught by "could destroy him" (p. 71). In the following weeks and months,

Copernicus is torn between giving in to the temptation of enjoying his new-found happiness, of liberating himself from the hegemony of the intellect by casting off the bonds of his body, and his self-imposed obligation to remain impervious to "the encumbering lumber of life" (p. 79). Profound though his feelings of love are, during that time they cannot bring him to address Girolamo by using the term of endearment 'thou'. Later on, he will diagnose the same about his relationship with Anna Schillings (p. 227). And so, finally, he wilfully abandons Girolamo, forfeiting one of the few opportunities in his life to discover his own humaneness: he goes cold and dead, and out of the wracked humiliated body his mind soars "slowly upward, into the blue", and he retreats back "into science as a refuge from the ghastliness of life" (p. 79).

The contrast between the two ways of being human, Girolamo's way of embracing life and Copernicus' of staying aloof, but likewise the existential conflict that Copernicus finds himself flung into on account of his relationship with Girolamo, and, lastly, also the thematic concern with those high cold heroes who renounce the world and human happiness to pursue the big game of the intellect — all these are with admirable mastery thrown into relief at the end of Part I. Before Copernicus and his friend, Girolamo, say their farewells in a filthy little inn, there are two scenes poignantly and potently juxtaposed. In fact they are set side by side in a contiguous fashion that the events delineated therein could be taken to occur simultaneously. In one, a girl, observed by Copernicus, performs an act of fellatio on Girolamo, "his head thrown back and his lips open in an O of ecstacy" (p. 82). In the other, Copernicus is described bent over his desk formulating the basic tenets of his theory and actually finding the solution to the cosmic mystery, which has come to him "like a magnificent great slow golden bird" (p. 84) in a creative leap that puts him in a situation where he experiences a very different kind of ecstacy: the ecstacy of the act of creation, of being able to turn the solution in his hands, so to speak, like a "flawless ravishing jewel". While Girolamo is immersing himself in the earthiness of life, Copernicus is immersing himself in the secrets of the sky.

The price he has to pay for this is immense. But not before it is too late is the full extent of his sacrifice borne home to him, when "his spirit ... [returns] to this bright place and he [finds] it all intact" (p. 86): the relationship, which he deliberately severed, to one of the only two people who meant anything to him in terms of human emotional commitment.

Perhaps there was yet another, a third person, apart from

Girolamo and Anna Schillings, namely Andreas. But strictly speaking, Andreas' relationship to Copernicus is of a different kind. While Copernicus does his best to "rid his life of everything that [may] bring him comfort" (p. 112), while he finds it "necessary to fend [everything] off, lest it should contaminate his vision ... and taint with earthiness the transcendent purity of his theory of the heavens" (p. 130), Andreas wallows in earthiness, as it were. He is clearly cast in the role of Copernicus' *alter ego*, representing "that mysterious self" that has eluded Copernicus always, and standing also for all that his brother seeks to remain uncontaminated by. Of him it is said that he "was handsomely made, very tall and slender, dark, fastidious, cold" (p. 9). He revels in the low life, whereas Nicolas' flesh "crawls at the thought" (p. 11); throughout, he enjoys to the full whatever life holds in store for him. Or perhaps it is not correct to suggest that he does so throughout; for the narrative does not in fact warrant such an assessment, describing Andreas' doings from a point of view that seems to be in sympathy with Nicolas' view.

In Nicolas' estimation, the life of the 'presence' which keeps haunting him from a distance (cf. p. 123), no matter where he seeks to hide himself from the world, is helplessly disintegrating (cf. p. 62). As if it were a fit punishment for his myriad sins, Andreas' face becomes horribly misshapen. On one of those dreaded visits from him, Nicolas is forced to notice that his upper lip is all eaten away on one side and that one of his ears is a mess of crumbled meat (cf. p. 100). "... it is the pox, brother, the *Morbus Gallicus*" (p. 101), Andreas explains. He may be despicable, but he is not "dead from the neck down", like his brother. Unlike him, "death-in-life, Poor Pol" (p. 101), Andreas can well say: "I have lived!" (p. 101), knowing that "our lives ... are a little journey through God's guts. We are soon shat" (p. 103), knowing, in other words, that life is an immeasurably precious thing that must not be squandered by being deprived of its essential quality. What that quality is, is revealed to Copernicus before his death only, when he has painfully been won over to embrace Andreas' view, when he repeats to Rheticus: "'Our lives —', he smiled, '— are a little journey through God's guts ...'" (p. 207).

Incidentally, the same will happen to Kepler, who as a dying man is searching too late for the life that he has missed, that his work has robbed him of,[21] and who realises in a dream, as hallucinatory as that of the dying Copernicus, that Tycho Brahe had shared a similar fate. It is Andreas' supreme task in the novel to teach Copernicus the truth about his life and the truth about the thing itself, the vivid thing. He comes to him as "the angel of redemption" and tells him:

I was that which you must contend with.

[...]

I was the one absolutely necessary thing, for I was there always to remind you of what you must transcend. I was the bent bow from which you propelled yourself beyond the filthy world. (p. 240)

*

While his sickness waxes and wanes, Copernicus asks himself: "[Is] redemption still possible ... even in this extremity?" (p. 228). For some reason, all his life he has been fascinated by *redemption* as "that greatest of all words" (p. 56). Searching for an answer to his question, his fevered understanding scavenges among the detritus of his life; but he can "find no sense of significant meaning anywhere" (p. 228). Indicatively enough, his mind, in wandering through the palaces of memory, focuses on that wonderful relationship with Girolamo and finds the past all intact, as he had known it to be when saying his farewell to his friend (cf. p. 86). But neither here, nor in his recollection of the linden tree and his youth in Torum can he find happiness. There is no answer, and despair blossoms in him (cf. p. 228). No less indicatively, he ponders on his relationship with Anna Schillings, and it strikes him that perhaps the fact that she had chosen to remain, had endured, was what she signified (p. 231). The compassion, the love and care she evinced for him is the important thing. He failed to realise this, having all the while been preoccupied with searching for what he mistakenly had considered to be "that thing which is itself" (p. 230). He failed even in discerning that thing, but the failure is a small matter, compared to the general disaster that was his life" (p. 232).

Then, when he knows for sure that he is dying, that he is unmistakably confronting what Henry James, on his deathbed, called "the distinguished thing",[22] he dreams Andreas comes as the angel of redemption, and the message Andreas brings is quite beautiful in its simplicity: "The world, and ourselves, this is the truth. There is no other ..." (p. 239). It is now that Copernicus realises:

If what you say were true, I should have had to sell my soul to a vicious world, to embrace meekly the hideousness, yes — but I would not do it! This much at least I can say, that I did not sell — (p. 240)

His words show that he is still putting up a fight against fully acknowledging the truth of Andreas' revelation. But the angel of redemption is insistent:

> With great courage and great effort you might have succeeded, in the only way it is possible to succeed, by disposing the commonplace, the names, in a beautiful and orderly pattern that would show, by its very beauty and order, the action in our poor world of the otherwordly truth. But you tried to discard the commonplace truths for the transcendent ideal, and so failed. (p. 240)

Moreover, he is quite outspoken about the true nature of "the thing itself, the vivid thing" (p. 241):

> It is that thing, passionate and yet calm, ..., fabulous and yet ordinary, that thing which is all that matters, which is the great miracle. You glimpsed it briefly in our father, in sister Barbara, in Fracastoro [i.e. Girolamo], in Anna Schillings, in all the others, and even, yes, in me, glimpsed it, and turned away ... Call it acceptance, call it love if you will, but these are poor words, and express nothing of the enormity. (p. 241)

And so, finally, Copernicus accepts; he becomes aware that it is not too late for redemption. In fact, he has redeemed himself. For the arguments broached by Andreas have after all been Copernicus' very own arguments. "It is not I who have said all these things", Andreas tells him, "but you" (p. 241).

At last he has managed to discern the thing itself; and in the end, it is the world, the voices of the evening, the herdsman's call, the cries of children at play, the rumbling of carts, the sea, the earth and the linden tree — in short, all that he did not want to sell his soul to which calls him away: "All called and called him, and called, calling him away" (p. 242). A similar notion of the power of redemption will occur in *The Newton Letter*, when the historian comes to speak about Newton's "two strange letters to Locke" (*The Newton Letter*, p. 50). "He wanted", the historian argues, "so much to know what it was that had happened to him, and to say it, as if the mere saying itself would be redemption" (p. 50)

Does *Doctor Copernicus*, then, suggest that the pursuit of the big game of the intellect should be given second place behind an opening up to life, compassion and love? The answer lies in what Andreas teaches Copernicus. Acceptance is one keyword. The world must be accepted in all its diverse manifestations, and not gainsaid. Another keyword is mutual dependence and it is hidden in Andreas' remark:

> I was the absolutely necessary thing, for I was there always to remind you of what you must transcend. I was the bent bow

from which you propelled yourself beyond the filthy world.
(p. 240)

The vivid "thing" is the world, and any attempt at discerning its secrets can only be successful if it is firmly grounded in encumbering life. Kepler will later discover the truth of this, when he comes upon the solution to the cosmic mystery at the height of a carousing night in the company of pox-ridden whores. The thing itself, the vivid thing — and this is the third key-thought — cannot be found by falling upward into the blue and by exploring the "marvellous grave gaiety" of the sky, but by disposing the commonplace in a beautiful and orderly pattern that will show by its very beauty and order the action in our poor world of the otherwordly truth. The world, then, is of the same utmost importance as are the attempts to come to grips with the chaos of life through systems of order and beauty. And little does it matter whether these systems represent supreme fictions. Perhaps supreme fictions are all we are capable of. The act of creation, of creating them, is the thing.

As Canon Wodka wisely warns Copernicus: "Beware these enigmas, my young friend. They exercise the mind, but they cannot teach us how to live" (p. 21). The historian in *The Newton Letter* will be subjected to the excruciating experience that the commonplace, "the *ordinary*", is the "strangest and most elusive of enigmas".[23] This enigma has to be solved first, as again the historian is constrained to learn, before the solution of any other enigma can be arrived at, if, that is, he who strives towards finding it does not want to become deprived of his humaneness.

*

To show whether or not Copernicus was a humane human being after all is partly the reason why the third part of the novel consists of a personal account by Rheticus of his life with the great astronomer. That part has other thematic functions, too, such as the treatment of why Copernicus took so long to publish his theory. But it is important to notice that it is a *personal* account.

Near the end of Part II, a shift in narrative perspective becomes conspicuous. By dint of certain narratorial comments that have a distinctly Fielding-like ring to them, the third-person point-of-view, prevalent up to this point, becomes superceded by an omniscient viewpoint which has a locquacious narrator push to the fore for the purpose of conversing with the reader, telling him for instance:

"How she [*i.e.* Anna Schillings] survived that awful period we shall not describe; we draw a veil over that subject ..." (p. 142; cf. also similar remarks on pp. 139-44). If these comments are meant as a crack at parody, of how for example in eighteenth-century 'histories' the narrators establish an intimate communicative relationship with the reader, they would have to be considered oddly out of place. There does not seem to be anything in the novel to warrant such a sudden, unexpected change into the parodic.[24] Perhaps it is more meet to see them as part of an attempt, which is assisted by the letters concluding Part II, to 'personalise' the narrative point-of-view in a very specific manner.

> I, Georg von Lauchen, called Rheticus, will now set down the
> true account of how Copernicus came to reveal to a world
> wallowing in a stew of ignorance the secret music of the
> universe. (p. 159)

Thus Part III begins. The historical Rheticus, Copernicus' only disciple, is known to have written the first biography of the great astronomer; it was never published and now is lost. Now, whether this part of *Doctor Copernicus* is meant as a fictional recreation of Rheticus' authentic eye-witness report is uncertain; it may just possibly have been inspired by the fact that such a report did once exist. The entire novel, though, is not, as may perhaps be surmised from having the implied narrator of the first two parts reveal his identity in the third, meant to be such a fictional recreation.[25]

Though Rheticus may state he will now set down a true account, towards the end of it, it becomes unmistakable that the motivating force is not a love of truth, of authenticity, but revenge: he wants revenge for not having been given what he believes to be his due. Everyone got a mention in *De revolutionibus orbium mundi* — Schoenberg is mentioned, and Giese — but, in spite of all the Herculean labour he performed on behalf of the book, "*there is no mention of [his] name*" (p. 216). Rheticus is not one to mince words. He has, he ardently admits, waited patiently "for this moment when I would have my revenge" (p. 216), and he does so by trying to pick holes in the majestic fabric of Copernicus' *orbium mundi*. Throughout his allegedly true account, he has the severest difficulties in holding his horses. Repeatedly, his bottled-up chagrin seeks to vent itself. "I hate them all", he once breaks out, "Giese with his mealy-mouthed hypocrisy, Dantiscus and his bastard, but most of them I hate — ah but bide, Rheticus, bide!" (p. 172). Shortly afterwards, the following statement occurs: "I can see it now, how cunning they were, the two of them, Giese and the Canon, cunning old conspirators..." (p. 174).

And then again, he is free to confess that, in spite of all and in retrospect, he *"was happy that summer at Löbau"* (p. 182), but only to own up on another occasion that he has, notwithstanding his initially expressed intention,

> not given here a strictly literal account of how I was inveigled into writing it [*i.e.* his *Narratio prima*], but have contented myself with showing how cunningly he worked upon my youthful enthusiasm and my gullibility in order to achieve his own questionable ends. (p. 187)

Rheticus, therefore, is an utterly unreliable narrator, who in his inscrutable deviousness — which he incidentally shares with the historian in *The Newton Letter* — is certainly on a par with Ford Madox Ford's narrator John Dowell, in *The Good Soldier*, that paradigm of unreliability. Dowell, in his confidential confession, makes it excruciatingly hard for the reader to decide whether the intimacy of the "four-square coterie" was "like a minuet" or whether it was "a prison full of screaming hysterics".[26] Like Dowell, who is permanently protesting that he does not know and that all is a darkness,[27] Rheticus is "to this day uncertain whether or not what [he is] about to relate did in reality take place" (p. 199).

On the other hand, he makes, in his account, much of a boy named Raphaël, with whom, it would appear, he entertained what his contemporaries tended to consider an unsavoury relationship, which finally was the reason for his fall from grace. Then, at the end, he divulges:

> The fact is, there never was a Raphaël. I know, I know, it was dreadful of me to invent all that, but I had to find something, you see, some terrible tangible thing, to represent the great wrongs done me by Copernicus. (p. 219)

Rheticus, then, comes across as an unreliable, revengeful and utterly conceited fellow. "Who else", he asks at one stage, "could have made such a compressed, succint account, in so short a time, of that bristling mesh of astronomical theory" (p. 188). When copying Copernicus' manuscript, he experiences the "malicious pleasure of correcting his slips" (p. 202). One such slip he thinks he has found in what seems to him "that nonsensical line in which he speculated on the possibility of elliptical orbits — *elliptical* orbits, for God's sake!" (p. 202). The world had, of course, to wait for Kepler to make that possibility an incontestable fact. Rheticus, with the full authority of his unfounded conviction to be "a greater astronomer" than Copernicus (cf. p. 205), utterly dismisses the idea. He even goes on to reveal that the printing of *De revolutionibus*, in which he was so exceptionally instrumental, was really only a ruse. For from that point in time onwards, Koppernigk had ceased to be a part of his plan, that plan consisting in Copernicus' making known his theory so that he can refute it and formulate his own "*true* system of the universe, based upon Ptolemaic principles" (p. 219).

Rheticus is, while penning his account, in exile, "to rot in this Godforgotten corner of Hungary that they call Cassovia" (p. 159), thus anticipating the historian in *The Newton Letter*, who is writing in the frozen wastes of some arctic region. There is a curious admission contained in the account that likewise prefigures the plight of Banville's Newton biographer.

> I was then [Rheticus remarks], and I am still, despite my loss of faith, one of those who look to the future for redemption, I mean redemption from the world, which has nothing to do with Christ's outlandish promises, but with the genius of Man. (p. 203)

The admission also recalls Copernicus' conversion to the belief in redemption, and it signals an uncanny transformation in some of the characters and their relationships in *Doctor Copernicus*. Shorn of all the inessential paraphernalia of character traits, Rheticus at bottom is made to correspond to Copernicus, as Copernicus is made to correspond to Brudzewski. Or more precisely, the relationship of Rheticus and Copernicus fundamentally equals the relationship of Copernicus and Brudzewski. Disillusioned about his success in ever discerning the thing itself and failing in health, Copernicus admonishes Rheticus:

> We must follow the methods of the ancients! Anyone who thinks they are not to be trusted will squat forever in the wilderness outside the locked gates of our science, dreaming the dreams of the deranged about the motions of the spheres — and he will get what he deserves for thinking he can support his own ravings by slandering the ancients! (p. 183)

Many years ago, Brudzewski had meant to curb the scientific enthusiasm of Copernicus by pointing out, in very similar words: "to him who thinks that the ancients are not to be entirely trusted, the gates of our science are certainly closed" (p. 37). Like Copernicus, Rheticus eventually comes to embrace the conviction that the world is absurd, a chaos (cf. p. 218), and this in spite of his erstwhile frenzy, which equals Copernicus' frenzy as a young man for his new science, to make known to the world Copernicus' theory, if only in order to advance his alternative views.

Rheticus ends up like Copernicus, with a solitary amanuensis, one

Lucius Valentine Otho, who, upon arriving at Cassovia, fell to his knees before Rheticus, as Rheticus himself had, actually or figuratively, done when meeting Copernicus for the first time. Rheticus confesses to having been struck by the coincidence that Otho, when he came to him, was the same age as he himself had been, so many years ago, when coming to Copernicus at Frauenburg (cf. p. 219). Strange recurrences, indeed, as strange as those that in multiple ways characterise *Mefisto* thematically as well as structurally.

Part III of *Doctor Copernicus*, as suggested above, serves not least to shed light on the puzzling circumstance of why it took Copernicus so extraordinarily long to publish his revolutionary *opus*. Rheticus' reception of the theory provides ample evidence of the enormity of the issues involved.

Tiedemann Giese is quoted in Rheticus' account as suggesting that fear lay at the bottom of Copernicus' procrastination, fear not doubt as to the validity of his conclusions made the great astronomer hesitate, "no — but fear. So it was, Herr von Lauchen: *fear*" (p. 177). Rheticus himself specifies that fear as fear of ridicule. The timid Canon, according to his amused amanuensis, was afraid of becoming a figure of fun for putting forward "new rules, yes, *but no proofs to support them*" (p. 185). This, however, is only half the truth, only one side of the cataclysmic coin. The other consists of the enormity of Copernicus' computational discovery. Rheticus hints at this issue, when he remarks:

> He was well aware that his theory ... would, if published, overturn the accepted notions regarding the movements of the spheres, and would therefore cause a hideous commotion, and he was not prepared *to lend his name* to the causing of such disturbance. (p. 185)

There is also the possibility that Copernicus postponed the publication of his theory because, at bottom, it was based on the Ptolemaic astronomy — that astronomy he had sought to overcome by his new science. Again Rheticus puts the matter poignantly. Contrary to his pretences, Copernicus was only too aware

> of having put forward a notion which, if he believed it to be true, made nonsense of his life's work (for, remember, whatever they may say about it now, his theory was based entirely upon the Ptolemaic astronomy — was indeed, as he pointed out himself, no more than a revision of Ptolemy ... (p. 186)

Arthur Koestler has called Copernicus "the last Aristotelian" and submitted that his absolute reliance not only on the physical dogmata, but on the astronomical observations of the ancients was the main reason for the errors and absurdities of the Copernican system.[28] (It required, for example, eight epicycles more than the Ptolemaic system.) The verdict would account for the Canon's late conversion to a belief in the ancients, as expressed by the admonition to Rheticus quoted earlier.

The disturbing enormity of the implications of *De revolutionibus* finds even more vivid expression in Rheticus' basic premise for advancing his own allegedly true system. His aim is to preserve the dignity of "old Earth", rescuing her from being banished to the status of an insignificant planet, "forever into darkness. It was sorrow", he writes, "sorrow that old Earth should be thus deposed, and cast out into the darkness of the firmament, there to prance and spin at the behest of a tyrannical, mute god of fire" (p. 180). His affiliation with Copernicus, devious as it may have been, never made Rheticus into a Copernican, or so the novel suggests; he remained irredeemably rooted in the Ptolemaic heritage, motivated by the unshakable conviction, twice stated by him (pp. 180, 220), "that this planet shall forever be the centre of all we know."

The despair shining through this adhering to the old concept is, above all, the despair of the common people on which Copernicus would have unleashed his dissentient view of the cosmos. Weeping, bowed down under the burden of despair with which he loaded them, they would have been asked to acknowledge that the universe was after all not created *propter nos*. We today have accustomed ourselves to the despairing thought, and some may have difficulty in seeing what the fuss was all about some three hundred years back. But that does not make the Copernican revolution a less momentous one.

The novel suggests that a major reason why Copernicus procrastinated was that he was afraid of pushing his contemporaries into despair. It may not be the authentic reason, but this cannot lessen the beauty of the suggestion.

*

This is not the place to deal *in extenso* with the various consequences, theological, ecclesiastical, epistemological and otherwise, of what has come to be known as the 'Copernican Revolution'. A few remarks must suffice, this especially in view of the fact that the novel is not about the 'Copernican Revolution', not about its impact upon the world, but about someone, a hero of science, who tries to come to terms with reality by dint of creating a supreme fiction. *Doctor Copernicus* is a parable about the Creative Imagination, as are the subsequent novels in the tetralogy. All make the point that truth in fact does not exist, that there are only workable versions of the truth which we contract to believe in, as Copernicus comes to learn when dying of a haemorrhage of the brain.

Copernicus was led to his heliocentric reform by his teleological conviction that the world had been created "*propter nos ab optimo et regularissimo omnium opifice*" and that in such a world, which had been created for the sake of man, there should exist no part that is not amenable to rational inquiry. This humanist rational-teleological anthropocentrism defended itself against the divisionary cosmology of Latin Averroism — the division into a sublunary and a supralunary sphere, about the latter of which only hypotheses can be put forward — with its complexity and the metaphysical sanctioning of the imprecise nature of astrological achievements. Instead Copernicus strove to preserve the metaphysical principle of the pervading rationality of the cosmos and, at the same time, establish man in the role of a *contemplator caeli* who, on account of his rational faculties, is capable of discerning the secrets of the sky.[29]

Goethe, in his *Materialien zur Geschichte der Farbenlehre*, puts the point pungently about the world-shaking enormity of this endeavour and its outcome.

> Unter allen Entdeckungen und Überzeugungen möchte nicht eine größere Wirkung auf den menschlichen Geist hervorgebracht haben, als die Lehre des Kopernikus. Kaum war die Welt als rund anerkannt und in sich selbst abgeschlossen, so sollte sie auf das ungeheure Vorrecht Verzicht tun, der Mittelpunkt des Weltalls zu sein. Vielleicht ist noch nie eine größere Forderung an die Menschheit geschehen: denn was ging nicht alles durch diese Anerkennung in Dunst und Rauch auf: ein zweites Paradies, eine Welt der Unschuld . . .; kein Wunder, daß man dies alles nicht wollte fahren lassen, daß man sich auf alle Weise einer solchen Lehre entgegensetzte, die denjenigen, der sie annahm, zu einer bisher unbekannten, ja ungeahneten Denkfreiheit und Großheit der Gesinnungen berechtigte und aufforderte.[30]

For Friedrich Nietzsche, Copernicus has become the metaphor of the nihilism of modern times: "Seit Kopernikus rollt die Menschheit aus

dem Zentrum in's 'x'". As a result of the 'fall of the theological
astronomy', he goes on to note, human existence has grown "noch
beliebiger, eckensteherischer, entbehrlicher in der sichtbaren
Ordnung der Dinge", and he asks: "Ist nicht gerade die Selbstver-
kleinerung des Menschen seit Kopernikus in einem unaufhaltsamen
Fortschritt?"[31]

Copernicus' contemporaries, or rather his peers among them,
were of course well aware of these consequences and were eager to
nip them in the bud. Osiander's preface to *De revolutionibus* offers
ample proof of this contention. The intention was to deprive the
Frauenburg Canon's *revolutiones* of the causticity of their
revolutionary nature; without the Canon's knowing it, Osiander
claimed that the conclusions of the new theory were only meant as
fundamenta calculi.[32] In *Doctor Copernicus*, Osiander explains to the
languishing astronomer:

> ... the Aristotelians and the theologians will easily be placated
> if they are told that ... the present hypotheses are not proposed
> because they are in reality true but because they are the most
> convenient to calculate the apparent composite motions.
> (p. 233)

In his opinion, they can only be "bases of computation".[33]

The result of this sly argumentative move is a return to the
epistemological orientation of scholasticism: the orientation from the
supralunary down to the sublunary sphere, from God in heaven down
to man on earth. As an inner scholastic event, the Copernican reform
was impossible. For it stipulated that the majority of orbital motions,
particularly the daily rotation of the fixed stars as well as the annual
rotation of the sun, represented the effect of a principle which was
operative "nicht von außen nach innen, nicht von oben nach unten,
sondern umgekehrt vom Innenraum des Kosmos aus, also ... von
unten nach oben".[34] Copernicus' reform was unacceptable also
because it postulated the possibility of explaining the phenomena,
instead of merely *salvare apparentia*. The main objection was that the
rational efforts of man were considered to be incommensurate to the
motions of the planets, the secrets of the universe. The hypothesis was
put forward by Nicolas of Oresme in a treatise published in the
second half of the fourteenth century and entitled *De commen-
surabilitate vel incommensurabilitate motuum caeli*. In it, he stresses the
incompatibility of the order of creation: "*rerum mundi proportiones
nosse praecisas humanum transcendit ingenium*".[35] Jorge Luis Borges, in his
story "Averroes's Search", has Averroes expound a similar notion in
the (to all intents and purposes) fictional study "*Tahafut-ul-Tahafut*

(Destruction of Destruction)": "the divinity knows only the general laws of the universe".[36]

The impact of Copernicus' revolutionary theory on the world, even the world of today, may be discerned from a dialogue exchange in Tom Stoppard's play *Jumpers*. Although the example may, given the context in which it occurs, somewhat smack of the facetious, it nonetheless puts the crucial issue nicely — an issue that is, incidentally, of the utmost significance for Banville's entire tetralogy:

> DOTTY: ... You're probably still shaking from the four-hundred-year-old news that the Sun doesn't go round *you*!
>
> GEORGE: We are *all* still shaking. Copernicus cracked our confidence, and Einstein smashed it: for if one can no longer believe that a twelve-inch ruler is always a foot long, how can one be sure of relatively less certain propositions, such as that God made the Heaven and the Earth ...[37]

The 'Copernican Revolution' has become what Blumenberg terms an "'absolute' cosmic metaphor": Copernicus' construct of the universe signifies the fundamental change in man's view of himself in the world.

Frequently it is suggested that the Canon took so long to publish his book because of a severe opposition by the church. That an opposition existed is clear from such efforts as are made by Osiander in his unauthorised preface. The condemnation of Copernicus was still virulent during the days of John Donne, who envisaged the astronomer in conversation with Lucifer in Hell, in the course of which he is quoted as pointing out to Lucifer:

> I am he, which pitying thee who wert thrust into the centre of the world, raised both thee, and thy prison, the Earth, up into the Heavens ... The sun, which was an officious spy, and a betrayer of faults, and so thine enemy, I have appointed to go into the lowest part of the world.[38]

Thus while the church was anything but happy about news from Frauenburg concerning a theory that devastatingly upset its theological as well as dogmatic apple-cart, one must, when considering the matter, not leave out the fact that — as Koestler has noted — the *Book of Revolutions* was not put on the Index until seventy-three years after it was published,[39] possibly as a result of Osiander's amelioratory preface. There is also, according to Koestler, some evidence of early benevolent interest in the Copernican theory shown by the Vatican.[40] Only when the 'heretic' Giordano Bruno radicalised the Copernican consequences, giving them a distinctly antichristian thrust, did Copernicanism become discredited in the eyes of the ecclesiastical rulers.[41] They tried to keep the people in pitiable ignorance, in spite of Kepler, Newton and others, by foisting upon them their own supreme fiction about the truth until 1822 and 1835, respectively, when *De revolutionibus* was deleted from the Index.

*

Doctor Copernicus, like most of Banville's work, is a finely wrought piece of fiction, betraying the hand of an artist who is immensely conscious of form. An effort to imbue the shape of the account with thematic significance is conspicuous everywhere in the book. There are, to begin with, an extraordinarily rich number of circular, or ring-like, patterns, which form part of the compositional design. They are mostly created by the strategies of repetition and variation. References to the linden tree open and close the novel, thus lending the whole a circular, closed shape. The concern with "the thing itself", also invoked at the start, purposely recurs throughout with subtle variation, as does the motif of the hawklike monstrous creatures flying on invisible struts and wires. Professor Brudzewski repeats Canon Wodka's words of warning that we are here and the universe, so to speak, is there, and Copernicus repeats to Rheticus Andreas' view of human life as a brief journey through God's guts. When a boy, Nicolas is called away by "the voice of sleep itself" (p. 5); when a dying man, Koppernigk is called away by "the voices of evening rising to meet him from without" (p. 242). The statement according to which the Turk impales his prisoners occurs at least twice (pp. 9, 99). The opening and ending of Part II are identical (cf. pp. 89, 155). Part III is likewise, by dint of repetition, coerced into a circular shape: the true purpose of von Lauchen's personal account, only hinted at the start, is fully disclosed near the end (cf. pp. 159, 216); Rheticus professes his scientific *credo* twice (pp. 180, 220). There are also those strange character transformations and recurrences in character constellation, involving Copernicus, Brudzewski, Rheticus, and Otho.

One could go on listing further examples; but the ones given here will prove the point about the circular patterns which permeate the novel. It is as if, with their help, Banville was aiming to effect a reiterative narrative progression that imitates the orbital motions of the planets, but likewise Copernicus' turning upon his obsession with "the thing itself", or, for that matter, Rheticus' turning upon his, no less obsessive, preoccupation with getting his revenge — in short, a progression that imitates Copernicus' world. As von Lauchen points out,

> [that] world moved in circles, endlessly, and each circuit was a repetition exactly of all others, past and future, to the extremities of time: which is no movement at all. (p. 204)

This passage is an example of Banville's inclination to incorporate into his books sly and subtle clues as to their shape. Rheticus' words suggest the *raison d'être* for part of the novel's structural design. *Kepler* contains a comparable intimation regarding its form in one of Kepler's letters,[42] and *Mefisto* divulges the intricacies of its structure in the very first and last paragraphs.

Perhaps because the compositional principle of repetition and variation is prevalent in the book, Banville has found it apt to remark that the form of *Doctor Copernicus* is musical, Part II for example being a theme and variation.[43] Maybe Robert Nye was justly reminded of a fugue when reading the book.[44] Yet one may have some doubts as to whether it is actually feasible to emulate musical patterns in fiction, notwithstanding the probability that Virginia Woolf's *To the Lighthouse* is a novel in sonata form, as E. M. Forster has it,[45] or that Anthony Burgess modelled his *Napoleon Symphony* on Beethoven's *Eroica*. But the matter is neither here nor there. What is beyond question is that with the help of those myriad correspondences as well as variations *Doctor Copernicus* acquires the shape of a harmonious whole.

Some critics have seen fit to deplore a void at the centre of the narrative. Seamus Deane, for one, has been critical: "There is a void at the heart of this novel which is, I think, caused by the author's failure to persuade us that his Nicolas Koppernigk is a genius."[46] Leaving the question aside whether the author in fact wanted to persuade the reader that his protagonist is a genius, one must point to the possibility that the said void may be intentional: to mimic in shape Copernicus' world not only with the help of circular patterns, but by a compositional feature that corresponds to the crucial deficiency of the Canon's vision of the universe. As Rheticus rightly remarks (p. 217) and Kepler was to discover later, Copernicus had placed in the centre of the world not really the sun, but the centre of the earth's orbit, "in order", as Kepler conjectures, "to save himself trouble and so as not to confuse the diligent readers by dissenting too strongly from Ptolemy".[47]

The Copernican world revolves relentlessly around a void, a nothingness, and Banville's fictional recreation of that world, most appropriate, also revolves around a hole, so to speak. That hole can be located almost precisely at the halfway mark of the account. There, both a void and a nothingness are mentioned in connection with Koppernigk, "the vigorous and able public man", within whom "there was a void, as if, . . ., all was a hollow save for one thin taut cord of steely inexpressible anguish stretching across the nothingness" (p. 132). This may not be exactly the void that Deane had in mind, nor should it be regarded as an object of criticism, being instead a formal device of enriching thematic significance.

Of no less significance is the general movement informing the book, if 'movement' is the appropriate term here. The entire account seems to obey an upward thrust, as if Banville had sought to mimic through this procedure Copernicus' severing himself from the clamour and chaos of the world, the stench of humankind by immersing himself totally in the splendour of those "blocks of glassy air in a clear blue unearly sky" (p. 19) and soaring upward into the heavenly bliss of his conviction to discern the thing itself. All is upward movement from that moment when Nicolas clambers up the winding stairs to Canon Wodka's observatory and observes how "all [tends] upward here, so that the tower itself [seems] on the point of flight". A foolish happiness instantly fills his heart, and he allows himself to "fall upward, into the blue" (p. 25). He remains aloof in matters scientific as well as human. The apex of the upward movement is, it would seem, reached in Part III, which is dominated by the sun, judging from the large number of references to it. Only at the end of his life and at the end of the novel is Copernicus drawn downward again and brought back to earth. No longer enthralled by the "marvellous grave gaiety" (p. 22) of the sky, he surrenders to the glorious clamour and chaos of the world, letting himself be called away by the herdsman's call, the cries of children, the rumbling of carts, the earth itself.

*

When he was languishing after having suffered a cerebral haemorrhage, paralysed down one side, deprived of his memory and mental vigour,[48] possibly at odds with his misspent life, lonely and forsaken, virtually ostracised, betrayed by Osiander and the extenuating preface, not even having seen a copy of De revolutionibus, the historical Copernicus jotted down a reflection upon a text by Thomas Aquinas in small, shaky writing on a bookmark:

Vita brevis, sensus ebes, negligentiae torpor et inutiles occupationes nos paucula scire permittent. Et aliquotients scita excuti ab animo per temporum lapsum fraudatrix scientiae et inimica memoriae praecepts oblivio.[49]

He may have seen in these words a fit summation of his own and all human life. Banville's fictional Doctor Copernicus, the maker of a supreme fiction, could sum up the aspirations of his life and, at the same time, characterise the narrative work in which he figures in terms of theme and structure in a remark from Beckett's *Molloy*:

All I know is what the words know, and the dead things, and that makes a handsome sum, with a beginning, a middle and an end as in a well-built phrase and the long sonata of the dead.[50]

CHAPTER 6
Kepler

An approximate idea of the magnificence of Banville's 'house of fiction' *Kepler* can be obtained from a closer look at its first paragraph. The reference to Henry James' term 'house of fiction' is quite intentional. For the opening of *Kepler* is indeed Jamesian inasmuch as, in the manner practised by James in *The Ambassadors*, it manages to introduce almost all the main thematic concerns of the book as well as to establish its most notable compositional strategies. One may recall in passing how this style of composition was operative in *Birchwood* and *Doctor Copernicus*, even in many of the stories in *Long Lankin*. In *Kepler*, the thematic issues adumbrated concern the astronomer Kepler on the one hand, and the man Kepler on the other. The two sides of Kepler's personality are finely juxtaposed and brought into illuminating relation, thus indicating from the outset the novel's perceptive treatment of their inter-dependence, while at the same time acknowledging the necessity of such a treatment for an adequate portrayal of the book's main character.

Kepler's idiosyncratic notion regarding the epistemological and astronomical discoveries; his ideas about the shape of the cosmos; the many wrong turns he took on his way towards arriving at his momentous laws; his marital difficulties and the family disharmony — these are some of the themes sounded at the start. And if one extends the focus of the analysis to include the next three paragraphs, further significant matters are brought into play with subtle compositional expertise, such as the financial destitution which characterised Kepler's entire life; the trials and tribulations he suffered on account of his religious belief, which include his repetitive, though fruitless, endeavours to obtain a professorship at the university of his beloved Tübingen; the political imbroglio that culminated in the

Thirty Years War; and finally, representing the numerous conflicts, quarrels and lawsuits Kepler had to endure, his altercation with Junker Tengnagel, Tycho Brahe's son-in-law, over Tycho's invaluable astronomical observations, which held up the publication of Kepler's *Astronomia nova* for years. The compositional characteristics revealed in the first paragraph are largely restricted to the complicated time-scheme underlying the narrative.

The first paragraph reads thus:

> Johannes Kepler, asleep in his ruff, has dreamed the solution to the cosmic mystery. He holds it cupped in his mind as in his hands he would a precious something of unearthly frailty and splendour. O do not wake! But he will. Mistress Barbara, with a grain of grim satisfaction, shook him by his ill-shod foot, and at once the fabulous egg burst, leaving only a bit of glair and a few coordinates of broken shell.
>
> And 0.00429.[1]

The novel begins, then, with Kepler dreaming; at the end of the book, fever-stricken and near his death, he is found dreaming again. This coincidence will have to be taken into more thorough account when discussing the structure of *Kepler*. Suffice it to suggest here that the dream-motif, which thus opens and closes the narrative, lends a ring-like compositional pattern to it. Kepler is dreaming the solution to the cosmic mystery. His life-long obsession with the mystery of cosmos that, significantly, found its first memorable expression in his *Mysterium cosmographicum* of 1596, is thereby evoked. But he has *dreamed* the solution. The implication of the opening sentence marvellously captures Kepler's opinion of how he came by his revolutionary discoveries concerning, first, the mystery and, later, the harmony of the heavens.

> I believe Divine Providence arranged matters in such a way that what I could not obtain with all my efforts was given to me through chance; I believe all the more that this is so as I have always prayed to God that he should make my plan succeed, if what Copernicus had said was the truth.[2]

This was the historical Kepler's comment on his first solution to the cosmic mystery, according to which the universe is arranged around the five Platonic solids. Later on, he remarked, in almost identical words, about his study of the Martian orbit which resulted in the first two of his planetary laws:

> I believe it was an act of Divine Providence that I arrived just at the time when Longomontanus was occupied with Mars. For Mars alone enables us to penetrate the secrets of astronomy

which otherwise would remain forever hidden from us.[3]
The recourse to Divine Providence may or may not be just a
rhetorical flourish. This possibility notwithstanding, the manner in
which Kepler arrived at many of his epochal findings lends
unmistakable support to the appropriateness of the suggestion that
Kepler *dreamed* the solutions to the tasks he set himself. Kepler made
quite a few of his discoveries by curious and devious routes. When,
for instance, he was working on the orbit of Mars, he committed a
series of mistakes which might have been disastrous, but which
miraculously cancelled each other out, so that with the uncanny
intuition of a dreamer, he found the right solution nonetheless.
Incidentally, the choice of his second wife was conducted along the
same lines,[4] and the result, for all we know, proved that it was the
right decision.

If *Kepler*, as some reviewers have submitted,[5] is about the nature of
the creative act, then the fact that Kepler is *dreaming* the solution to
the cosmic mystery can be of indicative impact. A creative act
demands a good deal of strenuous effort and a considerable amount of
unavoidable drudgery. And yet despite heart-rending exertions,
every so often the end-product of the creative act will be found not to
be so much the result of assiduous and painstaking work as of a sudden
unexpectable inspiration or an extremely fortunate flight of the
imagination. In fact, Kepler appears to have come by most of his
findings in such a manner. On the solution to the problem of the
world harmony, he reasons:

> When the solution came, it came, as always, through the back
> door of the mind, hesitating shyly, an announcing angel dazed
> by the immensity of his journey. (p. 182)

This announcing angel is evoked also in connection with all the other
discoveries of Kepler's the novel mentions.

The second sentence of the first paragraph moves towards
specifying Kepler's cosmic mystery. He holds the solution "cupped in
his mind". The image of the solution being held *cupped* in the mind
succinctly accommodates and aptly anticipates two important
aspects of Kepler's world system. Firstly, the cupped hands or the
globe-like shape of the mind within the human skull corresponds to
the individual spheres of the planets, holding, as if cupped, all other
planets nearer to the sun. Or the five regular solids that go to make up
Kepler's mysterious system could in a similar way be regarded as
cupping devices within cupping devices. More illuminating still is the
comparison of the cupped hands, or cupping mind, with that sphere
which Kepler considered the outer limits of his universe. He believed

in a finite cosmos, and he thought his fantastic construct of regular polygons within regular polygons to be contained within a glove constituted by the fixed stars.

The mystery is of "unearthly frailty and splendour". The unearthly frailty may refer to the fact that Kepler's solution was, as we know today, utterly wrong. There are, of course, not only six planets, the *conditio sine qua non* for Kepler's colossal heavenly fabric to make sense, but nine planets. The attribution of "splendour" to the cosmic design can be seen in connection with Kepler's obsession with order and harmony. As Banville rightly puts it, for Kepler the world was "a manifestation of the possibility of order" (p. 7), and "harmony was all" (p. 25). These notions are the logical consequence of his principal axiom

> that nothing in the world was created by God without a plan the basis of which is to be found in geometrical quantities. A man is godlike precisely, and only because he can think in terms that mirror the divine pattern ... Therefore his method for the task of identifying the cosmic design must be, like the design itself, founded in geometry. (pp. 25f.)

The next noteworthy aspect of the first paragraph is the shift in tense: from present perfect to simple present, then to simple future and back, as it were, to the past. The skilful manipulation of narrative time anticipates the manner in which the account moves backwards and forwards in time, as seen from a given focal point, so that patterns are generated which aim at emulating either the elliptical orbits of the planets or, at least in one instance, the form of a regular solid. It is by virtue of this intricate scheme of time-shifts and the resulting textures of narrative flow that much of the compositional splendour of *Kepler* is effected.

The "grim satisfaction" with which Mistress Barbara wakes the dreaming Kepler from his sleep is remarkable for two connotations. Besides slyly juxtaposing the astronomer Kepler and the man Kepler, the first half of the sentence brings into play the theme of marital antagonism between Kepler and his first wife; the "grim satisfaction" seems to point in this direction. But the sentence also hints at the disparaging attitude Kepler's wife, and incidentally also his family, entertained towards his work as an astronomer. After all, she causes the "fabulous egg" to burst. Out of a lack of interest, but more likely out of a lack of understanding, neither his wife nor his mother or brother cared for his achievements; his obnoxious father-in-law even derided them.

The "fabulous egg" is an unequivocal reference to Kepler's

famous 'egg-theory', which is taken up and briefly explained in Part IV of the novel, in a letter Banville has Kepler write to David Fabricius, the discoverer of the Mira Ceti, with whom the historical Kepler carried on a lively correspondence about all sorts of astronomical matters, for instance about how he discovered the first two planetary laws and how the *Astronomia nova* was taking shape. The 'egg-theory' plays a part in the *Astronomia nova*; it marks one particular phase in Kepler's struggle with the orbit of the most difficult planet — Mars. With the help of Tycho Brahe's observations and his own computations, Kepler, after several assaults on Mars, was finally able to conclude that the orbit was not a circle. "... it curves inward on both sides and outward again at opposite ends", he explains in *New Astronomy*, and he goes on to argue: "Such a curve is called an oval."[6] Next he tried to find a *raison d'être* for his oval, and fell back on the old quack remedy[7] of conjuring up an epicycle. The exact operations are numerous, and it would involve too much of a digression to explain them here. At any rate, the explanation seemed to work; it accounted for a very special oval: it had the shape of an egg, with the pointed end at the perihelon and the broad end at the aphelion.[8] Kepler was satisfied, or at least for the time being; it all seemed wonderfully plausible, as Banville, following the authentic documents, has him communicate to Fabricius (p. 151). The more, however, he pondered on his 'egg', the more doubtful the result of his analytical exertions appeared to him. When next he computed "180 sun-Mars distances" and added them together, repeating the operation forty times (p. 151), he felt constrained to discard his idea. The "bursting of the fabulous egg" in the first paragraph is thus a reference to this detour Kepler took on this way to discovering that the Martian orbit is an ellipse. He eventually came to realise the true shape of the orbit, when he found out that the two moonlets "lying between flattened sides of the oval and the ideal circular orbit, had a width at their thickest point amounting to 0.00429 of the radius of the circle" (p. 151). This is still Kepler explaining his discovery to David Fabricius. Again, to expound the subsequent steps Kepler took until he was able to affirm: "*The planets move in ellipses with the sun at one focus*" (p. 151) would go beyond the scope of this study. Banville has recounted them with enviable precision and simplicity. By introducing the number 0.00429 in a strikingly cryptic manner at the end of the first paragraph, or more precisely as the second paragraph, he has firmly installed the thematic issue connected with this number, and, moreover, has clearly emphasised its importance by allocating it the status of a paragraph, however quirkily brief.

The next paragraph, in addition to bringing more characters into play, is notable for mentioning Kepler's "borrowed hat". The necessity for a mathematician of Kepler's renown to borrow a hat because he could not afford one himself is an extraordinary dilemma. Precisely because of its unusualness, it will attract the reader's attention and, together with the "ill-shod foot" Barbara shakes (p. 3), acquaint him early on with the dire financial plight that over-shadowed Kepler's whole existence; his salary, first as "Mathematicus of the Province" of Styria and later as Imperial Mathematician, remained hopelessly in arrears; the printing of most of his books was delayed because the necessary finance was not available; and, probably the most absurd occurrence in his life, in order to collect the funds that were needed to see the *Tabulae Rudolphinae* into print as well as to obtain, at long last, the money Emperor Ferdinand owed his mathematician, Kepler took it upon himself to embark on an exhaustive and ultimately tragic journey; the saddening outcome of this mad enterprise was that he died of a mysterious fever before the trip was completed.

"The black bulk of woe that lowered over him all the way from Graz", in the next paragraph, evokes the theme of the tribulations Kepler had to suffer on account of his religious beliefs and of the political turmoil that formed the backdrop to his restless life. The mention in the same paragraph of Mästlin, who, among the many other of his so-called friends, "had failed him" (p. 4), relates, by way of anticipation to the numerous futile attempts on Kepler's part to return to his native Swabia and settle in Tübingen as a professor of mathematics or philosophy at his old university. Lastly, the characterization of Junker Tengnagel as a "caparisoned blond brute" (p. 4) points ominously to the squabble and wrangling between Kepler and Tycho Brahe's son-in-law over Tycho's astronomical observations without which Kepler would most certainly never have been in a position to make his famous discoveries.

*

One way of looking at Kepler's life, especially at the relation of his scientific accomplishments to his various activities as a private and public figure and also to the times in which the revolutionary discoveries were made, is to regard the whole complex as an elaborate, ultimately tragicomic paradox. Kepler held a profound and, in the main, unwavering belief in order. Moreover, he was almost pathologically obsessed with harmony of all sorts of forms. He considered — as Banville has him submit — "the world to be a manifestation of the possibility of order" (p. 7). His principal axiom was indeed "that nothing in the world was created by God without a plan the basis of which is to be found in geometrical quantities" (p. 25); and geometry was to him "the earthly paradigm of divine thought" (p. 26). These and related notions induced him to construct his plan of the cosmos around the five regular solids. They also led him "to see [everywhere] world-forming relationships, in the rules of architecture and painting, in poetic metre, in the complexities of rhythm, even in colours, in smells and tastes" (p. 48), even in the "eerie perfection of snowflakes" (p. 49), to which he devoted a separate study, *Strena seu de Nive Sexangula*, published in 1611. Finally, they made him hear "the hum of that great five-note chord from which the world is made" (p. 8), as expounded in *Harmonice mundi*. And yet his scientific quest for order and harmony was undertaken in times of excruciatingly severe political, theological disorder and disharmony, disorder and disharmony that were aggravated by the disorder and lack of harmony in Kepler's private and public life. When he completed his book on the harmony of the world, *Harmonice mundi*, in 1618, the empire was charging headlong to a war which was to last for thirty years. Furthermore, the myopic Kepler, whose eyesight had been weak ever since, as a child, he was inflicted with smallpox,[9] and who, consequently, must at times have had double or quadruple vision,[10] became the founder of modern optics. Lastly, Kepler, the indefatigable advocate of order and harmony, was plagued for most of his life by an inexorable and exasperating restlessness.

*

That man has in every way a dog-like nature. His appearance is that of a little lap-dog. His body is agile, wiry, and well-proportioned. Even his appetites were alike: he liked gnawing bones and dry crusts of bread, and was so greedy that whatever his eyes chanced on he grabbed; yet, like a dog, he drinks little and is content with the simplest food. His habits were similar. He continually sought the goodwill of others, was dependent on others for everything, ministered to their wishes, never got angry when they reproved him and was anxious to get back into their favour. He was constantly on the move, ferreting among the sciences, politics, and private affairs, including the lowest kind; always following someone else, and imitating his thoughts and actions. He is bored with conversation, but greets visitors just like a little dog. . . He tenaciously persecutes wrong-doers – that is he barks at them. He is malicious and bites people with his sarcasm. . . He has a dog-like horror of baths, tinctures, and lotions. His recklessness knows no limits, which is surely due to Mars in quadrature with Mercury, and in trine with the moon; yet he takes good care of his life. . . [he has] a vast appetite for the greatest things. . .

This man was born destined to spend much time on difficult tasks from which others shrunk. As a boy he precociously attempted the science of versifying. He tried to write comedies and chose the long poems to learn by heart. . . His efforts were at first devoted to acrostics and anagrams. Later he set about various most difficult forms of lyric poetry, wrote a pindaric lay, dithyrambic poems and compositions on unusual subjects, such as the resting-place of the sun. . . He was fond of riddles and subtle witticisms and made much play with allegories which he worked out to the most minute details. . .

In philosophy he read the texts of Aristotle in the original. . . In theology he started at once on predestination and fell in with the Lutheran view of the absence of free will. . . But later on he opposed it. . . Inspired by his view of divine mercy, he did not believe that any nation was destined to damnation.[11]

This is Johannes Kepler as he emerges from the horoscope he cast for himself. Banville has meticulously built his protagonist to make him accord with the original in large measure. Early in the book, at the close of an unpleasant conversation with his vituperative father-in-law, he asks forgiveness from his wife by admitting: "I am a dog, Barbara, a rabid thing; forgive me" (p. 19; cf. also p. 72). In a letter to his old and deeply revered teacher, Mästlin, he characterises himself in these terms:

> For it has always been thus with me, that I find it hard, despite all my efforts, to make friends, and when I do, I cannot keep them. When I meet those whom I feel I could love, I am like a little dog, with a wagging tail & a lolling tongue, showing the whites of my eyes: yet sooner or later I am sure to flare up and growl. I am malicious, and bite people with my sarcasm. Why, even I like to gnaw hard, discarded things, bones & dry crusts of bread, and have always had a dog-like horror of baths, tinctures & lotions! How, then, may I expect people to love me for what I am, since what I am is so base? (p. 146)

He was extremely vulnerable, easily offended, but also easily pacified, "a passionate & mocking character" (p. 115). It is a meritorious achievement that the author has captured most of Kepler's complex and contradictory personality in the first and second parts, which centre around Kepler's arrival at Tycho Brahe's castle, Benatek, near Prague, and, by concentrating on a few, carefully selected incidents in the short time the two great astronomers worked together, has described their precarious relationship.

Kepler had been driven to Prague as a result of the religious persecution he had to suffer in Graz. But this necessity was combined with Kepler's firm intention "to get his hands on . . . Tycho's treasure store of planet observations" (p. 62). He knew that in order to prove irrefutably the validity of his five-polygon construct of the heavens and, further, to erect his new, scientifically founded, edifice of astronomy, he was dependent upon Tycho's precise observational data. He was aware of Tycho's capacities as astronomer and the wealth of his material, but he also realised, with uncanny precision, Tycho's limitations. It appears that he saw his own chances arising precisely because and out of Tycho's shortcomings: he regarded himself as the executor of the supreme scientific feat of which Tycho himself was incapable:

> Tycho possesses the best observations, and thus so-to-speak the material for the building of the new edifice; he also has collaborators and everything he could wish for. He only lacks the architect who would pull all this to use according to his own design. For although he has a happy disposition and real architectural skill, he is nevertheless obstructed in his progress by the multitude of the phenomena and by the fact that the truth is deeply hidden in them. Now old age is creeping upon him, enfeebling his spirit and his forces.[12]

The historical Kepler expressed this view in a letter.

The relationship between the two men was under an unfavourable star from the beginning. The reasons are diverse. There was Kepler's vulnerability coupled with an unnerving sense of inferiority. When in the novel he arrives at Benatek, the situation he encounters accords in no way with his expectations. "Surely there should have been some better reception than this" (p. 5). At one point, he wonders whether he is being led "into the servants' quarters" (p. 4). Kepler feels slighted. "He was being treated as if he were a raw apprentice" (p. 10). Tycho does not bother to meet him upon his arrival, nor did he consider it his duty to come to Prague and accompany Kepler to his castle. ". . . the opposition at this time of Mars and Jupiter . . . encouraged me not to interrupt my work" (p. 8), he explains to the furious Kepler, and Kepler appears to accept the explanation. Yet what makes him almost mad with rage is the fact that, when finally the summons comes for Kepler to meet his host, Tycho ostentatiously takes more interest in his dead elk, which after drinking a pot of beer fell down a staircase and died, than in his celebrated guest.

The inappropriate reception and the calamitous days that follow make Kepler more and more furious and angry. He growls at Tycho for making "him a clerk, by God, a helper's helper!" (p. 5). Finally, after only a month at Benatek, turning a deaf ear to the entreaties of Baron Hoffman, Kepler, in a mad rush, leaves to stay at Prague. The authentic reason for Kepler's departure was an unwillingness on the part of Tycho Brahe to meet a number of demands Kepler had made for the improvement of his situation at Benatek. These demands are mentioned in the novel when Kepler and his wife recount to Baroness Hoffmann how he and Tycho came to blows. There is also the unmistakable hint that his anger was caused by his inability to get, as quickly as he wished to, access to Tycho's data, which the Dane, sensing to what brilliant use Kepler would put them, guarded over like a watchdog.

Yet, in spite of the severity of his frustration and anger, Kepler, as laid down in his horoscope, is anxious to get back into Tycho's favour. For this reason and also because his passion is aroused as quickly as it is pacified, by nightfall he returns to Benatek. Banville has deviated on this score from the historical facts, according to which Kepler remained in Prague for three weeks after the row,[13] until Tycho turned up there and drove him back in his coach. The deviation is important and, presumably, deliberate. It helps to put special emphasis on Kepler's shifts of mood. In Banville's version, Kepler does not reconcile himself with Tycho out of a realization that he is in the wrong. For, as he tells Mästlin in the same letter in which he characterises himself as a dog, if Tycho were resurrected and sent back to him, "there would be only squabbling" (p. 147). "I am trying to explain", he goes on, "how it is with me, that if I growl, it is only to guard what I hold precious, and that I would far rather wag my tail and be a friend to all" (p. 147). There is, then, a perverse dog-like tendency in Kepler's character, causing his behaviour to alternate between rage and humble submission.

It must be added in all fairness to Kepler, though, that Tycho Brahe was obviously a difficult man to live and work with. He was clearly envious of Kepler's achievements and intellectual brilliance. Besides, he was a stubborn and rancorous man. When inviting Kepler with the words 'do not hesitate, make haste, and have confidence' to escape his difficulties in Graz and come to live at Benatek, he requested in a postscript to the letter that Kepler write a pamphlet refuting certain claims by Ursus against Tycho; though Ursus was already dead, Tycho insisted on persecuting him beyond the grave. Additionally, Kepler was to write a refutation of a pamphlet by the physician to James of Scotland, John Craig, in which Craig had dared to doubt Tycho's theory about the comets.[14]

The situation was most certainly made worse by differences in opinion about the shape of the cosmos. "The flaw, I suggest", he lectures Kepler, "is that you have based your theories upon the Copernican system" (p. 9). Tycho remained a loyal follower of Ptolemy to his death; Kepler was a convinced Copernican. Explaining his squabbling with Tycho to Baroness Hoffmann, Kepler criticises Tycho for his wrong-headed notion about the heavens:

> ... it is misconceived, a monstrous thing sired on Ptolemy out of Egyptian Herakleides. He puts the earth, you see, madam, at the centre of the world, but makes the five remaining planes circle upon the sun! It works, of course, so far as appearances are concerned — but then you could put any one of the planets at the centre and still save the phenomena. (p. 60)

Tycho was the assiduous gatherer of information about the stars, Kepler the man of genius who revolutionised astronomy. Unlike Kepler, Tycho never made discoveries of an epoch-making sort. His discovery was that astronomy needed precise and continuous observational data; therein lies the Tychonic revolution in astronomical method. With his remarkable survey of the solar system and his remapping of the firmament, which comprised a thousand fixed stars, he paved the way for Kepler to discover his three laws. But he paved the way for Kepler in yet another sense. His proof that the *nova* of 1572 was a true star, and that the comet of 1577 moved in an orbit far outside the moon's put paid to the already shaken belief in the immutability of the skies and the solidity of the celestial spheres.[15] Copernicus found out that the earth, contrary to the prevalent theological dogma and astronomical opinion, was not the centre of the world; but neither the *Zeitgeist* nor Copernicus himself were prepared to accept the new theory that degraded the earth to the status of an insignificant planet among other planets. As a result of studies such as those by Tycho and a few other astronomers, Kepler was able to proclaim the validity of the Copernican theory some fifty years after Copernicus' death.

Whereas Kepler's experience with Tycho Brahe brings to the fore a hot-tempered, uncontrolled strain in his personality, his dealings with Galileo Galileus testify to patently opposite qualities in him. Surprisingly, they show Kepler as an essentially moderate, thoughtful, just and truth-loving character. It is surprising that Galileo should bring out this side in him, as, in spite of numerous attempts by Kepler to obtain approval of, and support for, his theories, the professor in Padua persisted in ignoring him, until, that is, Galileo himself was in need of support: for his discovery of Jupiter's moons. But Kepler, the self-professed tenacious persecutor of wrongdoers, neither barked at Galileo, nor did he bite him or show any malicious tendency towards him. Describing his experience with Galileo in a letter to Georg Fugger[16], he states:

> It has always been my habit to praise what, in my opinion, others have done well. Never do I scorn other people's work because of jealousy, never do I belittle other's knowledge when I lack it myself... Certainly, I had hoped for much from Galileo when my *Astronomia nova* appeared, but the fact that I received nothing will not prevent me now from taking up my pen so that he should be armed against the sour-tempered critics of everything new. (p. 123)

In the second letter to Fugger, he protests vehemently about the supposition that his *Dissertatio cum nuncio sidero*, written in defence of Galileo's *Siderus nuncius*, was a sly attempt to "*rip the mask from* [*Galileo's*] *face*"; previously he had utterly refuted the belief that he was trying to pull out Galileo's feathers (p. 123):

> How, you will ask, can I warm toward someone who will not even deign to write to me directly? But as I have said before, I am a lover of truth, and will welcome it & celebrate it, whatever quarter it may come from ... what a splendid & daring scientist he is! O, that I could journey to Italy to meet this Titan! I will not have him sneered at, you know, in my presence. (pp. 138f.)

At the same time, he confesses: "Galileo is difficult to love" (p. 138). Nor can Galileo's teasingly obscure anagrams, such as "*Smaismirmilmepoetaleumibunenugttauiras*",[17] by which he tried to communicate the true nature of his discovery to Kepler, persuade him to think differently. Kepler puzzled his head over the anagram for weeks. All he was able to offer in the way of a solution was a "barbaric Latin verse"[18] that did not make sense. Some time later, Galileo provided the decoded message: "*Altissimum planetam tergeminum observai.*"[19]

The reason why Kepler remained so benignly disposed towards Galileo, while he had emeshed himself in foolish, intemperate quarrels with Tycho Brahe, is that he had no occasion to develop an inferiority complex towards the Italian, or, at least, this is what

Koestler believes.[20] Banville's explanation is far more credible. It purports that Kepler had a dual personality, especially at times when his moods got the better of him and he was as incalculable in his reactions as a dog. At other times, his love of truth and his rational half, which clearly governed most of his actions, managed to keep his passionate *alter ego* in check.

*

All his life Kepler was a restless man, a waif and a stray. There were, of course, the political events and the concomitant religious controversies that drove him from Graz to Prague, from Prague to Linz, then to Sagan. But he was also impelled to an itinerant life by demonic inner forces, as if he had inherited the instability of his father. Father Kepler had led a turbulent life, verging on the criminal. With brief interludes spent at home with his family in Weilderstadt, Leonberg and Ellmendingen, he fought as a mercenary in the Netherlands, joined the hordes of the Duke of Alba, and later, as rumour has it, enlisted in the Neapolitan fleet and was never to return to his wife and children. Johannes Kepler's end is nearly comparable to his father's. In pursuit of the money he needed to print the *Tabulae Rudolphinae*, he set out, against the entreaties of his wife, Susanna, on an exhaustive journey that ended prematurely in Regensburg with his death.

The madness of Kepler's last journey is impressively brought out in the last part of the novel. His restlessness is also made to reflect the disorder, both private and public, of his age and its political as well as theological turmoil. Kepler does indeed emerge from Banville's fictional biography as "a bag of slack flesh in a world trained of essence" (p. 99). What is remarkable about the treatment of Kepler's disharmonious existence is the way in which the very first scene in the book, the arrival at Benatek, is filled with disorder of all sorts. The condition of Kepler's entire life is defined here with striking precision. Kepler arrives in the midst of bedlam; Benatek is resounding with clattering planks, crashing bricks, and the hammer-blows of masons who have orders from Tycho Brahe to turn the castle into "a new Uraniborg" (p. 4). Instead of gold-rooms, spontaneous applause, light and space, as he had expected, Kepler is greeted by deformities, confusion, and disorder (p. 6), a disorder immediately familiar to him, as it has been the condition of his life from the beginning. His early childhood had been characterised by too much noise from too many people, "packed together in that stinking little house" (p. 93) of grandfather Sebaldus. During a brief stay in his mother's house, in Part III, whereupon his arrival he again encounters bedlam (p. 89), such scenes of disorder from a receding past pass through Kepler's mind. He recalls, too, the repetitive beatings with which his father, when he was not away fighting a losing battle against his own inner restlessness, tried to pound the falling sickness out of his brother Heinrich (p. 95). Later in his life, the discord of his childhood was replaced by continual clashes with his father-in-law and his wife; one such clash, significantly, is the theme of the second chapter in the book. On top of it all was the tremendous havoc wreaked upon Kepler and his contemporaries by the jockeying for power of three emperors. Banville succeeds in summing up the dilemma of Kepler's life in one sentence: "If he managed, briefly, a little inward calm, then the world without was sure to turn on him" (p. 11). To Johannes Brengger, he confesses:

I think there are times when God grows weary, and then the Devil, seizing his chance, comes flying down upon us with all his fury & cruel mischievousness, wreaking havoc high & low. (p. 126)

Near the end of the letter, he even admits: "I fail sometimes to understand the ways of God" (p. 127), a telling admission for one who held such deep religious beliefs as Kepler did. In another letter he advises his step-daughter, Regina, how life should be mastered:

Life, so it used to seem to me, my dear Regina, is a formless & forever shifting stuff, a globe of molten glass, say, which we have been flung, and which, without even the crudest of instruments, with only our bare hands, we must shape into a perfect sphere, in order to be able to contain it within ourselves (p. 134)

Though he managed to provide a perfect, if illusory, shape for the world, he failed, for various reasons, to form his own life into a perfect shape.

One such reason was the religious atmosphere of his days and, in particular, the stance Kepler took. His insistence on tolerance, while around him a bitter war was being waged between the different theological parties, makes him into a kind of Quixotic figure. To the question of his father-in-law: "You said there would be hope if the Archduke were to ... pass on. Hope of what, may we ask?", he replies: "Hope of tolerance, and a little freedom in which folk may practise their faith as conscience bids them" (p. 15); and Banville has him, in an afterthought, disclose the absurdity of his hope:

"Ha! that was good. Jobst Müller [his father-in-law] had gone over
to the papists in the last outbreak of Ferdinand's religious fervour,
while Johannes held fast and suffered temporary exile" (pp. 15f.).
Perhaps it is correct to suggest that Kepler's difficulties on account of
his faith were the result of a certain amount of stubbornness. While
Banville plays with this idea, he is nonetheless perceptive enough to
treat the matter with greater circumspection. As accurately
described, Kepler's position is odd indeed. In a country where the
Lutheran creed was enforced, Kepler is regarded as a Calvinist who is
backed by the Jesuits for their own shady reasons (p. 49). For him, the
matter involved an issue of conscience; it was not empty stubbornness
that compelled him to exclaim, as Banville, in parodic manner, has
him do while realising that he is overdoing it: "*Here I stand!*" (p. 45); it
was a serious and entirely honest conviction, which Kepler was not
prepared to betray.

Much of the dispute between Kepler and the theological
authorities centred around the controversy about the Sacrament of
the Lord's Supper and the *ubiquitas* dogma.

> I hold it self-evident that matter is incapable of transmutation.
> The body and soul of Christ are in Heaven. God, Sir, is not an
> alchemist.

With these words, the renegade astronomer defends himself against
Matthias Haffenreffer, whom he has taken the trouble to see in
Tübingen on the matter of his excommunication. It is Kepler's last,
desperate attempt to end what is, probably, his most serious ordeal in
connection with his faith. Daniel Hitzler, chief pastor in Linz, had
been responsible for the whole unpleasant business, Kepler ruminates
in his mother's house; and he conjectures:

> Was there a link between his inner struggle and the general
> confessional crisis? Could it be his private agonising in some
> way provoked the big black giant that was stalking Europe?
> (p. 166)

Hitzler was a narrow-minded cog in the gigantic administrative
machinery which had branded Kepler a crypto-Calvinist, had denied
him a professorial post at Tübingen, and, moreover, had forced him
out of Graz to Prague, from Prague to Linz, and finally to Sagan.
Kepler was born in poverty and squalor, and he remained a misfit
both at court and in his family. One of the best and most striking
pieces of information in this respect is in the form of a single sentence.
At last confronted with the majestic and magisterial Dane, Kepler is
constrained to realise that he was "hopelessly of the class which
notices the state of servants' feet" (p. 8). There is, furthermore,

Kepler's penury. Speaking to the Hoffmanns about his quarrel with Tycho, he reflects:

> Damn it, Hoffmann knew nothing of what it was to be poor and an outcast, he had his lands and title and his place at court. (p. 58)

For most of his life, his hungry stomach looked up like a little dog to the master who once fed him, to use one of Kepler's authentic statements which is incorporated in a letter to Herwart von Hohenburg (p. 114).

How much a misfit Kepler was among the people at court is the subject of two masterfully realised scenes. The first scene is the one in which Kepler tries to persuade Duke Ferdinand to have his cosmic cup built. Since this cup had been designed to represent the world system made up of the five regular solids, he takes great pains to explain the plan to the Duke, his periwigs and gloomy barons, who can only raise a supercilious eyebrow at the panting Kepler. After his lengthy elaboration, all the Duke deigns appropriate to reply is: "That is clear, yes . . . what you have done, and how; but, forgive me, may we ask *why*?" (p. 36). The second scene features Tycho and Kepler in audience with the Emperor Rudolph. Rudolph engages Kepler in disquieting mathematical riddles and questions him on the subject of horoscopes, but soon loses all interests in the dwarfish astronomer, smiling vacantly at the admonitions not to put too much trust in "star magic" (p. 82). Kepler is annoyed, again quickly so, and he wonders in anger: "What did they expect of him? He was no crawling courtier to kiss hands and curtsy" (p. 83). On this occasion, too, his situation as a misfit at court is fully brought home to him: "In this empire of impossible ceremony and ceaseless show, Johannes Kepler fitted ill" (p. 83).

And yet he continually sought recognition at court. Boastfully he writes to his mother and brother: "Yet notwithstanding the shabbiness of my household and low rank, I am free to come & go in the Polz house as I please" (p. 120). Polz was Imperial Counsellor and First Secretary. Kepler closes his letter with an impressive list of the names of other worthies with whom, he asserts, he has influential connections. With some of them he did indeed have connections, but they did little to further his ascent of the social ladder. Nominally he was a famous man, he was Imperial Mathematician, and an astronomer of considerable renown, but all this did not prevent him from having to live for most of his life among unmannerly ruffians, in a badly roofed house, amidst filth and stink "that would drive back the Turk" (p. 119).

But not only with regard to his status at court was his life a "standing apology" (p. 161). With his family he was no less an outcast and a misfit. Part II serves to make the point well. The very moment he has crossed the threshold of his mother's house he feels out of place, a preposterously overdressed absurdity.

> Laughable, laughable — she had only to look at him, and his velvet and fine lace and pointed boots became a jester's costume. He was dressed only as befitted the imperial mathematician, yet why else had he carried himself with jealous care on the long journey hither, like a marvellous bejewelled egg, except to impress her? And now he felt ridiculous. (p. 91)

At another moment, the realization presents itself to him with even starker clarity:

> He had tricked himself out in imperial finery and come flouncing down upon his past, convinced that simply his elevation in rank would be enough to have caused the midden heap to sprout a riot of roses. And he had been hardly in the door before he realised that the trick had not worked, and now he could only stand and sweat, dropping rabbits and paper flowers from under his sprangled coat, a comic turn whom his glassy-eyed audience was too embarrassed to laugh at. (p. 91)

The glassy-eyed audience consists of his mother and brother Heinrich. How wide the gap is between Kepler and his mother, and in particular his brother, how incapable they are of even having an inkling of the significance of his work is finely established in one of the conversational passages in Part III, involving Kepler and Heinrich. Prior to the scene, Kepler recalls the situation at home during his time at Maulbronn. At fifteen he knew Latin and Greek, and had a grasp of mathematics. The family had been surprised by the changeling in their midst; they had considered all his learning ruinous to his health. "The truth was they saw his scholarship as somehow a betrayal of the deluded image the Keplers had of themselves then of study burgher stock" (p. 93). Now, some twenty years later, with the *Mysterium cosmographicum* as well as a number of other interesting studies to his credit and the *Astronomia nova* in the process of being published, brother Heinrich still holds on to the deluded notion that Johannes is printing a "storybook". Kepler's reply and Heinrich's subsequent comment are well worth quoting in full, as they bring into the open the implacable difference between the two men.

> "No, no", said Kepler, peering into his wine. "I am no good at stories. It is a new science of the skies, which I have invented." It sounded absurd. Heinrich nodded solemnly, squaring his shoulders as he prepared to plunge into the boiling sea of his

brother's brilliance. "... And all in Latin", Kepler added.

"Latin! Ha, and here am I, who can't even read in our own German." (p. 94)

Kepler was able to shape the heavens, but could shape neither his public nor his private life. His first marriage was a disaster; it was blighted from the start, make under a calamitous sky against the will of Kepler and his wife, or so he tells Regina (p. 129). Barbara of "a stupid, sulking, lonely melancholy complexion",[21] was of "an increasingly angry nature" (p. 129). Rather than taking an interest in Kepler's work, which was beyond her and for which she hated it, she ganged up with her insidious father and derided her husband and his stargazing. Querulous Barbara growled more at her 'dog-like' husband that he had a chance to growl and bark at her. The frequent disputes, carefully interspersed throughout most of the narrative, provided further fuel for Kepler's burning feeling of inferiority. The whole relationship between husband and wife was a hopelessly ill-matched affair. During the wedding celebration, Kepler concentrates on baiting his father-in-law as a way of avoiding his bride. Later that night, he gets himself deliriously drunk to stifle his fright. The first sexual encounter, in the gloriously funny manner Banville describes it, is an exquisite characterization of the unfortunate partnership and of Kepler's marital cup of sorrows:

> On the wedding night, in the vast four-poster in the bedroom overlooking Stempfergasse, they collided in the dark with a crunch. He felt as if he were grappling with a heavy hot corpse. She fell all over him, panting, got an elbow somehow into his chest and knocked the wind out of him, while the bed creaked and groaned like the ghost voice of its former tenant, poor dead Marx Müller, lamenting. (pp. 41f.)

Their years together did little to alter the state of affairs, and they remained "two intimate strangers lashed together by bonds not of their making" (p. 42), and soon "they began to hate each other, as if it were the most natural thing in the world" (pp. 42f.). After Barbara's untimely death from spotted typhus, or *Fleckfieber*, Kepler writes to his stepdaughter, explaining how, near the end, Barbara had grown stranger and more introverted than before. He also makes the bitter confession that not too much love came his way from Barbara, which is a literal quotation of an authentic Kepler statement. Nor did much material wealth come his way from her. For, as he adds in a *post scriptum*, she left him nothing in her will, which fact adds an ironic note to the squabbling over her inheritance. But the letter is also touchingly expressive of the guilt and remorse he felt after his wife's death for having himself been impatient and unnecessarily vituperative with her. Once more Kepler the dog-like creature and Kepler the lover of truth and persecutor of wrongdoers wrestle with one another for dominance.

Kepler and Copernicus were completely different personalities. Kepler was a gay dog, if we are to accept his self-characterization (p. 72), and Canon Koppernigk was a recluse and a sourpuss. But in Banville's treatment they have one noteworthy characteristic in common. When towards the end they clear their heads of all astronomical matters to reflect on the virtues and quality of their lives, both see their existence as having been totally devoid of happiness; both men are led to believe that, as a result of their inordinate interest in stargazing, they have forfeited the chance to fill their lives with human warmth. Most of the happiness Kepler got out of his life seems to have been in connection with his scientific discoveries. Especially the letters, in Part IV, communicate very well the satisfaction and enthusiasm about his successes. But it is a kind of happiness that is not the outcome of meaningful personal relationships. Letting his life pass through his mind, as he does in Part V and the excellent Part III, Kepler can hold on to only one moment and one person in his life that brought him happiness. The moment is the birth of his first son, which made "a great blossom of heedless happiness [open] up in [his] heart" (p. 43); unfortunately it was a moment of fleeting duration only. For the infant soon died of cerebral meningitis. The happiness gave way to heart-rending sorrow. The person is Regina, his stepdaughter. He loves her to such a degree that he experiences pangs of wild jealousy when she tells him she is going to get married. Soon afterwards she falls out with him when her husband prompts her to write imperious missives on the matter of her mother's inheritance. Happiness again gives way to feelings of disappointment and sadness. His second marriage was a moderately greater success than his first; but Kepler is too often away on business, leaving his family alone in Regensburg for long periods, to experience real domestic bliss.

The central section of the novel, Part III, is to a greater extent than the others devoted to Kepler's taking stock of the qualities of his life. "Was that ... happiness?", he asks himself, recalling a sunny Easter Sunday

long ago, when his grandfather was still alive, one of those days that had lodged itself in his memory not because of any particular event, but because of all the aimless parts of it, the brilliant light, the scratchy feel of a new coat, the sound of bells,

lofty and mad, had made altogether an almost palpable shape, a
great air sign, like a cloud or a wind or a shower of rain, that
was beyond interpreting and yet rich with significance and
promise. (p. 92)

Next he deliberates on his time at Maulbronn, at the age of fifteen,
and the life of bedlam in the house of Sebaldus that had in store for
him only "the frequent boxings which every inmate of the house,
even the youngest, inflicted on him when there was nothing worthier
at hand to punish" (p. 93). And he asks himself: "Where in all that
would happiness have found a place?" (p. 94). Then he thinks of his
father and concludes that there is not much to think of really: "a
callous hand hitting him" (p. 96). He wonders whether *he* had loved,
what impossible longings had driven *him* to leave his family for "the
brassy stink of fear and expectation of the battlefield at dawn"
(p. 96). Was happiness to be found in action of this kind? Lastly, after
answering for himself all previous questions in the negative, he
remembers Felix the Italian, Tycho Brahe's elk-keeper, "dancing
with his drunken whores in a back lane on Kleinseit". And once more
he concludes his musings with the question: "Was it possible, was
this, was *this* happiness?" (p. 108).

The question is left unanswered. What is made plain, though, is the
significance of Felix for Kepler in his effort to ascertain wherein the
essence of 'real life' resides. To him, the Italian is the embodiment of
"the splendid and exhilarating sordidness of real life" (p. 69). Kepler
knew sordidness in abundance, but sordidness of a different kind: dirt,
filth, persecution, social degradation and indigence, not the unbridled
enthusiasm with which Felix drank life's cup to the dregs. The first
time he associates Felix with this enthusiasm is after he has nursed
him through a disease, and he speculates about what he had expected
in reward for his Samaritan efforts:

Not love, certainly not friendship, nothing so insipid as these.
Perhaps, then, a kind of awful comradeship, by which he might
gain entry to that world of action and intensity, that Italy of the
spirit, of which this renegade was an envoy. Life, life, that was
it! In the Italian he seemed to know at last, however vicariously,
the splendid and exhilarating sordidness of real life. (p. 69)

But the "awful comradeship" is denied him, and the Italian spirit,
life, keeps eluding him, so that Barbara can, with some justification,
reproach him for its absence in him: "Are you alive at all, with your
stars and your precious theories and your laws of this and that and and
and ... (p. 78). Later, when he happens to meet Tycho's blinded
jester, Jeppe, who ran off with Felix to Italy and Spain and who tells

him how Felix died, he confesses: "There was much life in him ... I envied him that" (p. 178). This confession, which he recalls in his feverish delirium in Billig's house, and its expressive import for Kepler's attitude towards life is reminiscent of Canon Koppernigk's thoughts on the qualities of the interpersonal relationships he made, or rather failed to establish, during his life. Koppernigk chose to ignore Anna Schillings' feelings for him; Kepler is so concerned with his work that he turns a deaf ear to Barbara's anguished cries over the death of her third child; and he listens "in awe to his mind, of its own volition, thinking: My work will be interrupted" (p. 50). Where Koppernigk before his death had envisaged his brother, Andreas, visiting him and telling him the truth about his misspent life, Kepler, in a similar situation, remembers a visit from Tycho Brahe. He recalls the Dane standing barefoot outside his room, wearing a "forlorn and baffled look on his face, a dying man, searching too late for the life that he had missed, that his work had robbed him off" (p. 190). And he knows only too well that at this moment, when he is thinking of Tycho, the Billigs see the same look on his face (p. 190), the face of a dying man, who is likewise searching too late for the life that his work has robbed him of. The repetition of the motif seems to suggest that Banville considers scientific discoveries, or creative efforts, of the kind made by people like Copernicus or Kepler to be possible only at the expense of the discoverer, or creator, sacrificing his humaneness.

In yet another respect Banville's two protagonists are alike. Shortly before he dies, Copernicus is forced to admit that his life's work has been a failure. Kepler is, shortly before his death, assailed by almost identical thoughts:

> Everything is told us, but nothing explained. Yes. We must take it all on trust. That's the secret. How simple! He smiled. It was not a mere book that was thus thrown away, but the foundation of a life's work. It seemed not to matter. (p. 191)

The final verdict on his own work thus also involves a kind of redemptive despair, a form of acceptance of one's limitations, as in the case of Canon Koppernigk.

There is a last, interesting touch Banville adds to his admirable portrait of the man Kepler. This consists in the fact that, in addition to moulding him in accordance with the facts and bringing out the Quixotic side of his personality, he attributes a Hamlet-like quality to him. Again shortly before he dies, Kepler recognises his whole life summed up "in this picture of him, a little man, wet and weary, dithering at a fork in the road" (p. 187). The image of a procrastinating hero certainly points to a parallel with Hamlet. Furthermore, there are the two kinsmen of Tycho Brahe, the *grand seigneur* from the Hamlet country, who call on him one day to persuade him to come with them to England. Their names are Rosenkrands and Gyldenstjern (p. 187). The difference of spelling notwithstanding, the reference to the two attendant lords is unequivocal. Max Caspar's reliable and comprehensive biography, *Johannes Kepler*, does not mention any such persons in connection with Kepler; the two characters are Banville's invention.

*

> I am, I fear, no Columbus of the heavens, but a modest stay-at-home, an armchair dreamer. (p. 137)

Kepler was a dreamer, and is found to be so in the novel. But despite the claim to the contrary, he was a Columbus of the heavens. He discovered the first three 'natural laws', and he introduced scientific precision into astronomy. He regarded himself as a disciple of Pythagoras and Plato. *Kepler* pays due tribute to its protagonist's basic way of thinking. In a letter written to Herwart von Hohenburg, Kepler explains that the pure harmonies, of such momentous import for his world system, are contained in the soul as prototypes, or paradigms, of the harmonies perceptible to the senses. And he continues:

> And since these pure harmonies are a matter of proportion, there must be present figures which can be compared with each other: these I take to be the circle and those parts of circles which result when arcs are cut off from them. The circle, then, is something which occurs only in the mind: the circle which we draw with a compass is only an inexact representation of an idea which the mind carried as really existing in itself. (p. 149)

Kepler was an assiduous follower of Pythagoras and Plato in yet another sense, apart from holding that perceptible things are but representations of ideas contained in the mind. To Pythagoras and Plato the animating force of the deity radiated from the centre of the world outwards, until Aristotle banished the prime mover to the periphery of the universe. In the Copernican system, the sun again occupied the place of the Pythagorean central fire, but God remained outside, and the sun had no physical influence on the motions of the planets. In Kepler's universe, all mystic and physical powers are centred in the sun, and the prime mover is returned to the focal position, where it belongs.[22]

The wisdom of Kepler's dream is above all this: mind stands above matter, is of divine origin; and it is the mind which produces the harmonies; they are not to be gained from the material things, which simply provide the referential data; the mind puts these into relations and creates, by virtue of the innate ideas, harmonies; matter is dead without the mind of man.

Kepler was a Columbus of the heavens in that he was the first to put the Copernican system into effect; he was the first who did not want to save the phenomena, but truly and undeterredly to explain them.[23] His criticism of Copernicus is contained in Part I, where he analyses the flaws of the Canon's system (p. 24) and puts his finger on Copernicus' shrinking away from acknowledging fully the implications of his revolution and falling back on the dubious task of saving the phenomena (p. 25). Not so Kepler, who wants to explain in detail, scientifically. The famous eight minutes of arc, which trouble him in his computation of the Martian orbit, are a case in point (p. 79). They completely upset the apple-cart of one of his numerous hypotheses about this orbit. Kepler is in agony. But instead of following the normal practice of the age, which would have been to simply ignore them, he is prepared to discard a theory built in years of labour and torment, and declare his defeat. Though not for long, for soon he starts all over again until, after many detours, he is able to advance a theory which accounts for the eight minutes of arc. *Astronomia nova* is an impressive testimony to Kepler's labours and lays down the fundamental requirements of his science, namely, that hypotheses must be verified through observational data. His claim in the first letter, in Part IV, is totally warranted:

> No longer satisfied, as I believe astronomy has been for milleniums, with the mathematical representation of planetary movement, I have sought to explain these movements from *their physical causes*. (p. 112)

But not only as an individual was Kepler a divided personality, as an astronomer he was no different. Despite his belief in scientific precision, he *was* a dreamer. Some biographers have even called him a mystic. In Banville's book he realises at one point that "the demented dreamer in him rebelled" (p. 86). His harmonious model of the cosmos is essentially the product of a dreamer's mind. And so is his solution to the cosmic mystery. The notion of the planets being arranged around the sun so that the five regular solids fit into one another, as expounded in *Mysterium cosmographicum*, is, in Koestler's words, "one of the rare recorded instances of false inspiration, a supreme hoax of the Socratic *daimon*, the inner voice that speaks with such infallible intuitive certainty to the deluded mind".[24]

Kepler's proof of the validity of his concept consists in the deduction that God could only create a perfect world. Since only five symmetrical solids exist, they are obviously meant to be placed between the six planetary orbits. In truth, however, they do not fit at all, as Kepler was soon to discover for himself. In the notes to the second editon of *Mysterium*, he honestly acknowledges most of his errors. But the misguided belief in the five perfect bodies remains with him, in a modified version, to the end of his life. His gigantic cosmic cup, to be fashioned in accordance with his model of the universe, was no less a dreamer's idea. The mystic inclination in Kepler finds expression, for instance, in his theory of the earth as a living organism with a soul, a theory derived, partly at least, from the work of Giordano Bruno; it plays an important role in his attitude to astrology. The mystic in him may further be held responsible for some of his contentions regarding the function and significance of the sun. He maintained, for instance, that the sun was a symbol of God the Father. To some extent, Kepler represents a new Pythagorean synthesis of mysticism and science.

He saw his main aim as an astronomer in the task of laying bare the divine plan according to which the world had been created. He was able to succeed in this endeavour only because of his fundamental belief in order and harmony. Had the world been created a random and chaotic thing, any attempt to discover such a plan would have been doomed to failure from the start. Banville has managed quite a rare achievement in incorporating Kepler's ideas about order and harmony into his fiction in a manner which makes them fit naturally into the narrative account of Kepler's life and which makes them easily accessible even to the non-expert on matters of science as well as astronomy. They are further distributed throughout the book in such a way that they build on each other until, at the end, the whole gigantic Keplerian edifice of thought is defined. That some, perhaps even the majority, of the statements are quotations from Kepler's own writings, does not at all impair the brilliance of Banville's accomplishment. A few examples will make the strategy evident.

The first remark about his view of order Kepler makes to Tycho. "I hold the world to be a manifestation of the possibility of order" (p. 7), answers Brahe's enquiry about his philosophy. The chapter dealing with his miraculous discovery, on 19 July 1595,[25] while demonstrating a theorem out of Euclid to his pupils in Graz — the discovery that led to his five-polygon model — furnishes further information, such as the importance of harmony — "Harmony was all" (p. 25) — the role of geometry — "The world works by geometry, for geometry is the earthly paradigm of divine thought" (p. 26) — and, of utmost significance, his principal axiom:

> nothing in the world was created by God without a plan the basis of which is to be found in geometrical quantities. A man is godlike precisely, and only, because he can think in terms that mirror the divine plan ... Therefore his method for the task of identifying the cosmic design must be, like the design itself, founded in geometry. (p. 26)

Shortly after, he emphasises the importance of geometry in a conversation with his teacher Mästlin: "Geometry existed before the Creation, is co-eternal with the mind of God, *is God himself*" (p. 30). When, in temporary exile from Prague, he is staying with the Jew Wincklemann in Linz, he hears for the first time "that great five-note chord from which the world's music is made" (p. 48). He becomes obsessed with musical harmonies and begins to see "world-forming relations" everywhere. Later he will build the universe around that great five-note chord, in *Harmonice mundi*. And repeatedly, he comes back to the significance of geometry, whether in a letter to Röslin, where he asserts: "To enquire into nature, then, is to trace geometrical relationships" (p. 145), or to Professor Magini, at Bologna, to whom he explains a simplified version of his world system:

> The earth occupies the most distinguished place in the universe, since it circles the sun in the middle place between the planets, and the sun in turn represents the middle place at rest in a spherical space enclosed by fixed stars. And everything is regulated according to the eternal laws of geometry, which is one & eternal, a reflection of the mind of God. (p. 141)

And in the way of a fine summary of his Platonic ideas about epistemology as well as of his concept of harmony, he reflects, when near his end and thinking back on the "beauty" of his discoveries in *Harmonice mundi*:

> Years before, he had defined harmony as that which the soul creates by perceiving how certain proportions in the world correspond to prototypes existing in the soul. The proportions everywhere abound, in music and the movements of the planets, in human and vegetable forms, in men's fortunes even, but they are relations merely, and inexistent without the perceiving soul.

How is such perfection possible? Peasants and children, bar-
barians, animals even, feel the harmony of the tone. Therefore
the perceiving mind must be instinct in the soul, based in a
profound and essential geometry, that geometry which is
derived from the simple division of circles. (pp. 179f.)

Lastly, as quite an important instance, Kepler's edifice of thought
culminates in the idea of the world as a perfect work of art:

The solids describe the raw masses, harmony prescribes the fine
structure, by which the whole becomes that which it is, a
perfect work of art. (p. 182)

The quotation is important not so much for the astronomical *credo* of
the historical Kepler, but rather for Banville's novel, and it is so in at
least two respects. Firstly, it establishes a connection between the
nature of Kepler's discoveries and the nature of the creative act.
Neither the "raw masses" nor the "fine structure" Kepler speaks of
have any real significance. They are not there in the world but in the
mind, and he who discovers them creates them; the perceiver creates
form and structures just as an artist creates texture and form. It is
therefore that the scientific discovery of the Keplerian variety can be
likened to the creative act. Though one must hasten to specify the
term 'scientific discovery' to make the equation meaningful. What is
meant is not Kepler's true scientific findings, those that still have
validity because they are verifiable: the three laws, for instance.
Kepler is described as a creative artist only with regard to his models
of the world, the one built round the perfect solids, the other around
musical harmonies. They are both supreme fictions, creations of the
mind that have no counterpart in reality.

Kepler's scientific method was largely grounded on *a priori* reasoning
as the logical result of his "principal axiom". If God created the
world according to a plan "the basis of which is to be found in
geometrical quantities" (p. 25) and, moreover, if "man is god-like
precisely, and only, because he can think in terms that mirror the
divine pattern" (pp. 25f.), then it is only feasible to deduce the whole
plan of the creation by pure *a priori* reasoning, by reading the mind of
the Creator, as it were.[26] Kepler applied the deductive method not in
all of his scientific enterprises, but he did so with regard to his
exploration of the heavens. As well as the polygon model, the
harmony concept is conceived in the mind first and then tested for its
validity by means of inductive investigation. As the novel puts it, his
plans are the child of his "*cupiditas speculandi*" (p. 22), and his method is
mentioned in one letter, where he explains:

it seems to me that the real answers to the cosmic mystery are to be found not in the sky, but in that other, infinitely smaller though no less mysterious firmament contained within the skull. (p. 137)

According to Kepler, the world is enclosed by the sphere of the fixed stars. The absolute centre of the universe is occupied by the sun, the source of light and of the moving force. Around the sun, the six planets are arranged in geometrical order, an order determined by the five regular solids:

> ... between the orbits of Saturn and Jupiter I have placed the cube, between those of Jupiter and Mars the tetrahedron, Mars and earth the dodecahedron, each and Venus the icosahedron, ..., between Venus and Mercury the octahedron. (p. 36)

As there are only five regular polygons, it follows, according to Kepler's reasoning, that there can be only six planets. This being so, he knows, instantly, as he tells Professor Magini, that Galileo's newly discovered heavenly bodies cannot be planets, but "*moons circling other planets* as our moon circles the earth" (p. 122). He is right, they turn out to be moons of Jupiter, although his argument why they have to be moons is, of course, wrong. There are more than six planets, but Kepler could not know that. The sun, by means of the moving force emanating from it, moves the planets around it on elliptical orbits (p.152). The orbital motion is such that the radius vector of any planet will sweep out equal areas in equal time (p. 76). Moreover, the squares of the periods of revolution of any two planets are to each other as the cubes of their mean distances from the sun (p. 182).

The last three sentences contain Kepler's famous three laws. They represent the ultimate Kepler accomplished as a scientist and an astronomer. But obsessed by his ideas of harmony, he does not stop there. His *cupiditas speculandi* once more gets the better of him. He works out a relation between the extreme speeds of a given planet, in perihelon and aphelon, and assigns to it the proportional numbers and respective musical intervals. Next he does the same with the speeds of two planets, and again finds musical intervals corresponding to the relational quantities. Eventually he arrives at the supreme musical harmony of the cosmos. Koestler has characterised Kepler's *Harmonice mundi* as "a mathematician's Song of Songs 'to the chief harmonist of the creation'; it is Job's daydream of a perfect universe".[27] The last part of the characterization is of especial pertinence. For Kepler, in life, was a Job-figure, who, as portrayed by Banville, kept with him "a copy of that engraving by the great Dürer of Nüremberg, which is called Knight with Death & Devil, an image of stoic grandeur & fortitude from which [he derived] much solace" (p. 131).

There are, in the book, some excellent descriptions of how Kepler arrived at his discoveries. For instance, the moment, when he realises that the principle of uniform velocity is false, the principle which until then had governed the notion of orbital motion, is rendered with mastery and originality. Kepler has propped himself against a wall and, after too much wine, watches the goatish dancers before him circling in a pool of light from the tavern window, and while one of the whores is pawing him, the ragged fragment of a thought comes to him out of the fiddle music. The thought is "that *the principle of uniform velocity is false*"(p. 72). The fiddle music echoes the music of the heavens Kepler keeps hearing. Kepler himself, as if computing the orbit of Mars, is watching the goatish dancers, who correspond to the planets, circle in a puddle of light, which suggests the sun. And in the midst of life's merriment, from which he stands apart, while a whore is pawing him — could she represent life making its demands on him? — quite by accident, as actually happened in the case of his laws, he comes across one of his momentous discoveries. The subject matter of the entire book is thus metonymically expressed in one scene.[28]

*

Much of the brilliance of *Kepler* emanates from its superb structure, for which the specific time-plan underlying the whole narrative is of prime significance. Two different kinds of time have to be differentiated, one kind which, for want of a better term, could be called 'dramatic time', since it encompasses events shown in continual progression; the second variety may be labelled 'narrated time' as it accommodates incidents which are intercalated as remembrances into the dramatic time frame. The dramatic time in Part I spans a couple of hours, while the narrated time covers some seven years. In Part II dramatic time and narrated time are identical: two years. In Part III the dramatic time spans again a few hours, whereas the events remembered go back to Kepler's infancy, even as far back as his prenatal existence. Part IV possesses a time scheme similar to that of Part II, only here seven years are covered instead of two. Part V dramatises the occurrences of a few hours into which are interpolated incidents from the last eighteen years of Kepler's life. Like Kepler's *Harmonice mundi*, Banville's book is divided into five parts.

In one of the twenty letters which constitute Part IV, Kepler announces to Herwart von Hohenburg the compositional plan he has conceived of *a priori* for his projected opus *Harmonice mundi*:

> ... in the beginning is the shape! Hence I foresee a work divided into five parts, to correspond to the five planetary intervals, while the number of chapters in each part will be based upon the signifying quantities of each of the five regular & Platonic solids which, according to my *Mysterium*, may be fitted into these intervals. Also, as a form of decoration, and to pay my due respect, I intend that the initials of the chapters shall spell out acrostically the names of certain famous men. (p. 148)

Rather than giving some idea of the design of Kepler's book this is a precise, in-built characterization of the shape of *Kepler*, as the notion: "... in the beginning is the shape" precisely captures Banville's own idea of the process of artistic creation. The names spelled out acrostically are: Johannes Kepler, Tycho Brahe, Galileo Galileus, Isaac Newton. The five parts in *Kepler* do indeed correspond to the five regular polygons, with the number of chapters in each part being based upon the signifiying quantities of each of the five Platonic solids. And yet this intriguing compositional scheme contains only part of the entire intricately woven artistic design of the book. For it is held together as much by the laws of the world system Kepler laid down in *Mysterium cosmographicum* as by the complex time-plan, a first impression of which been given.

The whole narrative is contained in a circular, global frame, corresponding to Kepler's view that the planetary system is contained in a gigantic sphere constituted by the fixed stars. *Kepler* begins with a reference to dreaming, and it ends with a similar reference. Before the book closes, Kepler says to Hillebrand Billig: "Ah my friend, such dreams..." (p. 191). Moreover, most of Part V shows Kepler in feverish daydreams. Further evidence of the book's circular narrative shape is provided by the fact that the "borrowed hat" of the third paragraph (p. 3) and the theme of financial destitution it introduces are taken up again in Part V, especially in the first and last chapters: Kepler has come to Regensburg to obtain the money he has been waiting for in vain for most of his life. The theme of Kepler's religious persecution, evoked at the very beginning of the novel, is brought into prominence for the last time in the third chapter of Part V, thus supplying another circular pattern.

Like the novel at large, Part I displays a circular narrative movement. What is even more remarkable is that the middle chapter of its five chapters is likewise circular. The first chapter concerns

Kepler's arrival at Benatek on 4 February 1600. The second chapter goes backwards in time to the final year in Graz, 1599, with the regressive movement being triggered off by Kepler associating the disorder at Benatek with the disorder in Graz. Chapter 3 deals with the discovery of the solution to the cosmic mystery; it mentions the precise date of the incident at the outset, 19 July 1595, moves back to 1593, recounts Kepler's life in Graz, details some of the steps Kepler took towards arriving at the solution and ends, finally, with a brief description of Kepler's inventive feat while he was demonstrating a theorem out of Euclid on that famous day in July. From that point on, the events recalled progress in time. Chapter 4 deals with incidents from the first half of 1596, when the unfortunate bargain for Kepler's first marriage was made, to the birth and death of his first son in early 1598. The last chapter of Part I progresses in time until the events link up with those in chapter 1.

A number of thematic correspondences between chapter 1 and chapter 6 reinforce the circularity of the narrative movement. At the close as at the beginning, Barbara shakes Kepler out of his dream (cf. pp. 3 & 52). The borrowed hat is mentioned in the third paragraph and in the second but last one of the part. References to the summons Kepler is waiting for as well as to Tycho's elk occur on the first and last pages of the first section. And finally the number 0.00429, which makes up the peculiarly brief second paragraph, is mentioned again at the very end. Part I, thus, begins in 1600, moves backwards to 1593, as far as precisely determinable moments are concerned — there are a few flashbacks to childhood and student years — and then moves forwards to the same, or nearly the same, moment in 1600. The narrative movement describes a circle. And herein lies the explanation why the middle chapter, as opposed to the other chapters, is circular, too. In order to complete a circle, while going backwards and forwards in time, it is necessary that in the chapter where the account arrives at the most distant point in time it should, so to speak, pass through the same year twice, in this case 1595, so that the backwards movement, the solstitial point, and the subsequent forwards movement receive appropriate formal expression.

This might be overdoing it, but there is reason to regard the narrative movement as elliptical rather than as circular. Some support is given to such an idea inasmuch as the account does not regress and progress at uniform speed, which would be the corresponding expression of a circular 'orbit'. Though not in the regressive chapters, at least on the way forwards to 1600, in chapters 5 and 6, the motion becomes faster. When Kepler, as will be recalled, abandoned the principle of uniform velocity, he was able to detect the elliptical orbit of the planets and the law of orbital motion, according to which a planet moves faster the nearer it is to the sun, which occupies one focal point of the ellipse. The narrative focal point of Part I is in 1600, hence the speeding up of the account when approaching this point.

Banville has argued:

> time in each of the sections moves backward or forward to or from a point at the centre, to form a kind of temporal orbit. But no section comes back exactly to its starting point, since as Kepler discovered, the planets do not move in circles, but in ellipses.[29]

This appears to be a false description of what actually happens in the section. For Part I does come back to its starting point; it returns to it as closely as is possible without merely repeating sentences or whole passages; the thematic echoes suggest such a return. Besides, the movement Banville speaks of is that of a spiral, not that of an ellipse. While the time-plan underlying "Mysterium cosmographicum" may be said to be modelled on a circle, or an ellipse, the formal scope of the first part of the book, consisting as it does of six chapters of *mutatis mutandis* equal length, denotes the first of Kepler's regular polygons: the cube, to be inserted between the spheres of Saturn and Jupiter.

Part II, "Astronomia nova", offers a continuation of the focal incidents in Part I. Chapter 1 deals with the row and reconciliation between Tycho Brahe and Kepler on 5 April 1600, and, significantly, ends on a note anticipating future happenings: Kepler has been set the task of solving the problem of Mars, and he has a wager with Longomontanus that he will find the solution within seven days. Chapter 2 progresses to 1601; it shows Kepler still working on the Martian orbit, treats of — among other things — the death of his father-in-law, and the solar eclipse in May 1601, and likewise concludes by pointing to the future, when Jeppe predicts Tycho's death. Chapter 3 moves on to August 1601; Kepler, while on the spree, discovers in a drunken stupor that the principle of uniform speed is invalid; the rejection of uniform velocity, however, throws most of Kepler's world system into disarray, and when he discovers his "error of eight minutes of arc" and tries to solve the problem by means of his egg-theory, he is left for some time with a confusing number of coordinates. It is here that the anticipatory egg of the first paragraph is taken up and elaborated in the necessary detail. The chapter ends with Kepler being appointed Imperial Mathematician on 6 November 1601 after Tycho's death, and again aspects of

Kepler's future are brought into play; Kepler reflects: ". . . but where would he go?" (p. 78) The last chapter moves backwards in time to late 1600 or early 1601; Kepler and Tycho discuss the project of the *Tabulae Rudolphinae* with the Emperor Rudolph; at the end the future is once more anticipated through Kepler imagining that the future has found utterance in him (p. 86); but, on the other hand, his recollection of his squabbling with Tycho establishes a link with the beginning of "Astronomia nova", thus achieving, as in Part I, an overall circular narrative movement.

The four chapters are of equal length. The next polygon in Kepler's design is the tetrahedron, or the pyramid. The whole section comprises roughly two years, from 5 April 1600 to 6 November 1601, with each chapter ending on a future note. If chapter 1 represents the first side of the pyramid, then chapter 2 because of the future implications at the end of chapter 1, denotes the next side of the pyramid, as if one were walking around it, so to speak. Chapter 2, by way of its anticipatory ending, leads to the third side, to chapter 3, whose future implications point to the connection with the last side of the pyramid, while the last chapter's calling for a flashback to late 1600 or early 1601 seems to be an adequate formal expression of the fact that the fourth side is the underside; in terms of exploring the pyramid it would mean a form of regression.

If *Kepler*, in its constant shifts backwards and forwards in time, is somewhat reminiscent of Proust's *A la recherche du temps perdu*, then Part III is the most Proustian section of all. Dioptrice is that part of optics dealing with the refraction of light. "Dioptrice" is the most introspective part in the novel, where, appropriately, the present of Kepler's life is refracted through different moments in his past, while at the same time the future is being anticipated. Into the few hours Kepler spends in his mother's house on a particular day in 1609, there are intercalated numerous memories of, more or less, distinct periods of, and incidents in, his life as well as reflections on times to come. The reminiscences and the deliberations about the future are finely juxtaposed with the events that build up the dramatic present. Together they combine into an illuminating stock-taking by Kepler of his life and earthly happiness.

Part III has in common with the preceding sections a circular narrative movement. Chapter 1 shows Kepler entering his mother's house, and the last chapter has him leave it again. In between, he communicates with his mother and brother, but, more importantly, he reflects on the sense of his existence. These reflections span a period that comprises both the earliest scenes he is able to remember (cf. p. 95), even a notion of regressing into the womb, and the last, envisaged moments of his life before death. The most extreme stations in his life are tellingly united in one chapter — in chapter 5 of "Dioptrice". This particular chapter is of specific importance for the novel. Taking the entire scope of the book into account, chapter 5 of Part III contains the precise midpoint. Thematically, this point is occupied by Kepler falling asleep in his mother's house and imagining "the years . . . falling away, like loops of rope into a well" (p. 98). He goes further and further backwards in time, to his infancy, when Grandfather Sebaldus was "younger and more vigorous than Johannes remembered having known him" (p. 98), and finally back into the womb. The "warm water" of the well, the "incarnadine darkness" and especially the "great slow pulse" beginning to bear (p. 98) are unequivocally suggestive of the womb.

Part III is divided into twelve chapters of equal length. The number of chapters is based on the signifying quantities of the dodecahedron. Kepler asked for this polygon to be inserted between the spheres of Mars and earth. It is another of Banville's master-strokes that he devotes the very section of his novel that is modelled on the solid embracing the orbit of the earth to reflections on the true nature of earthly happiness.

Part IV, "Harmonice mundi" has a time-plan which, it may again be argued, entails an elliptical narrative movement. The first half of the twenty letters moves forwards in time from 1605 to 1612, and the second half goes backwards again to 1605. The seven years covered by the epistles are not traversed at uniform speed. If one took the accumulation of dates — for instance letters 13 to 16 are from the same years — as an indication of greater velocity, the speed would increase in the second half of the journey, roughly between 1602 and 1612. And if one considered the skipping of a year, on the way to and from the years between 1605 and 1609, as an indication of a slower movement, then the narration would move in an ellipse. Since the motion is fastest between 1609 and 1612, the narrative focal point would lie somewhere around 1610 and 1611.

The magnificence of "Harmonice mundi" is enhanced by another compositional pattern. The twenty letters are arranged in such a way that the second half is an exact mirror of the first. Because they are written to the same person and in the same year, the following letters are related to one another: 1 ≙ 20; 2 ≙ 19; 3 ≙ 18; etc. finishing with 10 ≙ 11. The structural design thereby established is an elaborate case of arch form. More precisely, it is suggestive of a compositional strategy known in music as retrograde canon or *canon cancrizans*, a canon in which the imitating voice gives out the theme not as the first voice gave it but with the notes in reverse order. What is important here is that Banville has based the construction of the part carrying the title of Kepler's mathematician's Song of Songs, *Harmonice mundi*, on a musical pattern. The solid Part IV resembles is the fourth in Kepler's cosmic edifice: the icosahedron.

Part V, "Somnium", is quite similar in design to Part I, portraying Kepler during a couple of hours in Regensburg, fever-stricken, recalling mainly events pertaining to his years in Linz and Sagan. Chapter 1 describes the arrival in Hillebrand Billig's house. Baking his chilblains at Billig's fire, he succumbs to brooding on when he first saw the Billigs; he remembers a scene from his childhood, his daughter's wedding on 12 March 1630, his own, second wedding in 1613, another scene from his childhood, and finally the three emperors he has known. From there his mind goes back, in chapter 2, to the last time he met the Emperor Ferdinand to present him with the *Tabulae Rudolphinae*. Banville has Kepler state that the meeting occurred "ten months to the day" (p. 159). The day of his arrival at Regensburg being 2 November 1630, the event would have taken place in January 1630. In truth, though, the meeting as well as the other events recounted in chapter 2 took place in 1627. This is not only proved by the historical facts, but the novel itself shows this to be the case at the end of chapter 7.

At the end of chapter 2 Kepler recalls his farewell to Linz. This recollection leads him in chapter 3 to ponder on his religious tribulations in Linz, the dispute with pastor Hitzler, which started in August 1612, his meeting with Haffenreffer in Tübingen in 1617. His religious difficulties make him think next, in chapter 4, of his mother's witch trial, from its beginning in 1616 to the actual trial in 1621. Then he remembers his friend Wincklemann, the Jew, as having possibly suffered a fate similar to that of his mother. Chapter 5 concerns his meeting with Jeppe in 1617, and it ends with a dream of "involuntary great dark plots" (p. 178). This dream leads to chapter 6, to his astronomical dream of the world harmony, as set down in *Harmonice mundi*, finished in 1618. Connected with chapter 6 by means of a thematic link concerning certain imaginary precipices, chapter 7 moves quickly from 1619, when *Harmonice* was printed, to 1627, when the *Tabulae* were completed and Kepler decided to present the first copies to Ferdinand. The end of chapter 7, therefore, ties up with the beginning of chapter 2, where Kepler arrives in Prague for this very purpose. Chapter 8 is similar to chapter 1 inasmuch as Kepler is again depicted in Billig's house, brooding, with interruptions that repeatedly bring the dramatic present of 1630 into play, on his time in Sagan as astronomer to Wallenstein; and gradually the events are brought up to the time when Kepler set out on his journey to Regensburg. Thus, as in Part I, a circular narrative pattern is generated. The circularity is, again as in Part I, reinforced by certain thematic parallels between the beginning and the end of "Somnium". The mention of his son-in-law, Bartsch (pp. 157 & 190), is one such parallel; so is Kepler's talk about the money he is owed (pp. 156 & 191), or the dream motif (pp. 155 & 191), and, lastly, the reference to the rain, which, upon Kepler's arrival in Regensburg, drifts slantwise through the November dusk (p. 155), and at the end of the book beats "upon the world without" (p. 192). Part V corresponds to the last of Kepler's solids: the octahedron, which he placed between the spheres of Venus and Mercury.

When explained in such detail, the almost mathematical precision of the compositional design of *Kepler* may seem sterile, even a mild form of lunacy. But while it may appear sterile and obtrusive in the analysis, it is extremely fertile and totally unobtrusive in the reading process. There, Banville's mastery of composition combines gracefully with his extraordinary, tenacious storytelling ability. As before in Banville's writing, the characteristic vintage Banville style of description serves the purpose of creating a marvellous piece of narrative discourse. It is that kind of style which is so ebulliently evocative, while never losing sight of the obligation, in the face of the meticulously woven interrelationship of form and content, to entertain the reader. Three examples, chosen more or less at random, will exemplify the particular quality of the style.

He selected three observations, taken by the Dane on the island of Hveen over a period of ten years, and went to work. Before he knew what had hit him he was staggering backwards out of a cloud of sulphurous smoke, coughing, his ears ringing, with bits of smashed calculations sticking in his hair. (p. 63)

Tycho, ill and half drunk, brought up again the sore subject of his lost elk, but in the midst of loud vituperation fell suddenly asleep into his plate. (p. 69)

The evening rested here, bronzed and quietly breathing, basking like an exhausted acrobat in the afterglow of marvellous exploits of light and weather. (p. 107)

*

There is, curiously enough, a counterpart to Banville's *Kepler* in German literature. In 1916 Max Brod published a novel under the title *Tycho Brahes Weg zu Gott*, which he dedicated to his friend Franz Kafka. The book is widely regarded as a historical novel, but as with *Kepler*, this classification appears to be inadequate since a deeply religious issue rather than an interest in a meticulous reconstruction of the historical facts lies at the centre of Brod's intention. Moreover, Brod chose to work out the attitude of Kepler towards Brahe in such a way that it would become a scathing comment on what Brod believed to be Kafka's condemnable attitude towards him. The constellation *Kepler-Brahe* is suggestive of the constellation *Kafka-Brod*. *Tycho Brahes Weg zu Gott* is a very different book from *Kepler*, not only in theme and subject-matter, but also in quality. Banville's seems to be the artistically more accomplished work. Whereas Banville focuses on Johannes Kepler, Brod centres attention firmly on Tycho Brahe, delineating Brahe's way to God — from despair to redemption. Yet Kepler plays an important role in Brod's account; he is portrayed as a scourge sent by God whose task it is to show Tycho the way to salvation.

What is striking about Banville's and Brod's very different treatments of the period in which the two majestic astronomers lived and worked together is that both writers start their accounts at precisely the same point in time — on 4 February 1600, when, Kepler, following Brahe's urgent invitation, is driving from Prague to Benatek, accompanied by Tycho's prospective son-in-law, Junker Tengnagel. The opening scenes of the two books are fairly similar as a result of certain themes and motifs they share. Their artistic purpose in the total design of the books is, however, very different. Unlike Brod, Banville uses these motifs and themes to anticipate the predominant issues as well as the structure of his whole novel, which is but one reason why *Kepler* is the better book.

Brod's characterization of Kepler is more in line with Banville's portrayal of Canon Koppernigk, while Brod's portrait of Tycho Brahe corresponds nicely to Banville's portrait of Kepler, especially as regards Tycho's notion about the harmony of the world and his belief in the power of his art. According to this belief Kepler's inventive feats are equivalent to the creative act of the artist, and Tycho's motto, as given in Brod's novel: "*Nec fasces, nec opes, solum artis sceptra perennant*"[30] could have been Kepler's.

CHAPTER 7
The Newton Letter

On September 16th, 1693, when he had passed his fiftieth birthday, Newton, sitting in the Bull in Shoreditch, wrote an angry letter to John Locke, accusing him of having endeavoured "to embroil [him] with women". The idea must have been excruciatingly upsetting to the great scientist, who is reputed to have died a virgin. Newton was at that time undergoing what followers of the Swiss Tweedledum and the Viennese Tweedledee would term a midlife crisis. *The Newton Letter*[1] is, to a considerable extent, reflective both of Newton's unfortunate missive and of his crisis. A brilliant exercise in literary derivation, with many quotations — from Marvell to Yeats, Henry Miller and Sartre — secretly woven into the text,[2] the narrative, on its most accessible level, masquerades as the letter of farewell to the science of history by an unnamed historian after he has abandoned his plans for a book on Sir Isaac Newton. Writing from somewhere in "the frozen wastes" of the Arctic region, the protagonist of the novella tries to communicate what happened to him while spending the summer in the country near Dublin. He had rented "the lodge" of a place called Fern House to put the finishing touches to his book, but very soon something had started to go wrong; like Newton, he had suffered a loss of sense and harmony, and had abandoned his book. Where Newton, however, had only imagined himself to have been embroiled with women, Banville's narrator actually became embroiled with women. He had begun an affair with Ottilie, the niece of Charlotte Lawless, who with her husband, Edward, owned Ferns. Then, gradually, he had fallen in love, even though his love remained unrequited, with Charlotte, and one night, while having sexual intercourse with Ottilie, he had imagined himself making love to Charlotte, so that in his spiritual adultery the two women merged into "Charlottilie".

What characterises the historian's experience at Ferns is, among other things, that he permanently misconstrues the nature of what he observes. Note the conspicuous use of such phrases as: "I had expected...", "I pictured her...", "I imagined...". He entertains illusions about the people at Ferns and weaves fictions around them. He imagines them to be patricians, landed Protestants, but has later to acknowledge that they are Catholics whose estate and business are going to seed and have to be sold. Edward he believes to be a boozer, an idler, a fortune hunter, a hollow man, and fails all the time to realise that he is slowly dying of cancer. Charlotte's seemingly aristocratic behaviour, her aloofness and occasional absent-mindedness are not, he is constrained to learn, the result of her character and social position, but of her being doped to the gills with valium. Or the child Michael is not, as he persistently conjectures, the off-spring of an illegitimate sexual encounter between Edward and Ottilie, but the son of a farmhand and a girl; Charlotte adopted him when his parents left Ferns. Thus the historian dreams up "a horrid drama and fails to see the commonplace tragedy that is playing itself out in real life" (p. 79).

It is, supposedly, a bit fanciful to read this thematic conflict between appearance and reality as a reference to one of Henry James' novels — to *The Sacred Fount*; and yet perhaps it is not. For Banville has admitted to a profound admiration for James' artistic achievements. *The Sacred Fount* is, in a sense, also about appearance and reality. The unnamed and unidentified narrator seeks to get to the bottom of how the people he meets at a weekend house party in Newmarch relate to one another. He reads what he can in and *into* relationships until he is brought up short. "Of course you could always imagine — which is precisely what is the matter with you", Mrs. Brisenden observes at one point as she deflates the narrator's theories.[3] And the narrator says to himself during dinner on the second night: "I remember feeling seriously warned not to yield further to my idle habit of reading into mere human things an interest so much deeper than mere human things were in general prepared to supply".[4] Yet since he has "little experience... in fact" but "much ... in fancy", he constructs a palace of thought that is no more than a collapsing house of cards, as the parallels suggested here between *The Newton Letter* and *The Sacred Fount* — the wish being father to the thought.

Still, it seems more sensible to suggest this novel of James' as a likely source than *The Europeans*, as Banville himself is inclined to do. In fact, how this fiction, in which James reversed the 'international situation'[5] by having two Europeans pay a visit to the United States, could have been an influence in the writing of *The Newton Letter* is a matter almost impossible to determine. True, there is a Charlotte in *The Europeans*, but Banville's Charlotte and James' Charlotte are as different as chalk and cheese. One could, with a good deal of unwarrantable fancy, see a faint similarity between the naiveté of Gertrude, in James' book, and that of Ottilie, but again, this character trait apart, the two personages have very little in common. Or one may want to submit that there is a parallel, of some sort, in the fact that whereas Eugenia is invited by Mr Wentworth to "live in the little house over the way', the historian comes to stay in the lodge; or even that the historian, in his habit of touching reality with soft feelers of imagination, somehow equals Gertrude in her reliance on her imagination. Yet all these parallels are scarcely more than pseudo-parallels. In plot, character constellation, thematic preoccupation, style — in almost everything, *The Europeans* is vastly different from *The Newton Letter*.

   The Newton Letter makes use of, and is (as far as certain thematic preoccupations are concerned) modelled on, yet another famous letter, this time a letter of fictitious status, but one that is reputed to be of the utmost significance for modern, or modernist, literature: Hugo von Hofmannsthal's "Ein Brief", or Lord Chandos' letter to Francis Bacon, which probably for the first time expresses the artistic predicament of the twentieth-century writer. Similar to what Lord Chandos experiences, Banville's principal character, in the end, is compelled to acknowledge that the "horrid drama" he has dreamed up about the people at Ferns utterly falls to pieces when measured against reality. He cannot truly make sense of what he sees either. Without so much dreaming up horrid dramas, Lord Chandos confesses to Francis Bacon that he can no longer fit the particulars of what he perceives and knows into a meaningful whole: "Es zerfiel mir alles in Teile, die Teile wieder in Teile, und nichts mehr ließ sich mit einem Begriff umspannen".[6] Formerly, before the devastating crisis that is responsible for what Chandos communicates to Bacon, things had been completely different:

> Mir erschien damals in einer Art von andauernder Trunkenheit das ganze Dasein als eine große Einheit: geistige und körperliche Welt schien mir kein Gegensatz zu bilden...
> (p. 463)[7]

More generally, though, the indebtedness of *The Newton Letter* to "Ein Brief" primarily concerns the tone and narrative ground-situation as brought about by the personal predicament of Banville's letter writer. For he has lived through a dilemma similar to that described by Lord Chandos. Like Chandos, he has "lost [his] faith in the primacy of text" (p. 1); words fail him;[8] he has been subjected to a severe scepticism about the possibility of expressing anything, truth least of all, through language; a scepticism shared also by Banville's Canon Koppernigk; he has abandoned his book and is now living in temporary "retirement from life" (p. 1) in a region whose icy climate mirrors his cold heart. Lord Chandos states in his letter:

> Es ist mir völlig die Fähigkeit abhanden gekommen, über irgend etwas zusammenhängend zu denken oder zu sprechen ... die abstrakten Wörter, deren sich doch die Zunge naturgemäß bedienen muß, um irgend welches Urteil an den Tag zu geben, zerfielen mir im Munde wie modrige Pilze. (p. 465)[9]

At the end of his missive, he explains why it is that he will never be able to write another book in either English or Latin:

> ... nämlich weil die Sprache, in welcher nicht nur zu schreiben, sondern auch zu denken mir vielleicht gegeben wäre, weder die lateinische noch die englische noch die italienische und spanische ist, sondern eine Sprache, von deren Wörtern mir auch nicht eines bekannt ist, eine Sprache, in welcher die stummen Dinge zu mir sprechen, und in welcher ich vielleicht einst im Grabe vor einem unbekannten Richter mich ver-antworten werde. (p. 472)[10]

These words are quoted by Banville's protagonist in slightly abridged form (p. 51) and said to be part of the second "strange letter" Newton wrote to Locke (p. 50). As a matter of fact, Newton wrote only one such letter to Locke, the one mentioned at the beginning of this chapter. Banville is only too aware of this, as he shows in a note pointing out that "the second Newton letter to Locke is a fiction, the tone and some of the text of which is taken from Hugo Von [sic] Hofmannsthal's *Ein Brief*" (p. 82).

But it is not only this loss of faith in the primacy of text that prevents Banville's Newton biographer from completing his book. Something else has afflicted him. "Real people keep getting in the way", he remarks, "objects, landscapes even" (p. 1). This situation may recall a particular scene in *Kepler*. When his son Heinrich dies of a fever of the brain, Kepler, standing by the bedroom window and hearing vaguely the anguished cries of his wife, thinks: "My work will be interrupted". But, more to the point, the situation recalls Lord Chandos' situation. Like Chandos, the historian has all of a sudden become overwhelmed by the minutiae of life, "by the *ordinary*, that strangest and most elusive of enigmas" (p. 11), in which he believes himself to have discovered an undreamed of significance. He has become interested in another kind of truth, a truth that "is nothing compared to the lofty verities of science" (p. 22), the truth about the small things in life, as incidentally Newton, too, is said to have been, when a fire in his rooms in Cambridge destroyed a bundle of his papers and he became aware that it did not matter, his scientific achievements did not matter, not as much as the figures of life anyway, which was why he occupied himself with observing such allegedly trivial matters as early morning light through a window, or his rescuer's one unshod foot and yellow toe-nails, while this man was dashing about, shirt-tails out, trying to extinguish the flames. Or Kepler, near the end of his life, while baking his chilblains at Hillebrand Billig's fire, searches too late for the life that he had missed, that his work had robbed him of. It is the theme of redemptive despair, so dominant in *Doctor Copernicus*, *Kepler*, and thus also in *The Newton Letter*.[11] Additionally, the historian's quest for truth, for an explanation of what happened at Ferns, is, in some way, reminiscent of Kepler's conviction that everything is told us, but nothing explained. Canon Koppernigk's and Kepler's entire scientific careers were based on a desire to explain, and, notably, the same desire is the moving force behind Gabriel Godkin's quest in *Birchwood*.

This sudden being stricken by the significance of the minutiae of reality likewise characterises Lord Chandos' situation. When the principal character of *The Newton Letter* speaks of commonplace objects, like drain-pipes and clouds, "requiring us far more desperately than I do them" (p. 2), then this is strikingly similar in tone and content to much of what Chandos states, for instance in this passage:

> Eine Gießkanne, eine auf dem Felde verlassene Egge, ein Hund in der Sonne, ein ärmlicher Kirchhof, ein Krüppel, ein kleines Bauernhaus, alles dies kann das Gefäß meiner Offenbarung werden. Jeder dieser Gegenstände und die tausend anderen ähnlichen, über die sonst ein Auge mit selbstverständlicher Gleichgültigkeit hinweggleitet, kann für mich plötzlich in irgendeinem Moment, den herbeizuführen in keiner Weise in meiner Gewalt steht, ein erhabenes und rührendes Gepräge annehmen, das auszudrücken mir alle Worte zu arm scheinen. (p. 467)[12]

Or when Banville's narrator exults in the physical memory of Ottilie by writing that "supernumerous existence wells up in my heart" (p. 79)[13], this once again finds an almost literal counterpart in the following statement by Lord Chandos:

Denn es ist ja etwas völlig Unbekanntes und auch wohl kaum
Benennbares, das in solchen Augenblicken, irgendeine
Erscheinung meiner alltäglichen Umgebung mit einer über-
schwellenden Flut höheren Lebens erfüllend, mir sich ankündet.
(p. 467)[14]

The Chandos letter is significant for *The Newton Letter* not least
because the predicament of the Newton biographer is reminiscent of
the predicament of Lord Chandos, which in turn, as was hinted
above, is suggestive of the creative dilemma of the writer and artist at
the beginning of the twentieth century.[15] In addition, Hofmannsthal's
own personal crisis[16] prefigures the personal crisis of Banville's
character, a crisis that in the former case goes hand in hand with a
crisis as a lyrical poet, and in the latter with a crisis as a scholar and
biographer. Furthermore, as H. Stefan Schultz has persuasively
shown, the reshaping of traditional material is a major characteristic
of Hofmannsthal's creative procedure in the Chandos letter as well as
in Hofmannsthal's larger works.[17] Banville's procedure is a comparable one: *The Newton Letter* largely consists in the reshaping of
traditional material, from Hofmannsthal, from Newton, from Henry
James, Andrew Marvell, Sartre, Yeats, Ford Madox Ford, and — as
will be argued shortly — Goethe.[18] The fact that Hofmannsthal
wrote an obituary notice, in the monthly *Moderne Rundschau* (1 April,
1891), on the French writer Théodore Faullain de Banville (14 March
1823-13 March 1891)[19] provides a nice piece of coincidence that
further unites the names of Hofmannsthal and Banville.

*

The historian, to add this aspect, finds himself in a predicament
exactly like the one in which Newton is said to have been caught:
embroiled with women, overwhelmed by the minutiae of life, and
robbed of his belief in absolutes. He is like Newton, furthermore, in
that he, too, has a "cold heart" (p. 68) and in his dealings with other
people does not "contract to be known" (p. 29) and does not seem to
care two hoots about his work.

*

The Newton Letter is indebted to Goethe, especially to *Die Wahlverwandtschaften* (*Elective Affinities*) for, among other things, the choice of
its characters as well as their relationships towards one another. The

names 'Edward', 'Charlotte', 'Ottilie', 'Mittler' suggest this indebtedness. All further parallels, it is important to observe, are mainly, if not exclusively, worked out through what the Newton biographer imagines. They are the result of his assessing reality by touching it with "soft feelers of imagination" (p. 42). This manner of assessing reality is likewise, at least partly, characteristic of Eduard in Goethe's novel, where it plays a major role in Eduard's conflict between duty and desire, moral obligations and personal inclinations.[20] In one respect, Banville's protagonist is cast in the role of Goethe's Eduard; his pining away for *die ferne Geliebte* unmistakably recalls Eduard's love for Ottilie. In his unbridled imaginings, Charlotte takes on the part of Goethe's Ottilie, whose renunciation of Eduard is echoed by Charlotte's aloofness. Whereas Goethe's Ottilie renounces her love, Banville's gives hers freely. The son whom Eduard, during his act of spiritual adultery, fathers on Charlotte in *Die Wahlverwandtschaften* finds its counterpart in the boy, Michael, surmised to have been fathered by Edward in an act of debauchery with Ottilie. Thus, in another respect, but once more only in the delusive assessment of the principal character in *The Newton Letter*, Edward is Eduard, and Ottilie is Ottilie.

What may already have become apparent is that the motif of spiritual adultery, as operative in Banville's novella, has its origin in *Die Wahlverwandtschaften*. Moreover, as Eduard is attracted to Ottilie according to the principle of elective affinities in chemical substances, expounded in chapter 4 of Goethe's novel, so Banville's historian is drawn to Ottilie and Charlotte.

Crudely put, *Die Wahlverwandtschaften* treats of conflict: not only between duty and desire, moral obligations and personal inclinations, but also between natural order and social order, nature and the demonic, or indeed between the ideal and reality, appearance and reality. The latter conflict in particular underlies *The Newton Letter*, too, namely with regard to the way in which the Newton biographer perceives and appraises the people and the events at Ferns.

The conflict between the ideal and reality, or appearance and reality, also significantly enough underlies Goethe's view of Newton as well as of Newton's theory of light and colours. According to Johann Peter Eckermann, Goethe would never have written his *Farbenlehre* if he had not regarded Newton's theory as a 'pernicious' error.[21] In Part II of *Farbenlehre*, Goethe occupies himself with what he terms "Enthüllung der Newtonischen Theorie, welche einer freien Ansicht der Farberscheinungen bisher mit Gewalt und Ansehen entgegenstand...".[22] Goethe likens Newton's theory to an old castle, and he decides to deconstruct it, so that, as he puts it,

> ... die Sonne doch endlich einmal in das alte Ratten- und
> Eulennest hineinscheine und dem Auge des verwunderten
> Wanderers offenbare jene labyrinthisch unzusammenhängende
> Bauart, das Notdürftige, das zufällig Aufgedrungene, das
> absichtlich Gekünstelte, das kümmerlich Geflickte.[23]

As elaborated in his *Geschichte der Farbenlehre*, Goethe moreover was of
the opinion that there are two classes of scientists. One of these, and it
is the class to which Newton belongs, accommodates people who are
'ingenious, prolific, fervent, and violent' and who create a world
entirely 'out of themselves' ("bringen eine Welt aus sich selbst
hervor"), without bothering whether this world corresponds to the
'real' world ("ohne viel zu fragen, ob sie mit der wirklichen überein-
kommen kann"):

> Entspringt [Goethe goes on to argue] in so einer tüchtigen
> genialen Natur irgendein Wahnbild, das in der allgemeinen
> Welt kein Gegenbild findet, so kann ein solcher Irrtum nicht
> minder gewaltsam um sich greifen.[24]

The fictitious writer of 'the Newton letter', interestingly, pertains to
the same class of people. Banville's two books that immediately
preceded the novella were about two of "those high cold heroes who
renounced the world and human happiness to pursue the big game of
the intellect" (p. 50). Newton was another of these heroes; he was a
scrupulous, punitive, austere, inhuman character, without passion or
desire, as Goethe has it, in short — a cold fish, like Canon
Koppernigk. And in this, the historian is like him. He senses that
Edward, Ottilie, and Charlotte are asking something of him, but he is
totally incapable of finding out what; he is fully aware that something
is expected of him, but whatever it is he is too cold-hearted to give it.
Like Canon Koppernigk and Newton, he lacks what John Marcher,
in Henry James' tale "The Beast in the Jungle", lacks — the power to
love.

*

The Newton Letter is the third in a series of four books. *Doctor
Copernicus* and *Kepler* are, to a large extent, about supreme fictions
concerning reality, the world. Newton's picture of the mechanistic
universe, as laid down in *Principia*, constitutes yet another supreme
fiction; it depends on the absolutes of space and time and motion.
Against Locke's challenge of these absolutes — which cannot truly be

absolutes since space, time, and motion can only be relative for us —
he held that such absolutes exist in God — a nice thought, but hardly
a true one. Banville's letter writer misconstrues reality partly
because, like Lord Chandos and Goethe's Eduard, he lacks absolutes
of judgement. He has failed in his efforts as an historian to write a
book on Newton, and his letter to one Clio is, in a sense, his letter of
farewell to the science of history; for 'Clio' may refer to a personage
of whom Banville's character asserts that she "has been [his] teacher
and [his] friend, [his] inspiration, for too long"; but the name may, at
the same time, refer to one of the nine daughters Zeus begot upon
Mnemosyne, and of course the historian "couldn't lie to [her]" (p. 2),
for she is the Muse of history.

Ultimately, perhaps, *The Newton Letter*, like *Doctor Copernicus* and
Kepler, is about the unknowable and ineffable nature of reality, or, in
other words, about the way in which any perception of reality is
conditioned and invalidated by the "wilful blindness" of the
perceiver, as most admirably thrown into relief at the end of *Kepler*,
for example, where the dying Herr Kepler, in utter desperation, but
with Dante-esque hopelessness, entertains, nay clings to the deluded
belief that he will "Never die, never die". The novella is about "the
ordinary, that strangest and most elusive of enigmas", a statement
which could be straight out of Lord Chandos' letter. Banville's
protagonist embarks on the writing of his letter in order to explain, to
understand, but in the end he is still a victim of wilful blindness. He
has not learned anything, even though he is aware that "some large
lesson seemed laid out here for [him]" (p. 19). He even believes that
he will take up his book again, while at the same time, echoing
Roquentin's final statement in Sartre's *La nausée*, he wonders whether
he will not have to go off once more, leaving his researches yet
another time.

Thus *Doctor Copernicus*, *Kepler*, and *The Newton Letter* — the latter in
two respects, first because of its reference to Newton and second
because of its principal character — are about people who, by dint of
an excessive idea, try to account for the quiddity of life; they seek to
make reality, the world, correspond to a concept of order and
harmony that they have thought up, but that in this form does not
exist at all. It is in this sense that Goethe becomes relevant to the
novella in yet another way. Even though he was all but a cold fish, he
was like Canon Koppernigk, Kepler, Newton, and the unnamed
historian of *The Newton Letter* in matters of scientifically accounting
for the phenomena that make up the world. That his forays into
physics, some of them at any rate, have not very much in common

with the study of physics as understood today should be of no concern for the moment, or perhaps only inasmuch as he, like Canon Koppernigk, Kepler, Newton, and the historian, proceeded from Platonic conceptions of the world, which he then sought to verify, or falsify, by what he was able to observe around himself. Or as Goethe said to Eckermann, on 26 February 1824:

> Hätte ich nicht die Welt durch Antizipation bereits in mir getragen, ich wäre mit sehenden Augen blind geblieben und alle Erforschung und Erfahrung wäre nichts gewesen als ein ganz totes vergebliches Bemühen.[25]

Like Kepler with his notion of *harmonia mundi*, Goethe regarded and sought the truth about the world as

> ... eine aus dem Innern am Äußern sich entwickelnde Offenbarung ... Es ist eine Synthese von Welt and Geist, welche von der ewigen Harmonie des Daseins die seligste Versicherung hat.[26]

Take Goethe's idea of "die Urpflanze", a totally untenable edifice of thought, as was Kepler's concept of the planetary system, or the Newton biographer's conjectures about the people at Ferns. Goethe noted about his idea:

> Mit diesem Modell und dem Schlüssel dazu kann man... Pflanzen ins Unendliche erfinden, die konsequent sein müssen, das heißt: die, wenn sie auch nicht existieren könnten und nicht etwa malerische oder dichterische Schatten und Scheine sind, sondern eine innerliche Wahrheit und Notwendigkeit haben. Dasselbe Gesetz wird sich auf alles andere Lebendige anwenden lassen.[27]

This also was essentially Canon Koppernigk's procedure, or Kepler's computing the universe according to his preconceived edifice of thought about the harmonious relations of the planets, or Newton's concept of the universe. Or take Goethe's theory of light and colour, again quite a hopelessly untenable theory, but one, admittedly, that is simple and charming, again like Kepler's fantastic edifice of the universe. As Erich Heller has pointed out with admirable clarity:

> Licht bedeutet für ihn den weißen Strahl eines Sonnentages und nicht jenen Strahl, den Newton destilliert, durch winzige Öffnungen forciert und mit komplizierten Mechanismen gefoltert hat. Daß das weiße Licht ein Gemenge von Farben sein soll, erschien Goethe als offenbare Absurdität. Nicht die Farben erzeugen das weiße Licht, sondern das weiße Licht die Farben. "Die Farben sind Taten des Lichts", schreibt er, "Taten und Leiden". Sie entstehen aus der Begegnung von Licht und

Finsternis. Also ist Finsternis nicht nur die Abwesenheit von Licht; sie ist eine selbständige schöpferische Kraft ... Nur zwei Grundfarben gibt es, Gelb und Blau; Gelb erscheint, wo das Licht gezwungen ist, erste Konzessionen an die Dunkelheit zu machen, und Blau, wo es dem Finstern wieder einigen Boden abgewinnt. Durch Steigerung und Mischung erhalten wir alle anderen Farben; lassen wir mehr und mehr Trübes ins Gelb eindringen, so erhalten wir Orange und Rot; helfen wir dem Licht in seinem Kampf mit dem Trüben, dann erscheinen Violett und Purpur. Mischen wir die zwei ursprünglichen Farben, Gelb und Blau, so ergibt sich Grün. Auf diese Weise gelangt Goethe zu seinem Farbenkreis, wo Gelb und Blau, Rot und Violett, Grün ind Purpur einander als Komplementärfarben gegenüberstehen.[28]

These are all rum arguments, as we well know today. But they, together with Goethe's history of science, as adumbrated in *Geschichte der Farbenlehre*, make one important aspect patently obvious; it is an aspect, it should be emphasised, which is of primary interest not only for *The Newton Letter* — in as far as it concerns Newton's theory as laid down in *Principia*, of the historian's 'theory' about Edward, Charlotte, and Ottilie — but equally to Canon Koppernigk's as well as Kepler's theories; and the aspect is this, as Heller has noted of Goethe's history of science:

> ... es ist vor allem die Erkenntnis, daß jede wissenschaftliche Theorie nur die rationelle Oberflächenform eines metaphysischen Substratums von bewußten oder unbewußten Glaubenssätzen über das Wesen der Welt ist.[29]

Exactly the same is true of the manner in which Banville's Newton biographer computes the world around him.

*

More similarities could be pointed out between Banville's novella and works by other writers. The historian may, in his obtuseness, owe something to John Dowell, in Ford Madox Ford's *The Good Soldier*; this is arguable. What is less arguable is that the novella has certain features in common with Banville's third book, *Birchwood*. For instance, both narratives exploit, in comparable terms, the big-house genre. Note that the Lawless family appears too in the earlier book, that there is some mystery surrounding the figure of Michael, with hints of an incestuous relationship; note also the drink-besotted master of the house, the decline of the family estate, and other similarities. Furthermore, there are a number of thematic aspects which *The Newton Letter* shares with Aidan Higgins' novel *Langrishe, Go Down*.

To make the extent of Banville's derivatory work near-complete, there would seem to be a more than purely accidental echo of Sartre's *La nausée* in *The Newton Letter*. Antoine Roquentin is also an historian engaged in the writing of a biography about a — to all intents and purposes — fictive personage: the Marquis de Rollebon. Roquentin does not communicate his life-changing experience in a letter, but in a diary, which he begins by a remark to the effect that something has happened to him while in Bouville (!), an interesting near-coincidence, this name. That something concretises itself as a feeling of existential nausea which makes him lose faith in his book, and eventually forces him to give up his biography and leave the filthy provincial town of Bouville (or rather Le Havre, where Sartre spent some time as a teacher) for the French capital. In one of his final entries, Roquentin notes that he will take up his pen again, not however to complete the abandoned work, as the Newton biographer envisages he will, but to embark on a new venture: a book of fiction, rather than of history.

Another small coincidence between Sartre and Banville is worth noting. The original cover of *La nausée* had Dürer's famous edging "Melancholia" on it. Neither the English nor the American editions of *The Newton Letter* followed Sartre's example, but, strangely enough, *Mefisto* did.

In the film version, *Reflections*, of *The Newton Letter* the historian has been given a name; he is called Willie Master. This identification may possibly point to yet another literary source for the novella: to Goethe's Wilhelm Meister novels, specifically to *Wilhelm Meisters Lehrjahre*. Like the historian, Wilhelm is cured through erring ("wird durch Irren geheilt"). His master subscribes to the maxim: "Der Irrtum [kann] nur durch das Irren geheilt werden" (VII, 5) ("errors can only be rectified by erring"). Again like the historian, Wilhelm falls victim to misjudging people. Thus, for instance, he mistakes Lothario's sister for a saint when in fact she is an amazon. Or Felix, whom he believes to be the son of Aurelie and Felix, turns out to be Wilhelm's own son.

*

Like all Banville's books, *The Newton Letter* is a densely wrought work
of fiction. A carefully selected number of textual reverberations,
expertly distributed throughout the account, establishes a circular
pattern of composition, which, by being thematically divided into
exposition, development, and recapitulation, could be likened to the
sonata form. And one should not forget to mention that, on top of all
that has been said here, *The Newton Letter*, by virtue of its brilliant
manipulation of language (a prose that falls on the page like sunlight,
to adopt Rebecca West's praise of *The Good Soldier*), is an extremely
fine book to read, splendidly elusive in the diversity of the readings it
calls for.

CHAPTER 8
Mefisto

In his article "Physics and Fiction: Order from Chaos"[1], Banville has made the challenging suggestion: "...imagine a Nabokov novel based on the life of a Gödel or an Einstein!" It may not be quite appropriate to assert that *Mefisto*[2] is that very novel, the last in the series of four about "those high cold heroes who renounced the world and human happiness to pursue the big game of the intellect"[3]. The life of its main character and narrator, Gabriel Swan, seems but loosely grounded on the life of Gödel or Einstein. And yet from early on, he has been a wizard with figures, a child prodigy with an extraordinary gift for numbers, and thus in a way may be regarded as *a* Gödel or *an* Einstein figure. In point of fact, precocious Swan does not truly resemble Einstein, who when young showed no visible signs of any special precocity and never developed any interest in mathematical puzzles.[4] Yet he is like Einstein inasmuch as his feelings about the mysterious order that seems to underly the apparent chaos of events — the discovery that nature appears to present itself as a mathematical riddle with remarkably simple and elegant solutions — were formed in his childhood.[5] Like Einstein, Gabriel is a creative genius, if of a particular sort. This feeling about the mysterious order governing the apparent chaos of things Swan, of course, shares with Copernicus, Kepler, and, to a lesser degree, the Newton biographer, in *The Newton Letter*.

Banville's fictions have always possessed a Nabokovian side to them, if by that term one means to denote an indefatigable interest in shape, in patterning; a magnificent mastery in using words to weave intricate storyteller's bookwebs and in using them in a most precise and dense, poetic manner, in creating 'worlds within the word'.[6] Banville appears to be prepared to subscribe to the definition of the "virtues that characterise all worthwhile art" as put forward by

Nabokov himself: "originality, invention, harmony, conciseness, complexity, and splendid insincerity"[7] — the ambidextrous insincerity of a Humbert Humbert, who was aware that he had "only words to play with".[8] In *Mefisto*, Banville has shown that he even shares with Nabokov a frivolous fondness for coincidences. And as with Nabokov's coincidences, so with Banville's: they are essentially not coincidences at all; they only appear so. What seems random, contingent betrays itself on closer scrutiny to be permeated by a sense of order. Chance resolves itself into order; order is won from chaos. Thus perhaps *Mefisto* represents one way of putting Banville's own challenging proposition into effect, after all.

*

The story in *Mefisto* is, in one respect, concerned with showing how Gabriel Swan comes into contact with a world in which Mefisto, or a Mephistopheles-figure, holds sway. He does not succumb to the myriad machinations, the titillating temptations of Felix, the Mefisto-*persona*:[9] he remains basically a looker-on, an eye-witness to how most other people around him fall prey to Mefisto's power. In another respect, the novel is about Gabriel's loss of belief in an all-embracing, unifying system by means of which the world can be explained. And in a third sense even *Mefisto* is about how Gabriel tries to discern sense and meaning in his life through the manner in which he recounts it in retrospect.

From early childhood on, Gabriel has been obsessed with numbers.

> Always [he remarks] I had thought of number falling on the chaos of things like frost on water, the seething particles tamed and sorted, the crystals locking, the frozen lattice spreading outwards in all directions. (p. 109)

That obsession makes him into a Pythagorean, so to speak, and this in turn brings Banville's narrative enterprise that has focused on principal stages of how man has tried to account for the world in epistemological terms full circle — back to the Greek era, and more especially to Pythagorean philosophy. Leaving out the "Dark Interlude", as Arthur Koestler calls it in *The Sleepwalkers*,[10] Banville started his tetralogy with Copernicus, who, by putting the sun in the centre of the universe where it belongs, put paid to the benighted attempts to 'save the phenomena'. He next concentrated on Kepler, who improved on Copernicus by, among other things, throwing out the misguided notions of circular orbits and uniform speed. Then

Newton and his mechanistic universe followed, but filtered through the Chandosean conscience of an historian who finds himself overwhelmed by the "*ordinary*, that strangest and most elusive of enigmas". [11] Now in *Mefisto*, he offers a Pythagorean protagonist who is compelled to acknowledge that the world cannot be known, the governing principle being chance. Gabriel Swan is thus a development on the fictional writer of the Newton letter, as Kepler was a development on Copernicus.

Gabriel equals his predecessors in that he, too, pursues a vision of a unifying nature. That is part of his Pythagorean heritage. What is even more Pythagorean about him is that he should base his vision on figures. To him, as to the Pythagorean brotherhood, numbers are sacred as the purest of ideas; numbers are eternal while everything else is perishable, or that is what he believes until he is constrained to admit that his vision is erroneous. Before that moment in his life, "all things are numbers", as they were to the Pythagoreans.[12] "I built up walls of numbers, brick by brick..." (p. 127), he notes. For the greater part of the book, he is trying to reduce reality to number series and number ratios, to contemplate the essence of reality by endeavouring to elucidate the secret of the dance of numbers.[13]

Gabriel is a Pythagorean, moreover, because his fate, or rather the fate of his vision, is comparable to that of Pythagorean philosophy. The Pythagorean vision was seriously impaired — although it was flexible enough to accommodate, or gloss over, the blow — by the discovery of irrational numbers. Gabriel's vision breaks down on account of the irrational: the irrational nature of chance. At the end, he decides to leave everything to chance, to *fatum*, as the Greeks did. The narrative series about "those high cold heroes" ends where the entire process of explaining the world scientifically in the only legitimate, because appropriate, manner began, in Greece, with the Pythagorean brotherhood and Philolaus, Herakleides, Aristarchus, and the sun-centred universe, before Plato and Aristotle rang in the Dark Ages with their deluded ideas, ideas that held sway until Copernicus and, even more so, Kepler turned the minds of the people back all the way to around 300 B.C.[14]

That Gabriel should have a special attitude towards the figure 10, that he should not be able "to see a one and a zero juxtaposed without feeling deep within the vibration of a dark answering note" (p. 18), this is quite in keeping with his Pythagorean bent of mind. For the Pythagoreans regarded the figure 10 as the 'leader' and the 'queen' of all figures.[15] It was the most sophisticated of all numbers, the most essential and most complete of all things, as Philolaus had it.[16] There is, further more, Gabriel's obsession with "the mystery of the unit", or *monas*, 'the beginning of all things', hence Gabriel's contention that "everything else followed from there" (p. 18).

Gabriel, in his preoccupation with numbers, may also bring to mind the inhabitants of Johann Valentin Andreae's utopian city Christanopolis, in *Reipublicae Christianopolitanae Descripto* (1619). These likewise believed that the Supreme Architect of the Universe did not make the mighty mechanism haphazard, but completed it most wisely by measures, numbers, proportions.[17] As Frances A. Yates notes, Andreae's city is unmistakably indebted to Campanella's City of the Sun.[18] Banville may have come across Andreae's notion when reading Yates' study.

Whereas Kepler thought in terms of geometrical patterns, Gabriel's epistemological tools are figures: they are, or rather, "were [his] friends" (p. 31), providing the basis on which he meant to erect his system of the world, before his experiences with Felix and above all with Kosok and his Dante-esque computer laboratory began to shatter and finally broke down his conviction. Kosok contends that there is no certainty, and he avails himself of the means of his computer to prove that nothing can be proved. At first, Gabriel still clings to his belief in "order, pattern, harmony" (p. 202); for a while he remains convinced that one has only to "press hard enough upon anything, everything, and the random would be resolved" (p. 202). In the end, though, he acquiesces in the notion that everything is governed by chance. "In the future, I will leave things, I will try to leave things, to chance" (p. 234). This is his final remark. The development he thus undergoes is similar to the development of Gabriel Godkin, in *Birchwood*. Both characters move from Cartesian certainty to Wittgensteinian despair. But whereas Godkin concludes: "There is no form, no order, only echoes and coincidences, sleight of hand, dark laughter. I accept it",[19] the concept of chance that Gabriel Swan eventually comes to embrace only *appears* to be negativistic. For ultimately he does not relinquish his faith in order. Chance does not mean complete randomness for Gabriel, and the specific nature of his concept becomes manifest through the particular shape of his autobiographical account.

*

"... under the chaos of things a hidden order endures" (p. 211), Gabriel points out. The idea has been with us ever since a particular school of thought in classical philosophy propounded it. Nietzsche had his Zarathustra pick it up; and quite recently it has acquired paramount significance in mathematics.

The atomistic world view of Democritus and Leucippus had it that the processes on a large scale come about because a multitude of irregular processes occur on a small one, to paraphrase the way in which none other than Werner Heisenberg puts it.[20] The Greek atomists held that behind the bewildering complex appearances of the forms of matter there lay a structure of atoms — indivisible particles — obeying simple laws which enable us to explain and correlate the experience of our senses.[21] Chance is the completion and manifestation of necessity, of order of a specific kind. This is to say that beneath the surface of apparently contingent, or chance, events there always is hidden a deeper necessity. In epistemological terms, chance represents the principle which dominates the surface, the appearance of things and events; it marks the starting-point for the recognition of necessity, the necessity which can only be discerned by analysing all seemingly random, contingent connections and thus uncovering their quintessential nature. Gabriel is not seriously convinced that the world is governed by chance. The world of *Mefisto*, like the world at large, is not at all based on chance. The manner in which Gabriel has put that world together makes this point plain. As will become obvious shortly, this manner is informed by Nietzsche's notion of "die ewige Wiederkehr der Dinge" — the eternal recurrence. There is a reference in the book to "*die ewige Wiederkunft*" (p. 223), thus providing the *raison d'être* for its shape — symmetrical and mirror-symmetrical relationships, sets of two, binary patterns.

Chance, then, is meant in the context of *Mefisto* as a camouflage for necessity, and "chaos is nothing but an infinite number of ordered things" (p. 183), as Gabriel contends, much in the sense of Schopenhauer's notion of "die Zufälligkeit" as a negation of stringency:

> Der Inhalt dieses Begriffes ist ... negativ, nämlich weiter nichts als dieses: Mangel der durch den Satz vom Grunde ausgedrückten Verbindung. Folglich ist auch das Zufällige immer nur relativ; nämlich in Beziehung auf etwas, das nicht sein Grund ist, ist es ein solches. Jedes Objekt ... ist allemal notwendig und zufällig zugleich: notwendig in Beziehung auf das eine, zufällig in Beziehung auf alles übrige.[22]

J. G. Hibben states the issue in more accessible terms: "Chance ... may be defined as a complex of casual elements, in which indefinitely various combinations are possible, and each combination yields a distinct result".[23] Chance is, as Kasner and Newman remark, "merely a euphemism for ignorance. To say an event is determined by chance is to say we do not know how it is determined".[24]

The notion of "die ewige Wiederkunft" is most readily associated with Nietzsche. People frequently overlook the fact that quite a similar concept underlay Democritus' atomistic world view. Democritus considered invariability to be the characteristic of the cosmos and his ideas concerning invariability denote precisely a network of perpetually recurrent events as well as the repetitive sequence of their combinations,[25] much to Aristotle's subsequent disapproval. Democritus and his forerunner Leucippus were the first to formulate scientifically the law of causality in nature, which was largely responsible for the introduction of the concepts of *heimarmene* and *fatum* by the Stoics, with the former signifying 'the successive causes of things', and the latter denoting *logos*, or divine order.

Gabriel Swan's very Greek idea of chance together with his Pythagorean fondness for figures and mathematical proportions would indeed seem to point to the intention on the part of the author of *Mefisto* to bring his investigation of how science has tried to come to grips with the world full circle: back to where it all started. At the same time, the concept of chance promulgated in the book may be intended as a reference to something eminently contemporary: to certain findings and ideas in modern mathematics — findings and ideas associated with the terms 'Mandelbrot set', 'dynamic systems', and 'fractals'. This is not the place for a detailed treatment of the phenomena designated by these words. Nor is this writer equipped with the knowledge necessary for doing so. The following, rather general, remarks must suffice here.

Mitchell Feigenbaum, experimenting with Verhulst's population growth model by changing the growth parameters, discovered that at a certain stage, when the parameter is extremely high in value, order turns into chaos. Comparably, the apparently random configurations of the Mandelbrot set betray themselves, when explored in detail, to consist of binary patterns. 'Fractals' are mathematical entities which, when printed out by a computer, produce graphs of mind-boggling beauty. These consist of an infinite number of structural patterns absolutely identical to the structure of the fractals themselves, chinese-box fashion: eternal recurrence. Or to offer one last and very simple instance of where apparent randomness, chance, resolves itself into "die ewige Wiederkunft". Take any number between 0 and 99. Multiply it by itself. Next take the last two digits of the result and multiply that figure by itself, and so on. Before too long the same series of figures will recur again and again. The figure 13, for example, will yield in the second operation the figure 63, next 21, 41, 81, and thereafter the series 61, 21, 41, 81 will repeat itself *ad infinitum*. Eternal recurrence, forsooth!

The world view advocated in *Mefisto* would seem to hold that the beginning and the end are marked by chance. This is incontestably suggested by the narrative itself. In between beginning and end there is chaos — a conviction that Gabriel Swan shares with Gabriel Godkin. But unlike his namesake, Gabriel Swan learns that "chaos is nothing but an infinite number of ordered things" (p. 183) and that the major principle informing the uncanny schema of order is eternal recurrence. That things repeat themselves is beyond question; the ratio of repetition, though, is unpredictable, beyond mathematical computation, beyond human knowledge; and because of this irritating fact, or rather in order to come to terms with it, humankind has found it convenient to believe that the ratio is governed by chance. All that can be known is a small, bounded stretch of the chaos, such as Gabriel's life, and this stretch betrays itself on close scrutiny as falling into symmetries, mirror symmetries, eternal recurrences.

Until the experiences he undergoes have radically changed his outlook, Gabriel Swan proceeds from the same epistemological premise as Johannes Kepler. In a letter written to his step-daughter, Regina, in September 1611, Kepler notes:

> Life . . . is a formless & forever shifting stuff, a globe of molten glass, say, which we have been flung, and which, without even the crudest of instruments, with only our bare hands, we must shape into a perfect sphere, in order to contain it within ourselves. That, so I thought, is our task here, I mean the transformation of the chaos without, into a perfect harmony & balance within us.[26]

Gabriel attempted to perform this task by dint of figures, until he was brought short and had to surrender to chance. But that is the Gabriel involved in the events narrated in the account, as distinct from the Gabriel involved in the telling, who assesses his life with hindsight. That Gabriel is not a mathematical wizard, but an artist figure.[27]

*

Gabriel Swan is an artist-figure not only in the sense in which Copernicus and Kepler are seen by Banville as artist-figures: their attempts to come to grips with the world are likened to the efforts made by an artist. The scientific imagination, as represented by

Copernicus and Kepler, is thought by Banville to operate along the same lines as the creative imagination does. In both cases, the overriding desire is to impose a sense of order and harmony, of giving a shape to the bustling mayhem that is life. Gabriel is an artist, like Copernicus and Kepler, inasmuch as his endeavours aim at discrimination and selection where life is "all inclusion and confusion".[28] Gabriel is an artist-figure, moreover, because he is presented in his endeavour to make sense of his life by accounting for it in written form, in the form of a sustained narrative, and by imposing upon his account a very specific design. That design has two noteworthy aspects to it. First, it follows Joyce's method of basing a narrative on a literary precedent — that method recommended by T. S. Eliot for others to pursue.[29] Second, it imbues this compositional approach with a sense of order of its very own.

*

The literary precedent for *Mefisto* is Goethe's *Faust*. But Banville being Banville, the book also contains thematically potent references, overt as well as covert, to Dante, Thomas Mann and a host of other writers. None of these should be overrated, not even the plentitudinous parallels to *Faust*. Heinrich Heine, communicating some details concerning his work on a *Faust* to Eduard Wedekind in 1824, remarked that he had no idea of rivalling Goethe but was putting his belief into practice that everyone should write a *Faust* of his own. *Mefisto* is, to some extent, Banville's *Faust*. Goethe's play fundamentally serves to provide a skeleton which Banville has fleshed out with distinctive substance. He has warned us not to take the similarities too seriously.[30] Even so — they are there, and they are so strikingly numerous that it is only possible here to list them in a shorthand fashion, with only the more significant ones being granted more prominent treatment.

Gabriel Swan is Faustian, although he is not intended as the Faust-figure, in that he strives to "see, with vision clear,/ How secret elements cohere/ and what the universe engirds..."[31] But then, so were Copernicus, Kepler, and Newton, even the fictitious biographer in *The Newton Letter* before him. All of Banville's 'high cold heroes" are Faustian because they strive, and in striving they err.[32] More specifically, *Mefisto* is indebted to *Faust* for the character of its different and yet so similar two parts. Before Mephistopheles, in Goethe's play, takes Faust to Auerbach's Cellar in Leipzig, he promises that they will "see both high and low, by lands and sea" (*Faust I*, p. 99), a somewhat unfortunate translation of the original line: "Wir sehen die kleine, dann die große Welt".[33] The 'small world' they see in *Faust I*, and the 'big world' in *Faust II*. Similarly, Part I of *Mefisto* betrays the small world of Gabriel's home town and Ashburn, whereas Part II shows him after his near-fatal accident in a large city, presumably Dublin, if the identification of the town is of any real import; he even meets a representative of a minister of state. Furthermore, *Mefisto*, like *Faust*, is informed and gains much of its structural coherence by repeating in its second part motifs, events and character groupings from its first part in a subtle and surreptitious manner. The drug-taking business in *Mefisto* as well as the scenes in the pub in Part II may be indebted to the Walpurgisnacht scenes. The principle characters are modelled on characters from Goethe: Faust-Kasperl/Kosok; Gretchen — Sophie/Adele; Mephistopheles — Felix[34]; Philemon and Baucis — Philomena and Ambrose/Liz and Tony. But then a somewhat different correspondence could be drawn up, particularly as concerns the Gretchen and Helena counterparts. Generally, each of the main characters in Goethe has a pair of *personae* in Banville to correspond with the pervading binary texture of the account. Thus Kasperl *and* Kosok are meant to represent the Faust figure. Sophie is clearly cast in the Gretchen role. Gabriel's mother also bears a resemblance to Gretchen; she, too, is a mother and a loser. Adele is a perverted Helena character. Her name spelled backwards reads 'Eleda', thus slyly hinting at the fact that Helena was the daughter of Leda. The second Helena *persona* could be Miss Hackett. She appears in Kosok's laboratory in as unannounced a manner as Helena in Faust's castle (*Faust II*, Act III), and she knows as little about computers as Helena knows about the Middle Ages (Cf. *Mefisto*, pp. 189ff. and *Faust II*, "Inner Courtyard of a Castle"). Kosok is unable to present Miss Hackett with satisfactory results; Faust is incapable of offering Helena appropriate answers. The laboratory scene and Wagner's attempt to create Homunculus find their counterpart in *Mefisto* in the laboratory scenes involving Kosok and his computer. The computer like Homunculus represents pure mind. That the Faust-figure in Part I should bear the name 'Kasperl' may be a covert reference to the fact that Goethe encountered the Faust-subject in the form of a puppet-show, which in German is often referred to as a 'Kasperletheater'. Furthermore, there was, as E. M. Butler has shown,[35] an association of some standing between Doctor Faustus and Casper, or Kasperle, in German puppet-plays.

But to continue on safer ground, Gabriel's descent into the laboratory underground and his sojourn there during "downtime" resembles, if loosely, Faust's descent into the underworld (*Faust II*, Act II). Faust's remark: "Two souls, alas, are housed within my breast/ And each will wrestle for the mastery there..." (*Faust I*, p. 67) may have inspired the use of the motif of twin brothers in *Mefisto*. Gabriel had a twin brother who died at birth. Yet he believes he is haunted and pursued by this phantom brother (p. 18).

Attempting to render the words of the Bible "in the loved accent of [his] native land", Faust wonders what may be "inferred" by the statement "In the beginning was the Word". Dissatisfied with the translation he substitutes for it first "In the beginning was the Thought", then "In the beginning was the Power", only to end up at the decision to write "In the beginning was the Deed". For Gabriel, that is the Gabriel writing his life-story, "chance was in the beginning" (p. 3). Felix is like Mephistopheles, "the spirit ... that endlessly denies". But there is a difference: whereas Goethe's Mephisto knows that he is "Part of a power that would/ Alone work evil, but engenders good" (*Faust I*, p. 75), Banville's Mefisto, for the greater part, achieves his aim to create evil. Both are alike insofar as they are "strange, sterile [sons] of chaos" (*Faust I*, p. 76). Goethe's Mephistopheles sings a song about a king who had a flea; Banville's Mefisto recites doggerel about King Flea, or *pulex irritans* (p. 112) — a flourish, no more; so is the parallel that a character called Brand, in a pub scene (p. 164), should sing Brander's rat song from the Auerbach's Cellar scene. Faust, on the mountain, in the "Forest and Cavern" scene, experiences a new lease of life; Gabriel undergoes a similar experience on top of a mountain. Both characters believe that quite a few riddles will now get solved. *Faust II* and Part II of *Mefisto* open with a comparable situation: Faust and Gabriel awake after a troublesome sleep. Gabriel's obsession with the fairy tale about the boy who learns to shudder recalls Faust's remark: "Das Schaudern ist der Menschheit bestes Teil", again rendered unfortunately in translation as "To feel the thrill of awe crowns man's creation" (*Faust I*, p. 78). Gabriel's visit to Mammy (pp. 228f.) counterpoints Faust's invocation of "ye Mothers", in the Baronial Hall scene in *Faust II*, Act I, and seems indebted to Goethe's Mother-myth. Faust says:

> In eurem Namen, Mütter, die ihr thront
> Im Grenzenlosen, ewig einsam wohnt,
> Und doch gesellig. Euer Haupt umschweben
> Des Lebens Bilder, regsam, ohne Leben.

Was einmal war, in allem Glanz und Schein,
Es regt sich dort; denn es will ewig sein.
Und ihr verteilt es, allgewaltige Mächte,
Zum Zelt des Tages, zum Gewölb der Nächte.
    (*Faust II*, lines 6427-6434)
[In your dread name, ye Mothers, where you throne
In infinite space, eternal and alone,
And yet at one, in presence that is rife
Which stir of lifeless images of life.
What once has been, in light and lustre vernal,
Is there astir: it seeks to be eternal.
And ye allot its fate, in sovereign might,
To day's pavilion, or the vault of night.]
    (*Faust II*, p. 85)
Goethe's Mother-myth must be seen in connection with the "Eternal
Womanhood" at the end of the play. There reference is made not to
God, but to the "Queen on high of all the World" (*Faust II*, p. 284):
Virgin pure in heavenly sheen,
Mother, throned supernal,
Highest birth, our chosen Queen
Godhead's peer eternal. (*Faust II*, p. 285)
The Mothers body forth "what once has been" and wants to be
eternal. As Buchwald notes: "[Sie dienen dem ewigen Sinn], indem
sie die Gestaltung und Umgestaltung vollziehen, die zur 'Unter-
haltung' des 'ewigen Sinnes' gehört, d.h. ihn aufrechterhalten und
verwirklichen".[36] The immortal part of every creature strives to
unite itself with the Mothers in order to be sent out into a new life. In
Mefisto, this whole idea has undergone a significant transformation.
Mammy lacks the Goethean implications; she is just a bloated old
woman who smells of peppermint and sits surrounded by the
remnants, the bric-a-brac of a life spent in utter seclusion.

A similar case of inversion concerns the relationship of Adele and
Gabriel. That relationship is modelled, or so it would seem, on the
relationship between Faust and Helena, albeit in reverse. It is not a
happy one, it does not bring about a Euphorion, but only entails the
profanation of a chapel and drug-taking. Philomena and Ambrose
likewise represent a case of inversion. They correspond to Philemon
and Baucis, the roles and the sex having been reversed. That
Philomena and Ambrose should be in the 'service industry' as it were,
she running Black's Hotel and he acting as chauffeur for Kasperl, is
quite in keeping with their classical precursors, who, according to
Ovid's account in *Metamorphoses*, act as host to Jupiter and Mercury,

waiting upon them with food and wine; and for this kind service they are spared the destructive fate of their godless neighbours. Banville's Philemon and Baucis become part of the godless neighbours; they do not act in ignorance of their guests' identity; moreover and more tellingly, their doings are designed to gain personal advantage. And lastly, they do not serve God, or a godhead, but Mefisto. They are not rewarded for the services rendered, but punished: Aunt Philomena loses the money she has invested in Kasperl's scheme at the instigation of Felix, and poor uncle Ambrose gets involved in a car accident as a result of which he goes soft in the head.

Lemures, Lamiae, and Empusa appear in *Faust II*, and they do in *Mefisto* as well, but as pain killers.[37] "Icarus, Icarus/ Full is the cup" (p. 232) is a straight quotation from *Faust II* (p. 208). Gabriel may be associated with Icarus because he tried to attain the impossible in his efforts to explain the world in terms of numbers. Tony is abducted by the sailors, who correspond to the three mighty fellows who haggle over money with Mephistopheles in a way similar to that in which the sailors talk about monetary matters in *Mefisto*. In the end, Felix gets Gabriel as little as Mephistopheles gets Faust, "Eternal Womanhood" having led Faust above. Felix, however, is convinced that "there's always another time" (p. 230) owing to the principle of eternal recurrence.

The world depicted in *Mefisto* is thus a Faustian world, but with a highly significant difference. Generally, it bears a Nietzschean imprint: God is, if not dead, at least absent, possibly paring his finger-nails. Significantly, in Mammy's room there is a coloured picture of Mary, the Mother of God, with a dagger piercing her heart (p. 229). There is no one in it "[whose] light [will] lead him [*i.e.* Gabriel] soon from despairing" (*Faust I*, p. 41). Gabriel's redemption and salvation is not, as with Goethe's Faust, a foregone conclusion, provided that his striving never cease. The strivings of Gabriel involved in the incidents seem to cease: he will leave everything to chance. Those of the Gabriel who is addressing the reader do not: his endeavours to establish a kind of order, to discern meaning and sense are undiminished and bring forth the extraordinary design of the account.

One may note in passing that *Mefisto* appears to be influenced, albeit in a general way, by Thomas Mann's *Doktor Faustus*. A comparable effort is conspicuous in both Mann and Banville to effect an inversion of motifs, characters and theme as one finds them in Goethe.[38] What Hans Mayer writes of Mann's novel could equally well be said of *Mefisto*:

In Grundriß und Ausführung strebt alles zum Gegenpol des klassischen deutschen Faust: *nicht zur Erlösung*, zur menschlichen Kraft und sozialen Utopie, sondern *zur Höllenfahrt*, zur menschlichen Ohnmacht und Untergangsbereitschaft.[39]

As well as influences due to Goethe and Mann, there are references to, and quotations from, an impressive number of other writers and works, such as Beowulf, Shakespeare, Bram Stoker's *Dracula*, and, not to be forgotten, Dante. The opening of Part II recalls the first canto of Dante's *Inferno*. "Midway this way of life we're bound upon", Dante wakes up "to find [himself] in a dark wood" after "the long horror of [a] piteous night".[40] And like Gabriel at the opening, Dante evokes the image of "a swimmer, panting" (p. 72); he hies onward through the desert and is confronted with the symbolic manifestations of the self-indulgent sins, the violent sins, and the malicious sins, before he meets Virgil, who takes him on his journey, whose first part is, significantly, through the kingdom of Dis. The 'big world' of Part II of *Mefisto* has an altogether Dante-esque, infernal character. When Gabriel learns that one of his fellow-patients in the hospital has died, he remarks: "... my Virgil. For this is hell, after all" (p. 135).

*

Gabriel's allusive and very Joycean mythopoeic method is a result of an obsessive concern with shape. It is a concern that ultimately forces all those literary derivations and allusions into symmetrical and mirror-symmetrical patterns within the two parts as well as between the two parts. As often in Banville, the first paragraph proffers crucial clues as to the dominant theme(s) and overall shape of the entire narrative:

> Chance was in the beginning. I am thinking of that tiny swimmer, alone of all its kind, surging in frantic ardour towards the burning town, the white room and Castor dead. Strange, that a life so taken up with the swell and swarm of numbers should start, like a flourish between mirrors, in the banal mathematics of gemination. The end was also chance. (p. 3)

The very first word, which is also the very last in the paragraph as well as in the book, introduces one of the novel's major themes. The reference to Castor points to the possible significance of matters Greek, such as the Pythagorean concern with numbers, which is further enhanced by the remark about "the swell and swarm of numbers". The mentioning of Castor as being dead suggests that the 'I' who is narrating is a kind of Polydeuces-figure, which in turn introduces the concept of twinship, so relevant for the shape of the book — the shape realised *in nuce* in the shape of the paragraph: the first sentence has the same number of words as the last one, and sentences 3 and 4 are, save for one word, also of the same length. The compositional principle of symmetry, of binary patterns, is thus hinted at. And the fact that the first and the last sentences, when taken as one unit, spell out a palindromic design, throws the structural device of mirror-symmetrical arrangements into relief.

The question is, of course, why Gabriel, or for that matter Banville, should have taken so much trouble to impose such a concept of order on his narrative. The reason is simply to prove that the Gabriel involved in the events is wrong in his ideas that chance was in the beginning and in the end as well. The narrator Gabriel notes: "I . . . have my equations, my symmetries, and will insist on them" (p. 4). In a manner different from his younger self, he too strives after order, harmony, "symmetry and completeness" (p. 19). But why this insistence on binary patterns, on the principle of duality? The question has already been answered earlier, with the consideration of Democritus' atomistic world view, Nietzsche's "die ewige Wiederkunft", 'fractals' etc. Furthermore, principles of duality would seem to be most appropriate ordering devices in an attempt to come to grips with the essential nature of the world because, as Martin Gardner and others have shown,[41] the phenomena that go to make up the world are largely built on the principle of duality, symmetry and palindromic patterns. The form of *Mefisto*, thus, bodies forth the order, harmony, symmetry and completeness underlying the seemingly contingent world of Gabriel's near-Faustian experiences in a Mephistophelean world. It is simply Swan's way of establishing sense.

*

In all this and much more besides, Gabriel Swan equals his namesake in *Birchwood*. It is as if Banville has, as it were, gone back in his career as a fiction writer and conscientious artist to creating not from history, but solely from imagination. Gabriel Godkin is in search of "time misplaced"[42] — that very Proustian of occupations. He is the first of Banville's fictional *personae* to be obsessed with harmony, order and in search of sense and meaning. Even when he is "midway upon [his] journey, stumbling in darkness" (*Birchwood*, p. 132) through the inferno of a famine-ridden Ireland, he still believes that life is "at least reasonable. The future must have a locus!" (*Birchwood*, p. 132). His quest for the "rosy grail" (*Birchwood*, p. 168) resembles the quest of an artist for perfection. The artist employs the faculties of his imagination in search of the grail of beauty and truth. Prospero, the magician, represents imagination, and Gabriel Godkin's very Proustian book is the product of the imagination. At the end of his efforts, Gabriel is constrained to acknowledge that he has failed. "There is no form", he writes, "no order, only echoes and coincidences, sleight of hand, dark laughter. I accept it" (*Birchwood*, p. 171). He fails because he is bound to fail. For the quest of perfection, for truth, in art is a never-ending one. This is his initiation.

In that sense, Gabriel Swan's endeavours, too, yield only an approximate success, in spite of the brilliant idea to build his world on dualities and make it conform with the notion of eternal recurrence. It is just one way of explaining the world by dint of a unifying system, but it is not the only and not the most perfect way, if indeed there is such a way.

The parallels between *Mefisto* and *Birchwood* abound. The world of Ashburn very much resembles the world of Birchwood. Both are inhabited by Dickensian oddities. The characters in the first part of *Mefisto* are quite similar to those in Part I of *Birchwood*: the mothers and the fathers; Jack Kay and Granda Godkin, especially in the deathbed scenes; the two Gabriels each have twin brothers, Swan's dead, Godkin's very much alive; Sophie is reminiscent of the milkmaid in *Birchwood*. Part I of *Mefisto* reads like a blend between a big-house novel, the Biblical expulsion from Paradise and a Faust-story set in a Birchwood landscape.

Gabriel Godkin, like Gabriel Swan, was "allowed to survive" (*Birchwood*, p. 3), both are lone survivors" (*Birchwood*, p. 70); and he, too, tries to come to terms with his life, "to discern a defensible reason for his labours" (*Birchwood*, p. 4) by remembering the "madeleines" that go to make up his past life and by committing them to paper. Significantly, he begins his "search for time misplaced" (*Birchwood*, p. 5) by wondering what he was doing "in the womb, swimming there in those dim red waters with my past still all before me" (*Birchwood*, p. 3). Gabriel Swan, in turn, commences his efforts by evoking the image of a tiny swimmer "surging in frantic ardour towards the burning town, the white room" and also of himself and his twin brother "together in [their] crowded amniotic sea", in the womb, "crooning and tinily crying" (p. 4). He was born first, his brother was a poor second: a spent swimmer, he drowned in air. At both Gabriel Godkin's and Gabriel Swan's birth there could be heard first a loud cry and then "another cry, weaker than the first" (*Birchwood*, p. 17).

Gabriel Godkin, as mentioned, is the first in a series of five to search for meaning, harmony, order. He hopes he will succeed in getting to the bottom of what those "extraordinary moments" mean, "when the pig finds the truffle embedded in the muck" (*Birchwood*, p. 3). His Proustian *recherche* is dominated by one principle question: "What does it mean? That is the question I am forever asking, what can it mean?" (*Birchwood*, p. 72). And when he goes on to suggest: "There is never a precise answer, but instead, in the sky, as it were, a kind of jovian nod, a celestial tipping of the wink, *that's all right, it means what it means*" (*Birchwood*, p. 72), then this not only anticipates the notion which Gabriel Swan finally comes to embrace, but also prefigures the convictions of Copernicus, Kepler, and the historian in *The Newton Letter*. After having surreptitiously observed his parents making love among the ruins of Cotter's cottage, Gabriel Godkin believes he has found "the notion of — I shall call it harmony" (*Birchwood*, p. 25). Seeing aunt Martha's son, Michael, juggling, he is overwhelmed by the beauty of it; his beloved puzzle turns into a paltry thing compared to this "harmony" (*Birchwood*, p. 37). Gabriel Swan's preoccupation with numbers is anticipated in *Birchwood*, albeit in an indirect way: Gabriel wins Rosie's heart with the help of mathematics (*Birchwood*, p. 63). The two parts of *Mefisto* resemble those of *Birchwood*, where the first, despite its "bleak comedy" of madness, spontaneous combustion, false teeth sunk into the bark of a birch tree and other unusual occurrences, is commonplace, while the second is eerie, nightmarish, otherworldly and interestingly entitled "Air and Angels". Part II of *Mefisto* bears the title "Angels".

Finally, Gabriel Swan is a narrator, a supreme weaver of fictions, like Gabriel Godkin — akin to God, of God's kin. He has his equations and symmetries and will insist on them, as when he lists the names of famous mathematicians so that the initial letters taken together spell out "Mephisto" (p. 24). It is, therefore, only appropriate that he should claim to be "omniscient, sometimes" (p. 27). But in his zest to come to grips with his life and the world by dint of a unifying system, he also equals Copernicus, and, above all, Kepler, who, like Nazareth, in Dante's *Paradiso*, quite frequently imagined that he "felt the beat/ Of Gabriel's wings",[43] announcing to him a particular aspect of the solution to the cosmic mystery.

*

Copernicus died in redemptive despair. He despaired at having misjudged the nature of the thing-in-itself. He comes to realise that instead of "the eternal truths, the pure forms that lie behind the chaos of the world",[44] he only saw *"a light in the sky"* (*Doctor Copernicus*, p. 239), the counterpart to Gabriel Godkin's "jovian nod". He learns too late that his stargazing robbed him of his humaneness. "The world, and ourselves, this is the truth" (*Doctor Copernicus*, p. 239), his *alter ego*, his brother Andreas, tells him. All his scientific discoveries, no matter how revolutionary, cannot offset the fact that, save for very brief periods, his life was devoid of human love and compassion, because he intentionally stayed aloof. His despair is redemptive because Copernicus accepts his failure and the quintessential nature of life, like Gabriel Godkin.

Kepler, even when near his death baking his chilblains at Hillerbrand Billig's fire, is convinced, despite the disorder and confusion of war and the disorder that was his life, despite even the hallucinatory image of Tycho Brahe as "a dying man searching too late for the life he missed, that his work robbed him of" (*Kepler*, p. 190) — an image of eminent stringency for Kepler's own life — that the world had been created according to a plan based on geometry and that it produced a music of heavenly harmony. He remains convinced that he will never die.

The writer of the Newton letter gives up history, together with his book on Newton, not only because words fail him the same way they failed Hofmannsthal's Lord Chandos, but also because — again as with Lord Chandos — the small things around him overwhelm him to such an extent that he finds himself unable to come to terms with them: he is forced to bear witness to the inappropriateness of his conjecturing, to the breaking down of his unifying system: supernumeries well up in his heart and drown him.

In *Mefisto*, this gradual process of disillusionment is completed. Gabriel Swan, like his Biblical namesake, is a witness to how Mephistophelean machinations have put paid to attempts to account for the world in terms of sense, reason and order. Or is it chance that puts paid to all this? The tetralogy comes to a close with an apotheosis of Heisenberg's 'uncertainty principle'. As Wincklemann told Kepler, "everything is told us, but nothing explained. Yes. We must take it all on trust. That's the secret" (*Kepler*, p. 191). What seems left as far as order, harmony, and completeness go, are symmetries, mirror-symmetries, and the Zarathustrian principle of 'eternal recurrence'.

CONCLUSION

John Banville's *oeuvre* to date constitutes an admirable whole. Like the symphonies of Gustav Mahler, say, each subsequent book picks up from where its predecessor left off, developing particular aspects, broadening the scope of interest by introducing new ideas and techniques. Thematically, the novels have concentrated on the search for sense and purpose, truth and beauty, *das Ding-an-sich*. The strain that runs through all the books is the tension between art and nature, ideas and life. *Nightspawn* and *Birchwood* are concerned with different, and yet so similar, ways in which the artistic imagination attempts to come to grips with the world. *Doctor Copernicus*, *Kepler*, and *The Newton Letter* shift the focus to the scientific imagination: the first two books centre on first-rate representatives of the natural sciences, the last one features an historian. *Mefisto* combines the two perspectives by presenting, in Gabriel Swan, a synthesis, as it were, of the artistic and the scientific imagination. Swan is a withered wizard of mathematics and an artist-figure.

In each case, the outcome of the labours is shown to represent a supreme form of failure. All that Banville's ardent artists and epistemological explorers have so far been able to achieve are supreme fictions, in Wallace Stevens' sense of the term. Every one of "those high cold heroes"[1] erects and puts forward unifying systems, literary or scientific, of sublime beauty and order. But they are systems that lack any foundation in fact. The artistic-figures fail as a result of the quintessential shortcomings of art; the scientists are defeated by their *a priori* belief in harmony and order, which, like the corresponding faith of the artist, the chaos of life defies.

The attempts of Ben White, in *Nightspawn*, are a desperate Beckettian effort to escape the suffocating void of silence, while at the same time representing a brave, though derivative, endeavour to

171

overcome exhausted conventions of narrative discourse and, by breaking them down, to create the prerequisites for a fresh start. Gabriel Godkin, in *Birchwood*, as if realising that a complete break with tradition is impossible, quite in Eliot's sense in "Tradition and the Individual Talent", intentionally falls back on older forms in his Proustian *recherche du temps perdu*. Mnemosyne, that lying whore, is as important to White as she is to Godkin. Canon Koppernigk's heliocentric system is as much a thing of the mind as is Kepler's notion of *harmonia mundi*, his world system based on the Platonic solids, or the "horrid drama" which the historian, in *The Newton Letter*, dreams up and which prevents him from seeing the common-place tragedy that is playing itself out in real life. Canon Koppernigk, Kepler and the historian learn too late that all their striving was "vanity, all vanity".[2] Obsessed with their supreme fictions, they forget that "we say only those things that we have the words to express",[3] and grow blind to the fact that their work robs them of their humaneness. All three contract not to be known; but, as Andreas tells his brother, Nicolas, "the world, and ourselves, this is the truth. There is no other."[4] All of Banville's 'heroes' end up in redemptive despair. Gabriel Swan, in *Mefisto*, is no exception; and yet perhaps he is. For he seems to accept the chaos of life, while at the same time, as an artist-figure, introducing a system of order that, contrary to the systems of his forerunners, does appear to have a basis in reality: his walls of numbers build up no more than a house of fiction; however, his concept of chance, governed by eternal recurrence, symmetries, mirror-symmetries and binary patterns is borne out by the world as we know it.

In addition to pursuing related thematic interests, Banville's *oeuvre* to date is held together by interlarding one book with references and allusions to the book that went before, quite in the manner of Beckett, who has the unnamable refer to Malone, Murphy and Molloy.[5] While the novels after *Nightspawn* rely more on thematic concerns they share, *Long Lankin* and *Nightspawn* are closely connected by what would appear to be purposive echoes. The Ben of "The Possessed" reappears as a fully-fledged writer in *Nightspawn*. At the end of the novella he announces that he will go away again, and *Nightspawn* finds him in Greece. "The memory of a drowned man seen long ago"[6] comes to White on one occasion. This is probably a reference to the drowned man in "Summer Voices". There is also the circumstance that White, just as the boy and the girl in that story, should have been "brought up in the depth of the country, living by the sea with a decrepit aunt"[7]. The story about Cain, in *Nightspawn*,[8] recalls Ben's problem regarding freedom in "The Possessed", and it echoes the Gide motto to the novella. The boy Yacinth and what he stands for in *Nightspawn* are incontestably derived from the Hyacinthus figure in the story which Ben tells Wolf near the end of "The Possessed". There is also the remarkably rich number of correspondences and parallels between *Birchwood* and *Mefisto*, which were discussed elsewhere in this study and need not be repeated here. These parallels in particular would seem to suggest that Banville has not offered a tetralogy — *Doctor Copernicus*, *Kepler*, *The Newton Letter*, and *Mefisto* — and two novels before it, but a series of five books, coerced into a harmonious whole by the first and last parts being so strikingly similar. Or it would, on the strength of the thematic correspondences between *Nightspawn*, *Birchwood* and the rest of Banville's work, be possible to maintain that the novels build up an intricately connected series of six.[9]

*

A tetralogy, in classical Greek literature, was a series of four dramas, three tragic (the trilogy) and one satiric, exhibited at Athens during the festival of Dionysus.[10] *The Newton Letter* is subtitled "An Interlude", and Banville seems inclined to regard the novella as corresponding to the satiric part of the classical tetralogy.[11] He has submitted that one purpose of the interlude was to send himself up and likewise part of his thematic preoccupations and stylistic mannerisms. The point may be valid. The problem, though, is that it may be valid first and foremost for Banville himself. For it is anything but easy to ascertain wherein the satiric really resides in the book. In fact, one has little difficulty reading the account without paying attention to, or becoming aware of, possible satiric elements. But then, as Dean Swift put it in the preface to *The Battle of the Books*:

> *Satyr is that sort of Glass wherein the Beholders do generally discover every body's Face but their Own; which is the chief Reason for that kind of Reception it meets in the World, and that so very few are offended with it.*[12]

Either this reader was too myopic to see the satire in *The Newton Letter*, or Banville's glass was too opaque to permit an appropriate view — a view other than the following one: Banville, writing about his disturbed historian realising that 'storytelling' is necessarily misleading, is himself telling a story and hence not to be trusted.

*

174 John Banville: A Critical Introduction

Thus we come to the last broken sentences. Johannes Kepler bids farewell to Hillebrand Billig saying: "Ah my friend, such dreams..." This study has sought to interpret dreams — the dreams of the writer John Banville. He may want to retort: "My song outspans/ Thy mortal wit, surpassing all thou know'st". The point is certainly valid. This has been only the first fully-sustained attempt to come to grips with the world of Banville's fiction. A good deal in it has still to be discovered. But there is form, order, echoes and coincidences, sleight of hand, dark laughter, artistic brilliance, and whereof I cannot speak, thereof I must be silent.

NOTES

Introduction

1. The present study does not follow what has, in some quarters, become a customary differentiation between Anglo-Irish literature, *i.e.* Irish literature in English, and Irish literature, *i.e.* Irish literature in Gaelic. The reason is simply that the decision to employ 'Anglo-Irish' in the sense given above is a rather unfortunate one. The term has distinct cultural as well as socio-political meaning, pertaining to a decisive period in the history of Ireland and it had this meaning prior to its altered usage.

2. Cf. Maurice Harmon, "Generations Apart: 1925-75", in: Patrick Rafroidi & Maurice Harmon (eds.), *The Irish Novel in Our Time* (Lille: PUL, 1975/76), pp. 49-65.

3. See Rüdiger Imhof, "'A Little Bit of Ivory, Two Inches Wide': The Small World of Jennifer Johnston's Fiction", *Etudes Irlandaises*, 10 (December 1985), pp. 129-44.

4. Robin Skelton, "Aidan Higgins and the Total Book", *Mosaic*, 10 (1976), pp. 27-37.

5. Cf. for example, Thomas Flanagan, *The Irish Novelists 1800-1850* (Westport/Conn.: Greenwood Press, repr. 1976, [1959]); John Cronin, *The Anglo-Irish Novel, vol I: The Nineteenth Century* (Belfast: Appletree Press, 1980); Barry Sloan, *The Pioneers of Anglo-Irish Fiction. 1800-1850* (Gerrards Cross: Colin Smythe, 1986); and the superb study by Klaus Lubbers, *Geschichte der irischen Erzählprosa, Bd. I: Von den Anfängen bis zum ausgehenden 19. Jahrhundert* (Munich: Fink, 1985).

6. A. Norman Jeffares, *Anglo-Irish Literature* (Dublin: Gill & Macmillan, 1982); Seamus Deane, *A Short History of Irish Literature* (London: Hutchinson, 1986).

7. Augustine Martin, *The Genius of Irish Prose* (Dublin: Mercier Press, 1984).

8. *Ibid.*, p. 120.

9. There is reason to hope that Klaus Lubbers will before too long publish volume II of his history of Irish narrative prose.

10. Richard Kearney, "A Crisis of Imagination", *The Crane Bag*, 3, 1 (1979), pp. 58ff.; Richard Kearney, *Transitions. Narratives in Modern Irish Culture* (Dublin: Wolfhound Press, 1988), esp. chapter 2-4.

11. Richard Kearney, "A Crisis of Imagination", p. 61.

12. *Ibid.*, p. 61.

13. Vivian Mercier is inclined to see Joyce in an Irish tradition: the Irish comic tradition; cf. Vivian Mercier, *The Irish Comic Tradition* (London, Oxford, New York: OUP, 1969), p. 236. This is, of course, not what is meant here. Besides, the evidence Prof. Mercier is able to proffer in support of his categorization is rather shaky.

14. It makes little difference that there are references to Ireland in Beckett's novels.

15. "Novelists on the Novel. Ronan Sheehan Talks to John Banville and Francis Stuart", *The Crane Bag*, 3, 1 (1979), p. 76.

16. *Ibid.*, p. 77.

17. *Hibernia* (4 October 1977), p. 27.

18. Seamus Deane, "'Be Assured I Am Inventing': The Fiction of John Banville", in: Patrick Rafroidi & Maurice Harmon (eds.), *The Irish Novel in Our Time*, p. 329.

19. John Banville, "Recent Fiction", *Hibernia* (30 September 1977), p. 25.

20. Seamus Deane, "John Banville, *Dr. Copernicus*", *Irish University Review*, 7, 1 (Spring 1977), p. 121.

21. Cf. Ulrich Broich & Manfred Pfister, *Intertextualität. Formen, Funktionen, anglistische Fallstudien* (Tübingen: Niemeyer, 1985).

22. Cf. Banville's remark, in: Rüdiger Imhof, "Q. & A. with John Banville", *Irish Literary Supplement* (Spring 1987), p. 13.

23. Annegret Maack, *Der experimentelle englische Roman der Gegenwart* (Darmstadt: Wiss. Buchgesellschaft, 1984).

24. The eight categories are: 1) the 'poetological' novel, or metafiction; 2) the renaissance of myths; 3) the adaptation of literary models; 4) variations on *Satyricon*; 4) future perspectives between *utopia* and science fiction; 6) metamorphoses of the detective novel; 7) historical fiction and fictitious history; 8) 'concrete' fiction and visual literature.

25. Ihab Hassan, *Paracriticism* (Urbana, Chicago, London, 1975), pp. 20f.

26. *Ibid.*, pp. 54ff.

27. Alan Wilde, "Modernism and the Aesthetics of Crisis", *Contemporary Literature*, 20, 1 (Winter 1979), p. 43.

28. Frank Kermode, *Continuities* (London, 1968), p. 24.

29. Cf. Larry McCaffery, *Postmodern Fiction — A Bio-bibliographical Guide* (Westport/Conn.: Greenwood, 1986).

30. Cf. Erhard Reckwitz, "Der Roman als Metaroman", *Poetica*, 18 (1986), pp. 140-64.

31. Cf. Rüdiger Imhof, *Contemporary Metafiction. A Poetological Study of Metafiction in English since 1939* (Heidelberg: Winter, 1986), *passim*.

32. Samuel Coale, "An Interview with Anthony Burgess", *Modern Fiction Studies*, 27, 3 (Autumn 1981), p. 444.

1. A *Principia* of Sorts

1. John Banville, "Fowles at the Crossroads", *Hibernia* (14 October 1977), p. 27.

2. *Ibid.*, p. 27.
3. *Ibid.*, p. 27.
4. John Banville, "It's Only a Novel", *Hibernia* (11 November 1977), p. 23.
5. John Banville, "Recent Fiction", *Hibernia* (16 September 1977), p. 20.
6. "Novelists on the Novel. Ronan Sheehan Talks to John Banville and Francis Stuart", *The Crane Bag*, 3, 1 (1979), p. 79.
7. *Ibid.*, pp. 81f.
8. John Banville, "Cracker-Barrel Philosopher", *Hibernia* (2 May 1975), p. 19.
9. John Banville, "Recent Fiction", *Hibernia* (30 September 1977), p. 27.
10. John Banville, "Enigma Variations", *Hibernia* (16 February 1978).
11. John Banville, "Saul Bellow's World", *Hibernia* (18 March 1977), p. 28.
12. John Banville, "Act of Faith", *Hibernia* (2 September 1977), p. 20.
13. *Ibid.*, p. 20.
14. John Banville, "Marquez: Fatal Lure of Action", *Hibernia* (29 April 1977), p. 21.
15. John Banville, "Saul Bellow's World", p. 28.
16. John Banville, "It's Only a Novel", p. 23.
17. John Banville, "The Only Begetter", *Hibernia* (10 June 1977), p. 24.
18. John Banville, "Beginnings", *Hibernia* (7 January 1977), p. 32.
19. Vladimir Nabokov, *Bend Sinister* (Harmondsworth: Penguin, repr. 1981), p. 103.
20. Cf. John Banville, "Native Talent", *Hibernia* (20 January 1978), p. 23.
21. John Banville, "No Real Blood", *Hibernia* (21 November 1969), p. 17.
22. John Banville, "Colony of Expatriates", *Hibernia* (6 October 1972), p. 18.
23. In a conversation with the present author in August 1984.
24. *The New York Book Review* (21 April 1985), p. 41.
25. John Banville, "It's Only a Novel", p. 23.
26. Cf. Rüdiger Imhof, "An Interview with John Banville. 'My Readers, That Small Band, Deserve a Rest", *Irish University Review*, 11, 1 (Spring 1981), p. 6.
27. *Ibid.*, p. 10.
28. *Ibid.*, p. 10.
29. *Ibid.*, p. 12; "A Talk", *Irish University Review*, 11, 1 (Spring 1981), p. 15.
30. Rainer Maria Rilke, *Duineser Elegien* (Frankfurt: Suhrkamp, 1975), p. 56; Rainer Maria Rilke, *Duino Elegies* (London: Chatto & Windus, 1981), p. 85.
31. John Banville, "A Talk", p. 16.
32. Cf. Martin Heidegger, *Der Ursprung des Kunstwerkes* (Stuttgart: Reclam, 1978), pp. 28ff., where Heidegger talks about the way in which van Gogh painted the shoes of a peasant.
33. John Banville, "Masterfully Maniac", *The Sunday Tribune* (20 September 1983), p. 5.
34. Letter of 3 March 1978.

2. Long Lankin

1. John Banville, *Long Lankin* (London: Secker & Warburg, 1970). All references are to this edition.
2. Francis J. Child, *The English and Scottish Popular Ballads*, vol. II (New York: Dover, repr. 1965), pp. 320–42.

3. Ed. by James Kinsley (Oxford: OUP, 1971), pp. 313ff.
4. One of the Leslies, earls of Leven and barons of Balwearie in Fife, which fact suggests that the ballad is of Scottish origin.
5. Cf. Elizabeth Mayor's comment in *The Glasgow Herald* (31 January 1970), or Ronald Hayman's remark in *The Sunday Telegraph* (25 January 1970).
6. John Banville, *Long Lankin* (Dublin: Gallery Books, 1984).
7. Rüdiger Imhof, "An Interview with John Banville. 'My Readers, That Small Band, Deserve a Rest", *Irish University Review*, 11, 1 (Spring 1981), p. 9.
8. The story replaces "Persona" in the revised edition of *Long Lankin*.
9. Cf. Banville's remark in: R. Imhof, "An Interview with John Banville...", p. 9.
10. Cf. Ciaran Carty, "Out of Chaos Comes Order", *The Sunday Tribune* (14 September 1986), p. 18.
11. Cf. Banville's comment in: R. Imhof, "An Interview with John Banville...", pp. 9f.
12. John Banville, *Nightspawn* (New York: W. W. Norton, 1971), p. 49.
13. Quoted in: Josef Kunz (ed.), *Novelle* (Darmstadt: Wiss. Buchgesellschaft, 1973), p. 63.
14. Benno von Wiese, *Novelle* (Stuttgart, 1964).
15. Cf. James George Frazer, *The Golden Bough: A Study in Magic and Religion* (London & Basingstoke: Macmillan, repr. 1976), p. 815.
16. *Ibid.*, p. 840.
17. *Ibid.*, p. 848.
18. *Ibid.*, pp. 849f.
19. *Ibid.*, p. 405.
20. T. S. Eliot, *Collected Poems 1909-1962* (London: Faber & Faber, repr. 1975), p. 17.
21. John Banville, *Doctor Copernicus* (London: Secker & Warburg, 1976), p. 29, *passim*.
22. Cf. Banville's admission in: R. Imhof, "An Interview with John Banville...", p. 9

3. Nightspawn

1. John Banville, *Nightspawn* (New York: W. W. Norton & Company, 1971), p. 159. All references are to this edition.
2. Seamus Deane, "'Be Assured I Am Inventing': The Fiction of John Banville", in: Patrick Rafroidi & Maurice Harmon (eds.), *The Irish Novel in Our Time* (Lille: PUL, 1975/76), p. 334.
3. *Ibid.*, p. 335.
4. *Ibid.*, p. 336.
5. *Oxford Mail* (4 February 1971).
6. *The Daily Telegraph* (1 February 1971).
7. *The Financial Times* (12 February 1971).

8. *The Spectator* (24 February 1971).

9. *Books & Bookmen* (May 1971).

10. Rüdiger Imhof, "An Interview with John Banville. 'My Readers, That Small Band, Deserve a Rest", *Irish University Review*, 11, 1 (Spring 1981), p. 6.

11. *Ibid.*, p. 6.

12. Cf. Banville's admission: "*Nightspawn* is very much influenced by Beckett", R. Imhof, "Interview with John Banville ...", p. 11.

13. Vladimir Nabokov, "Introduction", *Bend Sinister* (Harmondsworth: Penguin, repr. 1981), p. 11.

14. Cf. Rüdiger Imhof, *Contemporary Metafiction. A Poetological Study of Metafiction in English since 1939* (Heidelberg: Winter, 1986), *passim*.

15. Letter to W. W. Norton & Company. Miraculously, a copy of the letter lay in the copy of the novel I purchased in a second-hand shop.

16. "Tal Coat", *Three Dialogues. Samuel Beckett and Georges Duthuit*, in: Samuel Beckett, *Proust & 3 dialogues with Georges Duthuit* (London: Calder & Boyars, repr. 1970), p. 103.

17. "Bram Van Velde", *Three Dialogues*, p. 125.

18. R. Imhof, "An Interview with John Banville ...", p. 5.

19. *Ibid.*, p. 5.

20. *Ibid.*, p. 6.

21. *Caleb Williams* begins in the following way: "My life has for several years been a theatre of calamity. I have been a mark for vigilance of tyranny, and I could not escape. My fairest prospects have been blasted. My enemy has shown himself inaccessible to intreaties and untired persecution. My fame, as well as my happiness, has become his victim." William Godwin, *Caleb Williams* (Oxford: OUP, repr. 1978), p. 3.

22. P. N. Furbank, "Godwin's Novels", *Essays in Criticism*, 5 (1955), p. 214.

23. F. M. Dostoyevsky, *Notes from Underground & The Double*, transl. with intro. by Jessie Coulson (Harmondsworth: Penguin, repr. 1980), p. 15.

24. T. S. Eliot, "The Love Song of J. Alfred Prufrock", in: T. S. Eliot, *Collected Poems 1909-1962* (London: Faber & Faber, 1970), p. 15.

25. "The Love Song of J. Alfred Prufrock", p. 13.

26. Vladimir Nabokov, *The Annotated "Lolita"*, ed. with preface, introduction and notes by Alfred Appell, jr. (New York, Toronto: McGraw-Hill, 1970), p. 301.

27. Joyce Cary, *The Horse's Mouth* (Harmondsworth: Penguin, repr. 1979), p. 186.

28. Cf. Francis C. Molloy's critical remark: "While *Nightspawn* can certainly be called an experimental work, it is not completely successful. It is the product of a writer who had not learned to control his talents ... [etc.]." F. C. Molloy, "The Search for Truth. The Fiction of John Banville", *Irish University Review*, 11, 1 (Spring 1981), p. 37. The criticism may be valid. And yet compared to what has been put forward in the area of the narcissistic narrative since World War II (cf. R. Imhof, *Contemporary Metafiction, passim*), *Nightspawn* can well hold its own as a successful piece of writing.

29. Cf. here Francis C. Molloy's quite similar interpretation, "The Search for Truth. The Fiction of John Banville", *Irish University Review*, 11, 1 (Spring 1981), pp. 33f.

4. Birchwood

1. *The Observer* (25 October 1987), p. 27.
2. Banville has remarked in an interview: "*Birchwood* ... sold relatively well in America inasmuch as it sold ten thousand copies. I've always felt that the reason it sold was that Irish Americans mistook it for a novel about the 'big house'." "Novelists on the Novel. Ronan Sheehan talks to John Banville and Francis Stuart", *The Crane Bag*, 3, 1 (1979), p. 82.
3. *In Guilt and Glory* (London: Hutchinson, 1979), p. 271.
4. *Birchwood* (London: Secker & Warburg, 1973). All references are to this edition.
5. Seamus Deane, "'Be Assured I am Inventing': The Fiction of John Banville", in: Patrick Rafroidi & Maurice Harmon (eds.), *The Irish Novel in Our Time* (Lille: PUL, 1975-6), p. 337.
6. *Hibernia* (1 April 1977), p. 26.
7. Dante Aleghieri, *La Vita Nuova*, transl. Barbara Reynolds (Harmondsworth: Penguin, repr. 1986), p. 29.
8. *Four Quartets*, "Burnt Norton", in: T. S. Eliot, *Collected Poems, 1909-1962* (London: Faber, 1970), p. 189.
9. Johann Wolfgang von Goethe, *Faust. One*, transl. Philip Wayne (Harmondsworth: Penguin, repr. 1986), p. 44.
10. *Kepler* (London: Secker & Warburg, 1981), p. 191.
11. Marcel Proust, *Swann's Way* (Harmondsworth: Penguin, repr. 1984), p. 6.
12. Cf. here Roger Shattuck's illuminating comments on the form of *A la recherche*, in: *Proust* (Glasgow: Fontana, 1974), pp. 128ff.
13. In a letter of 3 March 1978, John Banville remarked: "Long before I came to Copernicus I was, it seems, fascinated by clockwork mechanisms."
14. Heraclitus, *Fragments*, cited in: *The International Thesaurus of Quotations*, comp. Rhoda Thomas Tripp (Harmondsworth: Penguin, 1976), p. 115-121.
15. Ludwig Wittgenstein, *Tractatus logico-philosophicus* (Frankfurt: Suhrkamp, 1971), p. 115.
16. Brian Donnelly, "The Big House in the Recent Novel", *Studies*, 64 (1975), pp. 133f.
17. Maria Edgeworth, *Castle Rackrent & The Absentee* (London: Dent, 1972), p. 3. All further references are to this edition.
18. Joseph Sheridan LeFanu, *Uncle Silas* (New York: Dover, 1966), p. 18. All further references are to this edition.
19. Cf. Banville's own comment in: "Novelists on the Novel...", p. 83.
20. Cf. for instance, Bruno Schleussner, *Der neopikareske Roman* (Bonn: Bouvier, 1969).
21. Samuel Beckett, *Molloy* (London: Calder & Boyars, repr. 1971), p. 39.
22. Francis C. Molloy, "The Search For Truth. The Fiction of John Banville", *Irish University Review*, 10, 1 (Spring 1981), p. 42.
23. Quoted in Molloy, pp. 42f.
24. Cf. Molloy, pp. 42f.
25. *Daily Telegraph* (8 February 1973).
26. "Novelists on the Novel ...", p. 82.

27. Cf. Molloy, p. 39.
28. As a matter of significant coincidence, the idea of a rose is associated with creative inspiration in *A Portrait*, when Stephen experiences "the instant of inspiration", feeling how "in the virgin womb of the imagination the word [is] made flesh". An afterglow deepens within his spirit, "whence the white flame had passed" and it deepens to "a rose and ardent light". (James Joyce, *A Portrait of the Artist as a Young Man* (London: Cape, repr. 1978), p. 221.)
29. Cf. Molloy, p. 38.
30. Cited in: Robert Hughes, "On Lucian Freud", *The New York Review of Books*, 34, 13 (13 August 1987), p. 56.
31. *Molloy*, p. 33.

5. Doctor Copernicus

1. Samuel Beckett, *Molloy* (London: Calder & Boyars, repr. 1971), 33.
2. John Banville, *Doctor Copernicus* (London: Secker & Warburg, 1976), 3.
3. The surname is variously spelt in documents as 'Coppernic', 'Koppernick', 'Koppernik', 'Koppernigk', 'Kopperlingk', 'Cupernick' and 'Kuppernick'. The most usual is 'Koppernigk' (the spelling adopted by Koppernigk's biographer Leopold Prowe; cf. L. Prowe, *Nicolaus Copernicus* (Berlin, 1883-4). He himself signed his name on different occasions as 'Copernic', 'Coppernig', 'Coppernik', 'Copphernic', and in later years mostly 'Copernicus'; cf. Arthur Koestler, *The Sleepwalkers. A History of Man's Changing Vision of the Universe* (Harmondsworth: Penguin, repr. 1977), 569, note 1.
4. Wolfgang Iser, *Der Implizite Leser* (Munich, 1972), 164.
5. In a letter to me of 9 January 1980.
6. Cf. James Joyce, *A Portrait of the Artist as a Young Man* (London: Cape, repr. 1968), 11, 15, 16.
7. Benjamin Lee Whorf, "Science and Linguistics", repr. in: *Language, Thought and Reality* (Cambridge, Mass., 1967), 212f.
8. John Locke, *An Essay Concerning Human Understanding*, collated and annotated by A. C. Fraser; vol. I, Bk. III, Ch. IX, 21, 119.
9. Cf. Gershon Weiler, *Mauthner's Critique of Language* (Cambridge, 1970), 9.
10. *Ibid.*, 15.
11. *Ibid.*, 32.
12. *Ibid.*, 177.
13. See the article on Mauthner in Edward's *Encyclopaedia of Philosophy*. I wish to express my indebtedness for these remarks to John Pilling's study *Samuel Beckett* (London, Henley & Boston, 1976), 128.
14. The conundrum is specified on pp. 19f. The solution is this: if 'x' stands for a black and 'o' for a white hat, the following seven combinations are possible:

    1 xxx
    2 oxx
    3 xox
    4 xxo

       5 xoo
       6 oox
       7 oxo

Of these, three must be ruled out as they do not fit into the scheme of the conundrum as set by Canon Sturm. The fifth possibility, for instance, is not feasible since A, seeing two white hats, would know that he is wearing a black one. The same applies to the seventh possibility, where B would see two white hats. The fourth possibility must equally be ruled out, for otherwise B would know the colour of his hat. He hears A say that A cannot tell whether his hat is black or white; he, therefore, knows that he, B, cannot be wearing a hat the same colour as that worn by C, which is white. Consequently, his must be black. Thus only these four possibilities are permissible:

       1 xxx
       2 oox
       3 xox
       4 oox

In each of them, C wears a black hat. This is no doubt a very unmathematical way of solving the conundrum. But even so — done! Harmonia.

15. Cf. Hans Blumenberg, *Die Genesis der kopernikanischen Welt* (Frankfurt, 1975), passim, esp. 70f.; Thomas S. Kuhn, *The Copernican Revolution* (Harvard, 1957).

16. Thomas Carlyle, *Sartor Resartus* (London, Melbourne: Dent, repr. 1984), 123.

17. Jeremy Bernstein, *Einstein*, p. 24.

18. John Banville, *The Newton Letter* (London: Secker & Warburg, 1982), 50.

19. John Banville, *Kepler* (London: Secker & Warburg, 1981), 50.

20. *The Newton Letter*, 29.

21. *Kepler*, 190.

22. Quoted in *The Faber Book of Anecdotes*, ed. by Clifton Fadiman (London, Boston, 1985), 305.

23. *The Newton Letter*, 11.

24. In a letter of 3 March 1978 to the present author, Banville has admitted that he is not happy about "the parodies at the end of part II".

25. John Banville's view expressed in a conversation with the present author.

26. Ford Madox Ford, *The Good Soldier* (London, Sydney, Toronto: Bodley Head, 1980), 17, 18.

27. *The Good Soldier*, 22, for instance, but also *passim*.

28. Cf. Koestler, *The Sleepwalkers*, 199.

29. Cf. J. Ritter & K. Gründer (eds.), *Historisches Wörterbuch der Philosophie*, IV (Darmstadt, 1976), col. 1094.

30. Johann Wolfgang Goethe, *Materialien zur Geschichte der Farbenlehre*, in: *Goethes Werke*, vol. XIV: *Naturwissenschaftliche Schriften II*. "Hamburger Ausgabe" (Munich: Beck, 1982), 81.

31. Cited in: Ritter & Gründer, col. 1097.

32. Cf. Hans Blumenberg, *Die kopernikanische Wende* (Frankfurt, 1965), 14.

33. That opinion, together with the conviction that hypotheses can only be *fundamenta calculi*, and not *articuli fidei*, was in fact expressed by Osiander in his

second letter to Copernicus of 20 April 1541; cf. Blumenberg, 92.

34. Cf. Blumenberg, 17.

35. *Ibid.*, 76.

36. Jorge Luis Borges, "Averroes's Search", in: J. L. Borges, *Labyrinths*, ed. by
     D. A. Yates & J. E. Irby (Harmondsworth: Penguin, repr. 1976), 180

37. Tom Stoppard, *Jumpers* (London: Faber & Faber, 1972), 74.

38. Cited in: Hiram Haydn (ed.), *The Portable Elizabethan Reader* (Harmondsworth:
     Penguin, repr. 1980), 42.

39. See Koestler, *The Sleepwalkers*, 154.

40. *Ibid.*, 155.

41. Cf. Jochen Kirchhoff, *Kopernikus* (Reinbek, 1985), 59f.

42. John Banville, *Kepler*, 148.

43. In a letter to the present author of 19 December 1986.

44. Robert Nye, "Heliocentric Universe", *Hibernia* (3 December 1976), 20.

45. E. M. Forster, "Virginia Woolf", repr. in: Claire Sprague (ed.), *Virginia Woolf*
     (Englewood Cliffs, N.J., 1971), 17.

46. *Irish University Review*, VII, 1 (Spring 1977), 120.

47. Quoted in Koestler, *The Sleepwalkers*, 258.

48. Thus Tiedemann Giese in a letter to Rheticus, cited in Koestler, *The
     Sleepwalkers*, 189.

49. "The shortness of life, the dullness of the senses, the numbness of indifference
     and unprofitable occupations allow us to know but very little. and again and
     again swift oblivion, the embezzler of knowledge and the enemy of memory,
     shakes out of the mind, in the course of time, even what we knew." Quoted in
     Koestler, *The Sleepwalkers*, 190.

50. Beckett, *Molloy*, 33.

6. Kepler

1. John Banville, *Kepler* (London: Secker & Warburg, 1981), p. 3. All references
    are to this edition.

2. Cited in Arthur Koestler, *The Sleepwalkers: A History of Man's Changing Vision of
    the Universe* (Harmondsworth: Penguin, repr. 1977), p. 250.

3. Cited in Koestler, p. 319.

4. Cf. Koestler, p. 405.

5. Cf. Brendan Glacken, "Head in the Stars", *Irish Times* (31 January 1981), p. 12.

6. Cited in Koestler, p. 333.

7. Cf. Koestler, p. 334.

8. Cf. Koestler, p. 334.

9. Kepler was not born with defective eyesight, as Koestler has contended
    (Koestler, p. 232); nor was his myopia plus polyopy the result of "frequent
    boxings", as Banville has it (*Kepler*, p. 93).

10. Cf. Koestler, p. 240.

11. Cited in Koestler, pp. 237f. & 242

12. Cited in Koestler, p. 308.

13. Cf. Koestler, p. 312.
14. Cf. Koestler, p. 314.
15. Cf. Koestler, p. 289.
16. Fugger's first name does not have an 'e' at the end, cf. *Kepler*, p. 123.
17. There appear to be two mistakes regarding the spelling of the message; it is quoted as "Smaismirmilmepoetaleumibunenugttaurias" (cf. pp. 138f.); the 'i' in the first part is neither in Koestler's study nor in Caspar's biography; and the very last part is identical with Koestler's version (cf. Koestler, p. 381), but Caspar gives it as "tauiras"; cf. Max Caspar, *Johannes Kepler* (Stuttgart, 1948), p. 232.
18. Cf. Koestler, p. 382.
19. "I have observed the highest planet in triplet form", cf. Koestler, p. 382.
20. Cf. Koestler, p. 366.
21. Cited in Koestler, p. 275.
22. Cf. Koestler, p. 263.
23. Banville's statement to this effect in "Novelists on the Novel. Ronan Sheehan Talks to John Banville and Francis Stuart", *The Crane Bag*, 3, 1 (1979), p. 79.
24. Koestler, p. 254.
25. The discovery was not made on 9 July, as Koestler asserts, cf. Koestler, p. 249.
26. Cf. Koestler, p. 264.
27. Koestler, p. 394.
28. In spite of the overall congruence between the real and the fictional Kepler, there are nonetheless deviations in the treatment. Some may regard it a worthwhile occupation to record these instances. Since an artist is absolutely free to manipulate the facts so as to make them suit his specific artistic aim, for after all a fiction writer is not a historian, the recording of these deviations seems to be of limited value only.

    The first deviation occurs in the very first paragraph in the novel. Banville's Kepler arrives at Benatek on 4 February 1600 in the company of his wife, Barbara, and stepdaughter, Regina. The historical Kepler made his first journey to Tycho Brahe alone; his family was in far away Graz. After the row with Tycho, Kepler did not return to Benatek by nightfall of the same day on which the quarrel happened, but three days later. Kepler did not boast that he would solve the problem of the orbit of Mars in seven (p. 62), but in eight days. His bad eyesight did not result from "the frequent boxings" which his sisters and brothers inflicted on him, but from the smallpox he suffered as a child around 1575. The first letter in Part IV was actually written to Herwart von Hohenburg. Because of an oversight in proof-reading, the title of the *Discurs von heutiger Zeit Beschaffenheit* has an 'r' at the end instead of a 't' (p. 117). It should be 'Wackher' instead of "Whackher" (p. 121), and 'Friederich' instead of "Freiderich" (p. 128). Kepler's stepdaughter, Regina, married in 1608, and not in 1609, as Kepler states in his letter to his mother (p. 119). Lastly, the conflict that led to the witch trial started between Kepler's mother and Ursula Reinbold in 1615; consequently Kepler could not have mentioned it in a letter dating from 1610 (p. 142).
29. Rüdiger Imhof, "An Interview with John Banville. 'My Readers, That Small

Band, Deserve a Rest'", *Irish University Review*, 11, 1 (Spring 1981), p. 6.
30. Max Brod, *Tycho Brahes Weg zu Gott* (Frankfurt/a.M.: Suhrkamp, repr. 1978), p. 266.

7. The Newton Letter

1. *The Newton Letter* (London: Secker & Warburg, 1982). All references are to this edition. This chapter uses material expounded by me in "*The Newton Letter* by John Banville: An Exercise in Literary Derivation", *Irish University Review* (Autumn 1983), pp. 162-67.
2. Cf. Banville's remark in *The Fiction Magazine*, 1, 3 (Autumn 1982), p. 31.
3. Henry James, *The Sacred Fount* (New York: Grove Press, repr. 1979), p. 313.
4. *Ibid.*, p. 156.
5. Cf. Leon Edel, *The Life of Henry James*, vol. I (Harmondsworth: Penguin, repr. 1977), p. 524.
6. Hugo von Hofmannsthal, "Ein Brief", in: H. von Hofmannsthal, *Erzählungen, erfundene Gespräche und Briefe, Reisen* (Frankfurt/a.M.: Fischer, 1979), p. 466. All further references in the text will be to this edition. The English translation reads: "For me everything disintegrated into parts, those parts again into parts; no longer would anything let itself be encompassed by one idea". [Hugo von Hofmannsthal, *Selected Prose*, transl. by Mary Hottinger & Tania & James Stern (New York: Pantheon Books, 1952), p. 134.]
7. The English translation reads: "In those days I, in a state of continuous intoxication, conceived the whole existence as one great unit: the spiritual and physical world seemed to form no contrast . . ." (*Selected Prose*, p. 132).
8. This, of course, is the prime aspect of Chandos' plight.
9. The English translation reads: "I have lost completely the ability to think or to speak of anything coherently . . . because the abstract terms of which the tongue must avail itself as a matter of course in order to voice a judgement — these terms crumbled in my mouth like mouldy fungi." (*Selected Prose*, pp. 133f.)
10. The English translation reads: ". . . to wit, because the language in which I might be able not only to write but to think is neither Latin nor English, neither Italian nor Spanish, but a language none of whose words is known to me, a language in which inanimate things speak to me and wherein I may one day have to justify myself before an unknown judge." (*Selected Prose*, pp. 140f.)
11. This theme, interestingly perhaps, is also of some importance in Samuel Johnson's *Bildungsroman Rasselas*, where the astronomer (!) ruminates, in chapter XLVI: "I have passed my time in study without experience; in the attainment of sciences which can, for the most part, be but remotely useful to mankind. I have purchased knowledge at the expense of all the common comforts of life; I have missed the endearing elegance of female friendship, and the happy commerce of domestick tendernesse."
12. The English translation reads: "A pitcher, a harrow abandoned in a field, a dog in the sun, a neglected cemetery, a cripple, a peasant's hat — all these can become the vessel of my revelation. Each of these objects and a thousand others

similar, over which the eye usually glides with a natural indifference, can suddenly, at any moment (which I am utterly powerless to evoke), assume for me a character so exalted and moving that words seem too poor to describe it." (*Selected Prose*, pp. 135f.)

13. This, incidentally, is an almost literal translation of the last two lines in the ninth of Rilke's *Duino Elegies*. In the original, these lines read:
    . . . überzähliges Dasein
    entspringt mir im Herzen.

14. The English translation reads: "For it is, indeed, something entirely unnamed, even barely nameable which, at such moments, reveals itself to me, filling like a vessel any such casual object of my daily surroundings with an overflowing flood of higher life." (*Selected Prose*, p. 135.)

15. Cf. Paul Kluckhohn, "Die Wende vom 19. zum 20. Jahrhundert in der deutschen Dichtung", *Deutsche Vierteljahresschrift*, 29 (1955), p. 5; see also H. Stefan Schultz, "Hofmannsthal and Bacon: The Source of the Chandos Letter", *Comparative Literature*, 13, 1 (Winter 1961), pp. 1-15

16. Cf. H. Stefan Schultz, *op. cit.*.

17. *Ibid.*, p. 10.

18. Cf. Banville's remark in *The Fiction Magazine*, 1, 3 (Atumn 1982), p. 31. As for Yeats, cf. the reference to the "chestnut-tree", the "great-rooted blossomer" of "Among School Children", one of Yeats' most famous symbols for Unity of Being, which, as F. A. Wilson [*Yeats's Inconography* (New York, 1960), p. 251.] and Frank Kermode [*Romantic Images* (New York, 1964), p. 94.] have suggested, was probably derived from a statement in Goethe's *Wilhelm Meister*. See also Marjorie Perloff, "Yeats and Goethe", *Comparative Literature*, 23, 2 (Spring 1971), p. 131. Banville's novella is related to Ford's *The Good Soldier* inasmuch as both fictions, in comparable terms, are related to *Die Wahlverwandtschaften*; cf. H. Robert Huntley, "*The Good Soldier* and *Die Wahlverwandtschaften*", *Comparative Literature*, 19, 2 (Spring 1967), pp. 133-41.

19. Cf. *Hugo von Hofmannsthal Bibliographie. Werke – Briefe – Gespräche – Übersetzungen – Vertonungen*, ed. Horst Weber (Berlin, New York: Walter de Gruyter, 1972), p. 412.

20. It would be interesting to read *The Newton Letter* with an eye to two thematic preoccupations in *Die Wahlverwandtschaften*, as noted by Jane K. Brown ["*Die Wahlverwandtschaften* and the English Novel of Manners", *Comparative Literature*, 28, 2 (Spring 1976), pp. 107f.]: the characters' loss of control over their lives and their inability to deal with one another in social situations. As for the reliance on the power of the imagination, this may recall Rilke again, especially his concern with the theme of 'inwardness' as realised in these lines:
    Nirgends, Geliebte, wird Welt sein, als innen. Unser Leben geht hin mit Verwandlung. Und immer geringer schwindet das Aussen . . .
    For this theme of 'inwardness' in *Duino Elegies*, see Erich Heller's excellent essay "Die Reise der Kunst ins Innere", in: Erich Heller, *Die Reise der Kunst ins Innere und andere Essays*, trans. by the author (Frankfurt/a.M.: Suhrkamp, 1966), pp. 121-97.

21. Cf. Johann Peter Eckermann, *Gespräche mit Goethe in den letzten Jahren seines Lebens*

(Wiesbaden: Insel, 1955), p. 455: "Wäre die Newtonische Theorie Goethen nicht als ein großer, dem menschlichen Geiste höchst schädlicher Irrtum erschienen, glaubt man denn, daß es ihm je eingefallen sein würde, eine 'Farbenlehre' zu schreiben?" This comment has been omitted in the Everyman edition of Johann Peter Eckermann, *Conversations with Goethe*, transl. John Oxenford, and ed. by J. K. Moorhead (London: Dent, repr. 1971). It is part of the conversation that took place on April 20th, 1825. Somewhat loosely translated it would read: "If the Newtonian theory had not appeared to Goethe to be a great and to the human mind most detrimental error, would anyone think that it had occurred to him to write a 'theory of colours'?" See also Goethe's remark of 4 January 1824: "Ferner bekam es mir schlecht, daß ich einsah, die Newtonische Lehre vom Licht und der Farbe sei ein Irrtum, und daß ich den Mut hatte, dem allgemeinen Credo zu widersprechen", *ibid.*, p. 509. The English translation reads: "It was also prejudicial to me that I discovered Newton's theory of light and colour to be an error, and that I had the courage to contradict the universal creed", *Conversations with Goethe*, p. 35.

22. Preface to *Farbenlehre*, in: *Zur Farbenlehre, Goethes Werke Band XIII: Naturwissenschaftliche Schriften I* (Munich: Beck, 1982), p. 317.

23. *Ibid.*, pp. 318f. As Erich Heller notes: "His [*i.e.* Goethe's] opposition to Newton, for instance, is ultimately based not on a conviction of his own *scientific* superiority, but on his commitment to values which he believed were threatened by man's adopting an exclusively mathematical-analytical method in his dealings with nature". (Erich Heller, *The Disinherited Mind* (London: Bowes & Bowes, 1975), p. 99.)

24. Johann Wolfgang Goethe, *Geschichte der Farbenlehre. Zweiter Teil* (Munich: Beck, 1963), p. 18.

25. Cited in Erich Heller, *Enterbter Geist*, transl. from the English by the author (Frankfurt/a.M.: Suhrkamp, 1981), p. 56. The English text reads: "If I had not carried, through anticipation, the world within myself, I would have remained blind with my eyes wide open, and all search and experience would have been nothing but a dead and vain effort." (E. Heller, *The Disinherited Mind*, p. 31.)

26. Cited in E. Heller, *Enterbter Geist*, p. 56. The English text reads: "... a revelation emerging at the point where the inner world of man meets external reality ... It is a synthesis of world and mind, yielding the happiest assurance of the eternal harmony of existence." (*The Disinherited Mind*, p. 31.)

27. Cited in E. Heller, *Enterbter Geist*, pp. 26f.. The English text reads: "After this model it will be possible to *invent* plants *ad infinitum*, which will all be consistent, that is, they *could* exist even if they have no actual existence; they would not merely be picturesque or poetic shadows or dreams, but would possess an *inner truth and necessity. And the same law will be applicable to everything alive.*" (*The Disinherited Mind*, p. 10.)

28. E. Heller, *Enterbter Geist*, pp. 44f. The English version reads: "Light for him is the bright, white radiance of a sunny day, not that ray distilled by Newton, forced through the tiniest holes and tortured by complicated mechanisms. That light should be a concoction of various colours is to Goethe a 'manifest absurdity'. It is not the colours which produce a white light, but the white light

which produces the colours. 'Colours are actions and sufferings of light', he says, the result of its meeting with darkness. This darkness is not merely defined as the absence of light, it is a creative force in its own right. Darkness interferes with light through all the shades of opaqueness provided by various media ... There are only two fundamental colours, yellow and blue, yellow emerging at the point where light has to yield some of its territory to darkness, and blue where light makes its first tentative inroad into blackness. By intensification and mixing one obtains all the other colours; allow more and more darkness to intrude into yellow and you get orange and red, and give light a better chance in its combat with black, and violet and bluish red appear. Mix the two elemental colours, yellow and blue, and you have green. Thus Goethe arrives at his colour-cycle where yellow and blue, red and violet, green and what he calls purple, face one another; they are complementary colours. It is all very delicate and very obvious...". E. Heller, *The Disinherited Mind*, p. 23.

29. E. Heller, *Enterbter Geist*, p. 49. The English version reads: "... the fact that every scientific theory is merely the surface realization of a metaphysical substratum of beliefs, conscious and unconscious, about the nature of the world." (*The Disinherited Mind*, p. 26.)

8. Mefisto

1. *The New York Times Book Review* (21 April 1985).
2. John Banville, *Mefisto* (London: Secker & Warburg, 1986). All references are to this section.
3. John Banville, *The Newton Letter* (London: Secker & Warburg, 1982), p. 50.
4. Cf. Jeremy Bernstein, *Einstein* (Glasgow: Collins, 1983), pp. 19, 68.
5. *Ibid.*, p. 19.
6. Cf. the title of William H. Gass' study *The World Within the Word* (Boston: Nonpareil Books, 1979).
7. Alfred Appel, jr., "Conversations with Nabokov", *Novel. A Forum on Fiction*, 4, 3 (Spring 1971), p. 210.
8. Vladimir Nabokov, *Lolita* (New York, Toronto: McGraw-Hill, 1970), p. 34.
9. Cf. John Banville's remark in: Rüdiger Imhof, "Q. & A. with John Banville". *Irish Literary Supplement* (Spring 1987), p. 13.
10. Arthur Koestler, *The Sleepwalkers. A History of Man's Changing Vision of the Universe* (Harmondsworth: Penguin, repr. 1977).
11. *The Newton Letter*, p. 11.
12. Cf. Koestler, *The Sleepwalkers*, p. 30.
13. Cf. Koestler's remark about Pythagoras, *The Sleepwalkers*, p. 37.
14. For these remarks I acknowledge my indebtedness to Koestler's *The Sleepwalkers*.
15. Cf. William Bauer, *Der ältere Pythagoreismus* (Hildesheim, New York: George Olms, repr. 1976), p. 13.
16. Cf. E. Frank, *Plato und die sogenannten Pythagoreer* (Darmstadt: Wiss. Buchgesellschaft, 1962), p. 310.

17. Cf. Frances A. Yates, *The Rosicrucian Enlightenment* (London, New York: ARK, 1986), p. 148.
18. *Ibid.*, p. 149.
19. John Banville, *Birchwood* (London: Secker & Warburg, 1973), p. 171.
20. Werner Heisenberg, *Das Naturbild der heutigen Physik* (Hamburg: Rowohlt, 1965), p. 25.
21. Cf. J. Bernstein, *Einstein*, p. 144.
22. Cited in *Wörterbuch der philosophischen Begriffe* (Berlin: Mittler & Sohn, 1930), *s.v.*: 'Zufall', p. 668.
23. *Ibid.*, p. 669.
24. *Mathematics and the Imagination* (Harmondsworth: Penguin, repr. 1979), p. 197.
25. Cf. S. Sambursky, *Das physikalische Weltbild der Antike* (Zurich, Stuttgart: Artemis, 1965), p. 230.
26. John Banville, *Kepler* (London: Secker & Warburg, 1981), p. 134.
27. Cf. Banville's remark in "Q. & A. with John Banville".
28. Cf. Henry James' dictum in the Preface to *The Spoils of Poynton*.
29. T. S. Eliot, "*Ulysses*, Order and Myth", *Dial*, 75 (November 1923), pp. 480–83; repr. in: Robert H. Deming (ed.), *James Joyce. The Critical Heritage*, vol. I (London: Routledge & Kegan Paul, 1970), pp. 268–71; here p. 270.
30. Cf. Banville's remark in "Q. & A. with John Banville".
31. Johann Wolfgang von Goethe, *Faust I*, transl. by Philip Wayne (Harmondsworth: Penguin, repr. 1986), p. 44. All references are to this edition.
32. *Faust I*, "Prologue in Heaven".
33. Johann Wolfgang von Goethe, *Faust. Der Tragödie erster und zweiter Teil*, ed. Erich Trunz (Munich: C. H. Beck, repr. 1976), line 2053. All quotations in German are from this edition.
34. Felix is clearly cast in the role of Mephistopheles, or a Satan-figure. Evidence of this fact abounds throughout the account. For example at the end of Part I (p. 116), he bids farewell to Ashburn by quoting half a line from Milton's *Paradise Lost*, where in Book I Satan is described lying on a burning lake and pondering upon what he has forfeited by his rebellion against God: "Farewell happy fields/ Where joy for ever dwells: hail horrors, hail", *Paradise Lost*, I, 249f.
35. E. M. Butler, *The Fortunes of Faust* (Cambridge, London, New York, Melbourne: CUP, 1952), pp. 106ff.
36. Reinhard Buchwald, *Führer durch Goethes Faustdichtung* (Stuttgart: Kröner, 1955), p. 141.
37. Banville's Lamia somehow recalls Keats' Lamia. She is a "palpitating snake" bemoaning her lot not to be able to "move in a sweet body fit for life"; she turns into a woman and beguiles and sings into sleep Lycius, who then "from death [awakes] into amaze", like Gabriel after the accident:

    And every word she spake enticed him on
    To unperplexed delight and pleasure known.
38. Cf. Hans Mayer's remark on *Doktor Faustus* in: *Thomas Mann* (Frankfurt/a.M.: Suhrkamp, 1980), pp. 286ff.
39. *Ibid.*, p. 289.

40. Dante Alighieri, *The Divine Comedy, 1: Hell*, transl. by Dorothy L. Sayers (Harmondsworth: Penguin, repr. 1983), p. 71. All further references in the text are to this edition.

41. Martin Gardner, *The Ambidextrous Universe* (Harmondsworth: Penguin, repr. 1982).

42. *Birchwood*, p. 5.

43. *The Divine Comedy, 3: Paradise*, IX, 138.

44. John Banville, *Doctor Copernicus* (London: Secker & Warburg, 1976), p. 238. All references are to this edition.

Conclusion

1. *The Newton Letter*, p. 50.

2. *Doctor Copernicus*, p. 240.

3. *Ibid.*, p. 240.

4. *Ibid.*, p. 239.

5. Cf. Samuel Beckett, *The Unnamable* (London: Calder & Boyars, 1975), pp. 8f.

6. *Nightspawn*, p. 20.

7. *Ibid.*, p. 123.

8. *Ibid.*, pp. 47f.

9. Cf. Banville's remark, in: Rüdiger Imhof, "An Interview with John Banville...", p. 9.

10. Cf. *Shorter Oxford English Dictionary*, vol. II, *s.v.*: 'Tetralogy'.

11. In a conversation with John Banville.

12. Jonathan Swift, "*A Full and True Account of the Battle...*", in: J. Swift, *A Tale of a Tub & other Satires* (London, Melbourne, Toronto: Dent & Sons, 1978), p. 140.

BIBLIOGRAPHY

I. Works by John Banville

"A Blackcurrant Rose" [extract from Birchwood], *Hibernia* (2 February 1973), p. 13.

Birchwood (London: Secker & Warburg, 1973; London: Panther, 1984).

(& Thaddeus O'Sullivan with Andrew Patmann), "*Birchwood*: Extracts from the Screenplay", *The Irish Review*, 1 (1986), pp. 65-73.

"De rerum natura", *Transatlantic Review*, 50 (1975), pp. 70-76.

"Die Liebenden", in: Frank Auerbach (ed.), *Shakespeare's Muse. Moderne Erzähler aus Großbritannien* (Stuttgart: Thienemann, 1983), pp. 407-17.

Doctor Copernicus (London: Secker & Warburg, 1976; Frogmore, St Albans: Granada, 1983; New York: W. W. Norton, 1976; Boston: Godine, 1984).

"Fragment from a Novel in Progress" [opening pages of *Kepler*], in: Peter Fallon & Sean Golden (eds.), *Soft Days: A Miscellany of Contemporary Irish Writing* (Portmarnock, 1980), pp. 170-76.

"From a Work in Progress" [extract from *The Newton Letter*], *Bananas*, 26 (April 1986), pp. 27f.

"From *Kepler: A Novel*", Ploughshares, 6, 1 (1980), pp. 97-104.

"From *Kepler: A Novel*", in: Andrew Carpenter & Peter Fallon (eds.), *The Writers. A Sense of Ireland* (Dublin: O'Brien Press, 1980), pp. 11-14.

"Gemini" [extract from *Mefisto*], in: Robin Robertson (ed.), *Firebird 4. New Writing from Britain and Ireland* (Harmondsworth: Penguin, 1985), pp. 11-27.

"Into the Wood", *Esquire*, 57 (March 1972), p. 126.

"Island", *The Irish Press* (January 1969).

Kepler (London: Secker & Warburg, 1981; London: Granada, 1983; Boston: Godine, 1983 & 1984).

Long Lankin (London: Secker & Warburg, 1970; rev. ed. Dublin: Gallery, 1984).

"Lovers", *The Irish Press* (July 1968); in: David Marcus (ed.), *New Irish Writings 1* (Dublin, 1970), pp. 20-30; transl. "Jugend und Alter", in: H. Petersen (ed.), *Erkundungen: 30 irische Erzähler* (East Berlin, 1979), pp. 260-68.

Mefisto (London: Secker & Warburg, 1986; London, Glasgow, Toronto, Sydney, Auckland: Grafton Books, 1987).

"Michael" [extract from *Birchwood*], *The Irish Press* (1 May 1971).

"Mr. Mallin's Quest", *Transatlantic Review*, 37 & 38 (Autumn-Winter 1970-71), pp. 29-34.

"Nativity" *Transatlantic Review*, 37 & 38 (Autumn-Winter 1970-71), pp. 35-39.

Nightspawn (London: Secker & Warburg, 1971; New York: W. W. Norton, 1971).

"Nightwind", *Transatlantic Review*, 35 (Spring 1970), pp. 5-13.

"Rondo", *The Irish Press (1976)*; repr. *Transatlantic Review*, 60 (1977), pp. 180-83.

"Sanctuary", *Transatlantic Review*.

"Summer Voices", *Transatlantic Review*, 28 (1968), pp. 99-107; repr. *The Irish Press* (24 January 1970), p. 7.

"The Birchwood" [extract from *Birchwood*], *The Times* (3 February 1973).

"The Day the Circus Came to Town" [extract from *Birchwood*], *The Irish Press* (3 February 1973).

The Newton Letter (London: Secker & Warburg, 1982; London: Granada, 1984; Boston: Godine, 1987).

"The Newton Letter" [extract from *The Newton Letter*], *Irish University Review*, 11, 1 (Spring 1981), pp. 18-28.

"The Party", *Kilkenny Magazine*, 14 (Spring-Summer, 1966), pp. 75-82

"Wild Wood", *Dublin Magazine* (Spring-Summer, 1969) pp. 25-30.

(A list of reviews by John Banville is contained in my "John Banville: A Checklist", *Irish University Review*, 11, 1 (Spring 1981), pp. 88-92. The checklist also offers bibliographical data of reviews of Banville's novels from *Long Lankin* to *Doctor Copernicus*.)

II. Theoretical Statements and Interviews

Banville, John. "A Talk", *Irish University Review*, 11, 1 (Spring 1981), pp. 13-17.

"'My Readers, That Small Band, Deserve a Rest'. An Interview with John Banville", *Irish University Review*, 11, 1 (Spring 1981), p. 5-12.

"Novelists on the Novel. Ronan Sheehan Talks to John Banville and Francis Stuart", *The Crane Bag*, 3, 1 (1979), pp. 76-84.

"Out of Chaos Comes Order. John Banville Interviewed by Ciaran Carty", *The Sunday Tribune* (14 September 1986), p. 18.

"Q. and A. with John Banville", *Irish Literary Supplement* (Spring 1987), p. 13.

III. Works by Other Authors

Allen, Findlay. "An Irish Devil", *The Literary Review* (November 1986), pp. 11f.

Banville, Vincent. "Goosing the Rational", *The Sunday Tribune* (4 January 1987), p. 4.

Bauer, William. *Der ältere Pythagoreismus* (Hildesheim, New York: Olms, repr. 1976).

Beckett, Samuel. *Molloy* (London: Calder & Boyars, repr. 1971).

Beckett, Samuel. *Proust & 3 dialogues with Georges Duthuit* (London: Calder & Boyars, repr. 1970).

Bernstein, Jeremy. *Einstein* (Glasgow: Collins, 1983).

Blumenberg, Hans. *Die Genesis der kopernikanischen Wende* (Frankfurt: Suhrkamp, 1975).

Borges, Jorge Luis. *Labyrinths*, ed. D. A. Yates & J. E. Irby (Harmondsworth: Penguin, repr. 1976).

Brod, Max. *Tycho Brahes Weg zu Gott* (Frankfurt: Suhrkamp, repr. 1978).

Broich, Ulrich & Manfred Pfister (eds.), *Intertextualität. Formen, Funktionen, anglistische Fallstudien* (Tübingen: Niemeyer, 1985).

Brownjohn, Alan, "A Matter of History", *TLS* (11 June 1982), p. 643.

Buchwald, Reinhard. *Führer durch Goethes Faustdichtung* (Stuttgart: Kröner, 1955).

Butler, E. M., *The Fortunes of Faust* (Cambridge, London, New York, Melbourne: CUP, 1952).

Cary, Joyce. *The Horse's Mouth* (Harmondsworth: Penguin, repr. 1979).

Cohen, I. Bernard (ed.), *Isaac Newton's Papers & Letters on Natural Philosophy and Related Documents* (Cambridge/Mass. & London, 1978).

Craig, Patricia. "A Rage for Order", *TLS* (10 October 1986), p. 1131.

Cruise O'Brien, Kate. "Pilgrim's Way", *The Listener* (22 July 1982), p. 24.

Deane, Seamus. *A Short History of Irish Literature* (London: Hutchinson, 1986).

Deane, Seamus. "'Be Assured I Am Inventing': The Fiction of John Banville", in: Patrick Rafroidi & Maurice Harmon (eds.), *The Irish Novel in Our Time* (Lille: PUL, 1975/76), pp. 329-38.

Delaney, Frank. "The Ones That Got Away", in: Tim Pat Coogan (ed.), *Ireland and The Arts* (London, n.d.), pp. 74-81.

Deming, Robert H. (ed.), *James Joyce. The Critical Heritage* (London: Routledge & Kegan Paul, 1970).

Donnelly, Brian. "The Big House in the Recent Novel", *Studies*, 64 (1975), pp. 133-42.

Dostoyevsky, Fyodor M., *Notes from Underground & The Double*, transl. by Jessie Coulson (Harmondsworth: Penguin, repr. 1980).

Driver, Paul. "Liza Jarrett's Hard Life", *The London Review of Books* (4 December 1986), pp. 24 & 26.

Eckermann, Johann Peter. *Conversations with Goethe*, transl. by John Oxenford (London: Dent, repr. 1971).

Eckermann, Johann Peter. *Gespräche mit Goethe in den letzten Jahren seines Lebens* (Wiesbaden: Insel, 1955).

Edel, Leon. *The Life of Henry James* (Harmondsworth: Penguin, repr. 1977).

Edgeworth, Maria. *Castle Rackrent & The Absentee* (New York: Dover, 1966).

Eliot, Thomas Stearns. *Collected Poems 1909-1962* (London: Faber & Faber, repr. 1975).

Fontenelle, "The Elogium of Sir Isaac Newton", in: I.B.. Cohen (ed.), *Isaac Newton's Papers . . .*, pp. 444-74.

Frank, Erich. *Plato und die sogenannten Pythagoreer* (Darmstadt: Wiss. Buchgesellschaft, 1962).

Frazer, James George. *The Golden Bough: A Study in Magic and Ritual* (London, Basingstoke: Macmillan, repr. 1976).

Gardner, Martin. *The Ambidextrous Universe* (Harmondsworth: Penguin, repr. 1982).

Gass, William H., *The World Within the Word* (Boston: Nonpareil Books, 1979).

Glacken, Brendan. "Head in the Start", *Irish Times* (3 February 1981), p. 12.

Godwin, William. *Caleb Williams* (Oxford: OUP, repr. 1978).

Goethe, Johann Wolfgang. *Faust*, ed. by Erich Trunz (Munich: Beck, repr. 1976).

Goethe, Johann Wolfgang. *Faust*, transl. by Philip Wayne (Harmondsworth: Penguin, repr. 1986).

Goethe, Johann Wolfgang. *Materialien zur Geschichte der Farbenlehre* (Munich: Beck, 1982).

Greacan, Lavinia. "A Serious Writer", *Irish Times* (24 March 1981), p. 8.

Heisenberg, Werner. *Das Naturbild der heutigen Physik* (Reinbek: Rowohlt, 1965).

Heller, Erich. *Die Reise der Kunst ins Innere und andere Essays* (Frankfurt: Suhrkamp, 1966).

Heller, Erich. *Enterbter Geist* (Frankfurt: Suhrkamp, 1981).

Heller, Erich. *The Disinherited Mind* (London: Bowes & Bowes, 1975).

Hemleben, Johannes. *Kepler* (Reinbek: Rowohlt, 1977).

Hofmannsthal, Hugo von. *Erzählungen, erfundene Gespräche und Briefe, Reisen* (Frankfurt: Fischer, 1979).

Hofmannsthal, Hugo von. *Selected Prose*, transl. by Mary Hottinger & Tania & James Stern (New York: Pantheon, 1952).

Imhof, Rüdiger. "'A Little Bit of Ivory, Two 'nches Wide': The Small World of Jennifer Johnston's Fiction", *Etudes Irlandaises*, 10 (December 1985), pp. 129-44.

Imhof, Rüdiger. *Contemporary Metafiction. A Poetological Study of Metafiction in English since 1939* (Heidelberg: Winter 1986).

Imhof, Rüdiger. "John Banville. A Checklist", *Irish University Review*, 11, 1 (Spring 1981), pp. 87-95.

Imhof, Rüdiger. "John Banville's Supreme Fiction", *Irish University Review*, 11, 1 (Spring 1981), pp. 52-86.

Imhof, Rüdiger. "*The Newton Letter.* An Exercise in Literary Derivation", *Irish University Review*, 13, 2 (Autumn 1983), pp. 162-67.

Imhof, Rüdiger. "Swan's Way, or Goethe, Einstein, Banville — The Eternal Recurrence", *Etudes Irlandaises* (1987), pp. 113-29.

Iser, Wolfgang. *Der implizite Leser* (Munich: Fink, 1972).

James, Henry. *The Sacred Fount* (New York: Grove Press, repr. 1979).

Jeffares, A. Norman. *Anglo-Irish Literature* (Dublin: Gill & Macmillan, 1982).

Joyce, James. *A Portrait of the Artist as a Young Man* (London: Cape, repr. 1978).

Kearney, Richard. *Transitions. Narratives in Modern Irish Culture* (Dublin: Wolfhound Press, 1988).

Kilroy, Thomas. "Teller of Tales", *TLS* (17 March 1972), pp. 301f.

Kirchhoff, Jochen. *Kopernikus* (Reinbek: Rowohlt, 1985).

Koestler, Arthur. *The Sleepwalkers. A History of Man's Changing Vision* (Harmondsworth: Penguin, repr. 1977).

Kuhn, Thomas S., *The Copernican Revolution* (Harvard: Harvard U.P., 1957).

Kunz, Josef (ed.), *Novelle* (Darmstadt: Wiss. Buchgesellschaft, 1973).

LeFanu, Joseph Sheridan. *Uncle Silas* (New York: Dover, 1966).

Lernout, Geert. "Looking for Pure Vision", *Graph. Irish Literary Review*, 1 (October 1986), pp. 12-16.

Levin, Bernard. "Scouring the Heavens", *The Sunday Times* (25 January 1981), p. 41.

Maack, Annegret. *Der experimentelle englische Roman der Gegenwart* (Darmstadt: Wiss. Buchgesellschaft, 1984).

Manuel, Frank E., *A Portrait of Isaac Newton* (London: Muller, 1980).

Martin, Augustine. *The Genius of Irish Prose* (Dublin: Mercier Press, 1984).

Mayer, Hans. *Thomas Mann* (Frankfurt: Suhrkamp, 1980).

McCaffery, Larry (ed.), *Postmodern Fiction — A Bio-Bibliographical Guide* (Westport/Conn.: Greenwood, 1986).

McCormick, David. "John Banville: Literature as Criticism", *The Irish Review*, 2 (1987), pp. 95-99.

McMahon, Seán. "The New Irish Writers", *Eire-Ireland*, 9 (Spring 1974), pp. 136-43.

McMinn, Joe. "An Exalted Naming: The Poetical Fictions of John Banville", *The Canadian Journal of Irish Literature*, 14, 1 (July 1988), pp. 17-27.

McMinn, Joe. "Reality Refuses to Fall into Place", *Fortnight* (October 1986), p. 24.

Mercier, Vivian. *The Irish Comic Tradition* (London, Oxford, New York: OUP, 1969).

Milne, Tom. "The Golden Pendulum", *The Observer* (1 April 1984), p. 20.

Molloy, Francis C., "The Search for Truth: The Fiction of John Banville", *Irish University Review*, 11, 1 (Spring 1981), pp. 29-51.

Nabokov, Vladimir. *Bend Sinister* (Harmondsworth: Penguin, repr. 1981).

Nabokov, Vladimir. *The Annotated "Lolita"*, ed. with preface, introduction and notes by Alfred Appell, jr. (New York, Toronto: McGraw-Hill, 1970).

O'Brien, George. "Irish Fiction since 1966. Challenge, Themes, Promise", *Ploughshare*, 6, 1 (1980), pp. 153f.

Proust, Marcel. *Swann's Way* (Harmondsworth: Penguin, repr. 1984).

Rafroidi, Patrick & Maurice Harmon (eds.), *The Irish Novel in Our Time* (Lille: PUL, 1975/76).

Reckwitz, Erhard. "Der Roman als Metaroman", *Poetica*, 18 (1986), pp. 140-64.

Rilke, Rainer Maria. *Duineser Elegien* (Frankfurt: Suhrkamp, 1975); *Duino Elegies* (London: Chatto & Windus, 1981).

Schleussner, Bruno. *Der neopikareske Roman* (Bonn: Bouvier, 1969).

Shattuck, Roger. *Proust* (Glasgow: Fontana, 1974).

Skelton, Robin. "Aidan Higgins and the Total Book", *Mosaic*, 19 (1976), pp. 27-37.

Stoppard, Tom. *Jumpers* (London: Faber & Faber, 1972).

Vaughan, Stephen. "Music of the Spheres", *The Observer* (25 January 1981), p. 29.

Wandor, Michelene. "Valedictions", *The Listener* (16 October 1986).

Weber, Horst (ed.), *Hugo von Hofmannsthal Bibliographie* (Berlin, New York: Walter de Gruyter, 1972).

Weiler, Gershon. *Mauthner's Critique of Language* (Cambridge: CUP, 1970).

Wilde, Alan. "Modernism and the Aesthetics of Crisis", *Contemporary Literature*, 20, 1 (Winter 1979).

Wittgenstein, Ludwig. *Tractatus logico-philosophicus* (Frankfurt: Suhrkamp, 1971).

Yates, Frances A., *The Art of Memory* (London, Melbourne & Henley: ARK, Routledge & Kegan Paul, repr. 1984).

Yates, Frances A., *The Rosicrucian Enlightenment* (London, New York: ARK, 1986).

INDEX

198 John Banville: A Critical Introduction